DATE DUE

A Gestalt Institute
of Cleveland
publication

HERE NOW NEXT

Here
Now
Next

*Paul Goodman and
the Origins of Gestalt Therapy*

———

Taylor Stoehr

Jossey-Bass Publishers • San Francisco

A Gestalt Institute of Cleveland publication

Substantial discounts on bulk quantities of Jossey-Bass books are available to corporations, professional associations, and other organizations. For details and discount information, contact the special sales department at Jossey-Bass Inc., Publishers.
(415) 433–1740; Fax (415) 433–0499.

For international orders, please contact your local Paramount Publishing International office.

Manufactured in the United States of America. Nearly all Jossey-Bass books and jackets are printed on recycled paper containing at least 10 percent postconsumer waste, and many are printed with either soy- or vegetable-based ink, which emits fewer volatile organic compounds during the printing process than petroleum-based ink.

Selected quotations from *Gestalt Therapy* by Frederick Perls, M.D., Ralph F. Hefferline, Ph.D., and Paul Goodman, Ph.D., copyright © 1951, 1979 by Frederick Perls, Ralph F. Hefferline, and Paul Goodman, are reprinted by permission from Crown Publishers, Inc.

Library of Congress Cataloging-in-Publication Data

Stoehr, Taylor, date.
    Here now next : Paul Goodman and the origins of Gestalt therapy / Taylor Stoehr. — 1st ed.
        p. cm. — (Jossey-Bass social and behavioral science series)
    Includes bibliographical references and index.
    ISBN 0-7879-0005-2
    1. Goodman, Paul, 1911–1972—Contributions in gestalt therapy. 2. Gestalt therapy—History. I. Title. II. Series.
RC489.G4S76 1994
150.19'82'09—dc20   94–9711
                                       CIP

FIRST EDITION
HB Printing   10 9 8 7 6 5 4 3 2 1   Code 9478

Contents

vii

CONTENTS

To Geoffrey Gardner, friend and counselor

Preface

THE STORY TO BE told in this book is twofold: first, Paul Goodman's role in establishing the principal ideas of Gestalt therapy, and after that, the way in which Goodman's own practice as a therapist changed him and ultimately led him to a new vocation, which might be called socio-therapist of the body politic.

As one of Goodman's younger friends I was witness to much of his later career, and as his literary executor and biographer I have become familiar with the facts of his life and their contexts in a way that no friend or even family member could know them. I am only a layman with regard to psychotherapy, however, and was never a member of any Gestalt group. Except for Goodman himself, I knew no therapists and few patients during the early days of the Gestalt Institute. I did meet Fritz Perls once—on the same occasion when a friend first brought me to Goodman's Manhattan apartment, one night in February 1950. This was the very time Perls and Goodman were working on *Gestalt Therapy*, but I was a naïve eighteen-year-old, and had no idea that the grey-looking man with the accent and the vivid man who kissed me at the door—much to my amazement—

were writing a great book together. I left the East Coast soon after that and never lived in the same city with Goodman, but I kept in touch and our friendship grew, especially during the sixties. Over twenty years elapsed before I met another Gestalt therapist, Goodman's protégé George Dennison. We had heard of each other from Goodman, but when we finally met it was at Goodman's graveside in 1972, after which we became close friends. Although Dennison had worked as a therapist for only a short time, he had a lot to tell me about his training with Goodman and the way Goodman ran his groups. After I decided to write Goodman's biography—a larger undertaking than the present volume—I began to meet other therapists, who had been part of the original institute and could report their versions of its founding. I am grateful to those who shared their memories. Without their help, my story would have been too dependent on Goodman's own point of view, so fully revealed in his letters and journals and lecture notes for the training sessions he ran. It is important to know how his colleagues and patients saw him from their unique perspectives.

The book I now offer concentrates on Goodman's contributions and indebtedness to the Gestalt therapy movement. Very little is said of his earlier interest in psychoanalysis, his absorption and championing of Wilhelm Reich's ideas, or his own self-analysis which immediately preceded his work with Perls. The line had to be drawn somewhere. And there are other omissions and, no doubt, some distortions because of them. While the ideas and practice of psychotherapy were certainly central for Goodman during the ten years I am reconstructing here, other concerns took as much or more of his attention—his deepening engagement in the politics of non-violence, his ambivalent love affair with the Living Theatre, his devotion to his art and his efforts to get his work published, and his absorption with his family and with the circle of friends and disciples that constituted his community. All these points of contact come into play in the story of Goodman as Gestalt therapist; sometimes one or another of them threatens to become the center of attention and to push psychotherapy into the background. I try to keep a strong figure before the reader, for the sake of vitality and closure, but I am aware of unfinished business in the corners. It is a problem of perspective Gestalt therapists will appreciate. I hope my other readers, too, will find some poignancy in this portrait of a man in the very quick of his existence, facing the great turning point of his life. This is not something that could be captured in a tidy summary of Goodman's role in inventing a new psychotherapy.

The expression "here and now" has quite rightly been associated with Fritz Perls, whose life and whose practice as a therapist were so focused on the present moment. I call my book *Here Now Next* to emphasize Goodman's particular contribution to the theory of Gestalt therapy, his insistence that awareness can develop fully only in an *ongoing* present. Lively engagement with the unpredictable world of the *next* moment was what being in the vital present really amounted to for Goodman. It was what he meant when he gave his half of *Gestalt Therapy* the title "Novelty, Excitement and Growth." The phrase "here now next" might even be considered an adverbial translation of that title, taking it out of the static realm of abstract nouns. And of course Goodman used the phrase often in his later writings when he wanted a shorthand way of saying what was important in making contact with experience.

Furthermore, I mean to suggest by my title something of the political dimension of Goodman's view of psychotherapy. Indeed, one might say that the here now next of *my* book is the movement from Goodman as theorist, to Goodman as therapist/patient, to Goodman as prophet. In this sequence Gestalt therapy may be seen as the necessary groundwork for Goodman's later career as a social critic and political philosopher. My book then is not simply a history of the Gestalt therapy movement and its antecedents, nor a biographical study of Goodman's own participation in its founding and development, but also an examination of the psychological import of that great upheaval of the sixties known as the New Left. More than any other person Goodman articulated the point of view, at once utopian and practical, of that remarkable political movement. And at every point Gestalt insights and therapeutic experience informed his ideas. Almost a whole generation later, we have perhaps arrived at another crossroads, for the health of the body politic and the here now next of our culture. I think we could do worse than to look to Goodman for advice and inspiration.

Cambridge, Massachusetts   Taylor Stoehr
June 1994

Acknowledgments

MANY PEOPLE HAVE aided my work by sharing their memories and understanding of Paul Goodman and the Gestalt therapy movement and by other forms of advice and support. I wish to thank Diva Agostinelli, Rogers Albritton, Robert Anderson, Rose Mary Anderson, David Andree, Gregory Bateson, Karl Bissinger, Burt Brooks, Holley Cantine, Jonathan Croall, George Dennison, Mabel Dennison, Honore Valincourt Elkus, Howard Frisch, Isadore From, Jane Gapen, Frieda Gardner, Geoffrey Gardner, Betty Gomory, Naomi Goodman, Percival Goodman, Sally Goodman, Susan Goodman, Marilyn Hamilton, Toby Huff, Karen Humphrey, Alexander Katz, Richard King, Richard Kitzler, Lawrence Kornfeld, David Koven, Edmund Leites, Abba Lerner, Glenn Lewis, Diana Liben, Meyer Liben, Nilo Lindgren, Alexander Lowen, Judith Malina, Ilse Mattick, Paul Mattick, Robert Merideth, Richard P. McKeon, Jackson MacLow, Arthur Nelson, Benjamin Nelson, Edwin Nevis, Jim Nixon, John Oatfield, Laura Perls, Erving Polster, Miriam Polster, Virginia Pond, Leo Raditsa, Dachine Rainer, Jerome Raphel, Raymond Rosenthal, Michael Rossman, David Sachs, Oscar Shaftel, Elliott Shapiro, Myron

Sharaf, Lottie Weisz, Gordon Wheeler, Eleanor Rackow Widmer, David Wieck, Joe Wysong. Among these people, many of them good friends, there are some who have not lived to see this book. I trust they knew my gratitude for counsel that cannot be replaced.

For permission to quote passages from published and unpublished sources, I wish to thank the following persons and institutions: Marie Coleman, Mabel Dennison, Sally Goodman, Alexander Katz, Ena Neill, and Zoe Readhead; the Rare Book and Manuscript Library of Columbia University, for letters from Goodman in the Benjamin Nelson Papers; the Beinecke Rare Book and Manuscript Library of Yale University, for letters from Alexander Katz in the Dwight Macdonald Papers; the Houghton Library of Harvard University, for materials in the George Dennison Papers and the Paul Goodman Papers. I wish particularly to thank Elizabeth Falsey of the Houghton Library for many years of generous assistance.

Portions of this book were presented as a talk to the New York Institute for Gestalt Therapy, and as an address to the 1991 Annual Conference of the *Gestalt Journal*. The latter address, along with other parts of this book, was published as "Paul Goodman and the Political Dimensions of Gestalt Therapy," in the *Gestalt Journal* (Spring 1993), 16, pp. 55–90.

A number of friends whose judgment I especially value have read and commented on earlier versions of the book, or portions of it. I want to thank Mabel Dennison, John Dings, Isadore From, Geoffrey Gardner, Naomi Goodman, Sally Goodman, Susan Goodman, Robert Nichols, Ruth Perry, Lewis Petrinovich, Gordon Wheeler, and Joe Wysong.   —T. S.

The Author

TAYLOR STOEHR is Paul Goodman's literary executor and is writing Goodman's biography. Born in Omaha, Nebraska, in 1931, Stoehr attended the public schools there and graduated from the University of Omaha. He studied at the University of California, Berkeley, where he received his Ph.D. degree (1960) in English and American literature. He has taught at Cornell University; the State University of New York, Buffalo; and the University of California, Santa Cruz. Since 1971 he has been professor of English at the University of Massachusetts, Boston.

In addition to editing over a dozen volumes of Goodman's work, Stoehr has also written five books and many articles on such literary figures as Dickens, Lawrence, Hawthorne, and Thoreau, as well as cultural studies of utopian communities, the free love movement, pseudoscience, and other countercultural experiments in nineteenth-century America. His most recent books are *Decentralizing Power*, a collection of Paul Goodman's social criticism, *Format and Anxiety*, a collection of Paul Goodman's writings on the media, and *Crazy Hope and*

Finite Experience, which brings together Goodman's final essays, framed as a credo.

Taylor Stoehr has five children and a stepson. He lives in Cambridge, Massachusetts, with his wife, the feminist scholar Ruth Perry.

CHAPTER ONE

At the Crossroads

GESTALT THERAPY came into existence in the very middle of the century now drawing to its close, our own epoch. Of its originators, the person chiefly responsible for formulating Gestalt theory, putting it into words, was Paul Goodman. At that time Goodman was not yet a therapist himself but a literary man, the very breed that Freud had once said made the best psychoanalysts. Indeed it did make him the right person to write *Gestalt Therapy*, the founding text of the new movement. And yet, today, anyone who knows Goodman's name is not likely to remember him in either of these callings, therapist or author, but as the social critic whose championing of the disaffected young in *Growing Up Absurd* inaugurated the intergenerational struggles of the sixties and whose critique of the "Organized System" was taken up by the political radicals of the New Left.

The starting point for Gestalt therapy was in fact a turning point for Goodman, who had come to the great crossroads of his life. A decade earlier he had high hopes as a poet, playwright, and novelist, as well as promise for a brilliant scholarly career in the universities, had he wished it. A decade later he would be famous for his books on public issues and social change. But in 1950 he stood between these two careers, quite at a loss. He felt he had failed as a writer, for although he had already written a dozen splendid books, nobody wanted to read them. Twenty years of hard work and extraordinary creativity had won him almost no reward and little notice. He was about ready to give up. The academic community offered no alternative, not even an economic last resort. He had been fired by three different schools, because he insisted on his right to fall in love with his students.

Goodman understood that he had brought much of this situation on himself, but he also believed that the world he lived in and wrote for, especially the conformist society that was taking shape in America after the Second World War, simply could not accept a person such as he. His audience had become his enemy. The public that preferred to be entertained by Hollywood and Madison Avenue was also content to be governed from Washington, was grateful for employment at an Office in a Skyscraper, was ready and willing to commute to the Suburbs, enjoyed shopping at a Mall, and was happily raising a Family in the American Way. The story of how Goodman became a prophetic figure in his country's political history, instead of a famous poet or novelist, is also the story of how America came more and more to need his critique of its trivial culture, which values the standard of living over the quality of life, vulgar riches over decent poverty, and full employment and high GDP over worthy tasks and public goods. But however urgent the message he brought, Goodman's passage from neglected author to influential social critic did not happen overnight and would require much labor and change in his character. Gestalt therapy was the pathway Goodman followed from one career to the other, for it was during his decade of work as a theorist and practitioner that he slowly and painfully came to terms with the failure of his art to attract an audience, and found the will to serve his fellow citizens in a new way. In this opening chapter I want to set forth these social needs and personal motives, starting point and crossroads, fully enough to allow the reader to see what was at stake for Goodman, for Gestalt therapy, and for our culture as a whole. Later chapters will say more about his choices and what came of them.

After the Second World War the victors East and West turned from the "war against Fascism" to create their own versions of the same all-encompassing superstate they had been reducing to rubble—except that from now on totalitarianism would have other names and a smiling face. Orwell called it Big Brother. In the West it was also called the permanent war economy, democratic socialism, the Communist conspiracy, and the Great Society, depending on one's allegiances. For critics of the American version like Goodman, the name that stuck was the system, or less neutrally, the organized system.

The idea was an old one, though it had been sheer fancy in earlier times, a utopian dream or even a satire, that human society could be rationally analyzed and planned. Now the idea was being enacted in deadly earnest. The great imperialisms of the twentieth century were reimagining Plato's republic on a scale that would bring peace and happiness—and above all, civil order—to the entire planet. Whether in "great leaps forward" or in finely tuned annual increments, the universal expansion of industrial production and mass consumption now guaranteed an ever-higher standard of living and a longer, healthier life to enjoy it in. Mastery of technology and a sophisticated new social science would permit benevolent state authority to install this perfection everywhere.

There was soon a revulsion from such grandiose and hubristic schemes, which of course entailed new kinds of economic and cultural conquest and coercion, not only in the "underdeveloped" nations of the Southern hemisphere and Asia, but also within the already industrialized and systematized world powers competing for control of future bliss. Resistance to the new imperialism of progress came in many forms, not always perceived as resistance. Ties to traditional values and ways of life remained intact in many places, since even the scorched earth of two world wars could not kill the roots of self-reliance and mutual aid on which human culture ultimately depends. Everywhere, too, there was a new nationalism, which took its energy from a resurgent sense of community and selfhood, especially in the most beleaguered societies and former colonies. But these impulses were quickly commandeered by various ideological elites and put to work to construct states on the Western model, borrowing the infrastructure that invents and manipulates scarcity, defines standards and needs, and harnesses whole peoples to the machinery of production and consumption. Given the nature of the human raw materials, the overnight transformation of traditional cultures into modern states could be only partially accomplished, so that most of these new societies now freakishly resemble a richly armored Don Quixote astride a starving Rocinante. The unassimilable masses are not simply poor and oppressed but have also lost touch with their traditional modes of life. Waves of nativist revival confirm this loss without doing much about it, for modernization is as irreversible as any other form of cultural evolution. No doubt there are viable combinations of old and new taking shape in the caldron, but at the moment the outlook in many parts of the world is either very bleak or very bloody for ordinary people.

The destruction of the social fabric took a different course in the already modernized states. In the United States, for instance, it had begun early in the century with urban growth, the automobile and paving of roads, electronic communications, the incorporation of business, the standardization of goods for mass production, the development of consumer marketing, and other such foretastes of what was to come. Progress became first a serious promise, then suddenly a runaway fact of life. The Great Depression and the Second World War put much of this into a framework of governmental regulation and support since the construing and servicing of people's needs could be practiced on a gigantic scale during these periods of crisis. After the war, with much of the machinery now in place, the final undermining of traditional culture was chiefly engineered by an onslaught of media that promoted new consumerist values and usurped the place of older forms of cultural exchange. Floods of entertainment swamped popular art while the grinding uniformities of mass education deadened sensibility. Survivals from the past were mummified in schools and museums, and the cult of newness and fashion held sway. Although some people obviously gained more than others (most of us were losing a great deal), none of this was the result of any conspiracy. We did it to ourselves.

The sketch of the modern state I am presenting here will be familiar enough to many readers (some will think it a travesty or caricature), but perhaps my emphasis on the Second World

War as the great watershed will seem too much an epochal, not to say apocalyptic, exercise of historical imagination. In attempting to characterize the pivotal moment at the very middle of the twentieth century I am of course describing a set of relations and a condition of life, not presenting a chronology. I am speaking polemically from the vantage point of the end of the century and telescoping processes, which were at work before the century began and which continue to this day, in order to dramatize what I do indeed believe was a greater crisis for the world than the war itself.

It is easy to see what our current problems are—war, poverty, racism, pollution, urban blight and rural decay, consumerism, media swamping, and so on. Although there are always those who believe that solutions lie just around the corner, in enlightened planning and improved technical capabilities, it is more and more apparent that the opposite is the case, and many of our problems stem from putting too much hope, and too much power, in the hands of planners and managers, taking responsibility and decision making away from the people who will actually live with the consequences. It is as simple, and as hard to reform, as that.

The modern state with its centralizing and homogenizing drive has substituted itself for the historical tradition and indigenous culture that people need in order to believe in themselves and be self-reliant. This is at least as true for the imperialist and cosmopolitan West as it is for the recently decolonized parts of the world. The question is not so much one of how to repair or prevent social damage—the poverty and blight and managerial breakdown endemic in almost every major city, East or West, North or South—but rather whether anything can be done to give people back their culture and tradition. That is, how can we reestablish the conditions of social health? Obviously this is not a simple matter of teaching courses in "Western civilization" in the schools, as certain neoconservatives vociferously maintain. But it is also true that in the West the Western tradition is the only tradition that there is. We are shaped by it, whether or not we know it; we need it if we are to have any roots at all, and perhaps the best way to reconnect with it is precisely to examine and criticize it, to take responsibility for its failures and disasters as well as its glories.

The backlash of the sixties revealed the extent of resistance still left in the country but also the weakness and confusion of that resistance. Among the American young in high school and college there was a strong sense of the worthlessness of their education, especially in light of the emptiness and alienation that awaited them in the workaday world, but their moral outrage did not explode until exacerbated by the call to fight in yet another war. Even then their resistance had little weight of traditional values or even firsthand experience behind it. Thus doubly cut loose from the past, many of the student activists never really trusted the intellectuals of the previous generation, most of whom were "part of the problem," as the students' slogans claimed. Their heroes were guerilla fighters in foreign uniforms. Paul Goodman was one of the exceptions, and his appeal to the young was partly based on his puzzling mixture of rebellious rejection of the status quo and attachment to traditional values and knowledge. What was it, the students wondered, that made him keep harping on the importance of the liberal arts and sciences if he agreed with them that the educational system was bankrupt? "It would be woeful," he said, "if the great moments of the spirit did not survive." But he admitted that he did not have a method to teach these moments—for "to know them in our terms, it is first necessary to make the abnegation of learning them in their terms. And the less culture one has to begin with, the harder this is to do."[1]

U.S. youth tended to be divided between consumers of popular media on the one hand and would-be renegades from that prefabricated world on the other, enthusiasts for Eastern religion and civil disobedience, a counterculture with its own drugs and music, its vegetarianism and back-to-the-soil communitarianism. Given the "plastic" future they saw ahead of them, it is not hard to understand the impulse of the young to create alternative institutions, but not much of this effervescence would maintain itself for long. It was easily coopted by the dominant culture, either as style or as menace, and the radical young were too often entranced by their own images on the screen, so that it was hard to separate authentic feeling from role-playing. Some of their pursuits had long traditions in one part of the world or another, but aside from the civil rights movement in the South there was no ongoing body of indigenous cultural experience that could stand up to the spread of the organized system in the United States. Neither in the sixties nor today has there been the necessary coherence of community values or solidarity with past and future generations (that is, culture and tradition) to support even the most obvious remedies for our social ills.

Probably "remedy" is the wrong word, part of the vocabulary of progress and mastery. In Goodman's critique of the organized system and its follies, which is the basis for much of the account I have been offering here, he took pleasure in proposing little makeshift remedies for social problems, but he always insisted that small changes were better than big ones. The main goal should be to diminish anxiety, so that you could once again trust people to know their own good and do for themselves. Radical or conservative, any large-scale schemes for the future made him uneasy. "I am squeamish," he said, "about masses of people enthusiastically building a New Society."[2]

Since Goodman's time, things have gotten steadily worse. In my view the public figures who have taken his place have good reason to be less hopeful than he tended to be, and yet they exemplify the same faith in ordinary people and small truths. I am thinking particularly of a few international prophets and artists like Ivan Illich, or Peter Schumann, of the Bread and Puppet Theater, whose views of traditional culture and the modern state are similar to Goodman's (Illich was profoundly influenced by Goodman)—but whose way of facing into present realities has been rather different. Illich and Schumann have been much more devoted to exploring and revivifying popular wisdom and spiritual knowledge of the past, and perhaps most relevant to our hubris and hastening fate, they solemnly remind us of the necessity of suffering and the Dance of Death, lessons from the Middle Ages and the Black Forest. It is certain that the solutions to our problems must come from a deeper source than social science or systems analysis; changes in attitude and desire do not begin as policies calculated on high. Perhaps a first step toward the modesty and compassion that we lack could be an awareness of our own mortality.

The psychoanalytic movement went through its own version of these midcentury transformations. Sigmund Freud's legacy was built on conceptions of psyche and society that were being undermined by history. The primacy of the father in Freud's theories and the centrality of his borrowings from Western tradition, all the way back to Sophocles' Oedipus and the Hebrew myths of the Garden—none of this could survive the collapse of the Victorian ideal of the family and the accelerating erosion of Western values. Much of this structure of belief and practice had already begun to come apart after the First World War, and one reason Freud lost his most gifted disciples—Carl Jung, Otto Rank, and Wilhelm Reich—was that they intuited the necessity of breaking free from an orthodoxy so thoroughly bound up in the splendid Viennese culture that had flourished at the turn of the century but was now crumbling away. And yet after the Second World War there was a great surge of interest in psychoanalysis, particularly among American intellectuals. Among its causes were the emigration of many refugee analysts to New York at the very moment of U.S. intellectuals' disillusionment with socialism, their great secular faith of the prewar years. And the trauma of the war itself had to be worked through somehow.

Whatever forces may have propelled it, the midcentury wave of psychoanalysis broke and fragmented on the hard reality of the postwar social order that was requiring every institution to make a choice: either become part of the organized system or resist it by offering some alternative way of life. Neo-Freudians like Erich Fromm and Karen Horney, the most widely published and influential of the younger generation of psychoanalysts, led the majority of analysts in developing criteria of "social health" and fostering "adjustment" to the new mass culture with its base in industrial society. Psychoanalysis would contribute its mite to the superstructure of universal schooling, media indoctrination, and expert managing of "the good life."

Of course all the elements of this new social order were put in a framework of representative democracy, in which the individual's freedom and spontaneity were supposedly protected and the interests of society and private persons would completely mesh by virtue of the sensitivity and intelligence of the new social organization. Psychotherapy was for persons who did not fit into this thoroughly rationalized world. In retrospect one is tempted to speak ironically and say that some such project of social hygienics was necessary to make up for the losses: family bonds and neighborhood continuity, patterns of work that gave satisfaction and a sense of worthiness as well as livelihood, enterprise attuned to local tastes and genuine necessities, pleasure and passion embodied in classical and popular arts passed on from generation to generation, religious feeling and faith— in short, most of the fabric of daily life. There was a lot to adjust to in an hour a week of psychotherapy.

Some resistance to the new psychology appeared within the ranks of the old guard itself, partly a clinging to Freud's great edifice, partly a prior commitment to other forms of revisionism, the renegade therapies of Jung, Rank, and Reich. For the most part the struggle went on quietly, often by ignoring the position and arguments of one's opponents; the political implications of the new emphasis on social hygiene were wrapped in silence. The single exception was an article titled "The Political Meaning of Some Recent Revisions of Freud," which appeared in the July 1945 issue of the radical magazine *Politics*. The author was a young anarchist writer of fiction and poetry, Paul Goodman.

Goodman dismissed the pious talk about democracy and individualism in the psychoanalysts' new orthodoxy and pulled out of Erich Fromm's popular book *Escape from Freedom* some sentences that betrayed adjustment psychology's true colors: "The irrational and planless character of society must be replaced by a planned economy that represents the concerted effort of society as such. Society must master the social problem as rationally as it has mastered nature." And why was such a rationalized society necessary? "Only in a planned economy in which the whole nation has mastered the economic and social forces, can the individual share responsibility and use creative intelligence in his work." First, mastery through the system, then freedom within it. Goodman's comment was, "This is simply false," and he accused Fromm of Stakhanovism, the Soviet form of "rationalized labor" under state control. Suspicious as we are today of "mastery" of all sorts, Fromm's argument is likely to raise our hackles, but then it was not always so easy to see through such bland formulations of the good society. In 1945 no one else was challenging this conception of the mission of psychoanalysis, which, as Goodman complained, had no other aim but "the continued and more efficient working, without nervous breakdowns, of the modern industrial system, war and peace."[3]

Against the weight of the neo-Freudian orthodoxy Goodman's article championed the work of Wilhelm Reich, not Reich's current theories of orgone energy but his earlier crusade for an activist psychotherapy, the radicalism of which (contraceptives and sex counseling for working-class youth for example) had gotten him thrown out of both the International Psychoanalytic Association and the Communist Party. In Goodman's view, Reich's position was precisely the opposite of Fromm's: psychotherapy in the current social order had the aim of restoring people "to sexual health and animal spirits," and if it did, they would no longer "tolerate the mechanical and routine jobs they have been working at, but turn (at whatever general inconvenience) to work that is spontaneous and directly meaningful." The ultimate result would be "a different kind of society."[4] Alas, however eager he was to pit such ideas against those of the adjustment psychologists, Goodman's campaign was vitiated by the fact that Reich himself now wanted to steer clear of political controversy for the sake of his new researches. In any case the deeper crisis at midcentury was not really addressed by Reich's theories of Fascism and the "little man"; none of Reich's books, early or late, paid much attention to the breakdown of traditional culture that accompanied, as both cause and effect, the spread of the new social order. Reich was fixated on his own confrontation with the state. As Goodman phrased it in *The Empire City*, a novel he was writing during this period, the dilemma was this: "If one conforms to our society, he becomes sick in certain ways. . . . But if he does *not* conform, he becomes demented, because ours is the only society that there is."[5] Reich's work in the nineteen thirties had dealt with the first horn of this dilemma; his apocalyptic tracts in the forties and fifties, *Listen, Little Man!* and *The Murder of Christ*, would take up the second, upon which he himself was finally impaled when the U.S. Food and Drug Administration had him indicted and sent to prison as a medical quack who violated injunctions against marketing his orgone accumulators.

Insofar as orthodox psychotherapy recognized the dilemma of conformity, it was seen as a problem of the individual neurotic patient, not a crisis of the body politic. But most of the fuss and bother in the profession was merely sectarian—which school or institute was in, which was out. People like Reich were "demented," and those who held similar views about the relations of therapy and politics were regarded with disdain as a lunatic fringe. One of the unquestioned assumptions of the professional consensus at midcentury was that only the Freudian heritage constituted a vital tradition, and each of the revisionist schools claimed to have the true interpretation and appropriate modern emphasis of this tradition. Psychoanalysis was a doctrine of no great age or coherence, already fraying and fragmenting. As in the realm of political economy, there was much lip service to the hallowed past at the same time that serious ties to it were being cut in the name of social science.

The general cultural situation was mirrored in the state of psychoanalysis. Gestalt therapy reflected the desire to make a new synthesis. True enough, a line can be traced from Freud through Reich to Fritz Perls and Paul Goodman, but in fact the theory Goodman constructed in Gestalt therapy's founding text was an extremely eclectic one, drawing on a rich and peculiarly various set of sources. It was a synthesis of different traditions rather than a modern systematic model. The Freudian influence was itself quite variegated and filtered because so many disciples had gone off on their own, like Reich. And there were strands of thought in Gestalt therapy that came from surprisingly far-flung places—Taoist attitudes from ancient China, Enlightenment ideas from Immanuel Kant, modern existentialist conceptions found in the religious thought of Martin Buber, along with an Aristotelian simplicity and clarity. Although these borrowings might prove intellectually satisfying in a number of ways the hybrid could hardly have the authority of familiar experience or faith. Still, it was better than the rootless platitudes of the new adjustment psychology.

The eclecticism of *Gestalt Therapy* was not merely a function of the times; it was also a result of the intellectual character of its two primary authors, Frederick (Fritz) Perls and Paul Goodman. Perls was a magpie if there ever was one. Indeed, his borrowings in an earlier book, *Ego, Hunger and Aggression*, would seem like grasping at straws were it not for his crashing self-assurance. He took bits and pieces from Salamo Friedlaender, Jan Christian Smuts, Alfred Korzybski, Franz Alexander, Jacob Moreno, and an assortment of other theorists with no evident commonality. Only slightly more fundamental in this early attempt at synthesis were the Gestalt psychologists with whom both Perls and his wife Lore Posner (Laura Perls) had worked in Frankfurt in the twenties.

Perls had a marvelous talent for collecting ideas that he could use for his own purposes, but it usually took a while for them to cohere. Some thinkers who at first seemed promising were later discarded (Friedlaender, Smuts, and Korzybski) while others (like Moreno and the Gestalt psychologists) were so totally absorbed they became part of Perls's own thinking—and then they too were no longer mentioned.

Goodman's habits of mind were quite the opposite. Although he was a wide-ranging, cosmopolitan thinker few could rival, what he once fitted into the framework of his learning was rarely dislodged, nor did the relative balance alter very much as he made new discoveries. Even the ideas of Reich and Perls, the enthusiasms of Goodman's middle years, never displaced what he had taken from Freud much earlier. This comprehensiveness and coherence in Goodman's thought influenced Gestalt therapy in two crucial ways.

First of all, despite the eclecticism, which Goodman certainly contributed to, there is a single prominent idea at the center of *Gestalt Therapy*—a view of human nature that can be traced all the way back to Aristotle, with ramifications in both the Gestalt psychologists of Frankfurt and the functionalists who followed William James in America. This central conception (to be considered more thoroughly in a later chapter) reflected Goodman's own philosophical training and his commitment to the Western tradition—the Greeks, the Enlightenment, the natural science of Faraday, Darwin, and Freud. To put it briefly and schematically, Goodman's view assumed that human experience took place at the boundary of organism and environment (conceived as a single whole—of breathing and air, eating and food, seeing and light, and so forth—all of which was full of both novelty and familiarity, as well as pleasure, growth, and animal faith) and that this field of action and function was not only physical but social, with a history and a culture. None of these aspects of the unity of our nature could be understood in isolation from the others or the whole. It was this holistic psychology that refuted the positivist view of human nature that had come to power after the Second World War.

Second, and ultimately based on this understanding of what it is to be human, Goodman did not view psychotherapy as a discipline closed off from the rest of life, just one more professionalized service industry in the planned society. Goodman's experience as an artist gave him his model for the therapist. Filled with love and longing like any other human beings, the artist and the therapist were each somehow balked in the direct expression of such feelings, yet able to make contact with the world, in ways that had their own risks and satisfactions, through the creative imagination and through compassion for others. For the therapist living in the age of the organized system this meant attempting to revivify face-to-face community and to reclaim traditional values, endeavors that were moral and political as much as they were physicianly or pastoral. Goodman's conception of therapy began with the awareness that healing could not occur in isolation from culture and, further, that in our times culture itself was in need of healing.

It was part of the Gestalt attitude to regard each patient as a kind of trainee or apprentice, in a guild of everyday life if not literally in the therapeutic calling, to make community wherever one found oneself, working with the ordinary materials of experience rather than with schemata and protocols. From this close perspective, neurosis could no longer be viewed as a weed patch to be rooted out or treated with chemicals; it too had its ecological meaning and uses in the patient's life. No matter how contorted or misapplied, neurotic behavior always began as the defensive strategy of a creative organism coping with desperate situations. Since the modern world had become a chronic low-grade emergency situation it was not surprising that most patients manifested symptoms of neurotic anxiety, hard to treat in the orthodox therapies but sometimes relieved by Gestalt techniques. The principle of organismic self-regulation, which Perls and Goodman agreed was Reich's most important contribution, provided a rationale for the Gestalt attitude toward neurosis and health. If we remove or relax the unnatural pressures of coercive institutions, and replace them with face-to-face community and mutual aid, the individual organism may heal itself—or at least find its limp and pain easier to bear. "Help each one down his own slope!" was the slogan Goodman proposed in a comic scene in *The Empire City*.[6] He meant this quite seriously. It was a matter of relieving anxiety and nurturing self-awareness and initiative. "Relent! Remedy!" was another motto in Goodman's fiction.[7] We must give the young a chance to grow up without being either adjusted or deformed.

Goodman thought the therapist ought to play an active part in the lives of patients in pursuit of such ends. This was not merely a question of whether to be directive or nondirective during the therapeutic hour; it meant rethinking the whole institutionalized framework—the hour, the couch, the fee, the transference—all the decorums that kept patient and therapist rigidly in their roles. Of course there must be arrangements and routines too. But in Goodman's view psychotherapy could never make up for the loss of community and traditional wisdom, the advice and counsel of friends and neighbors on which people had always relied. Since it was the obvious, normal human inclination to be a friend to the patient, a fellow citizen and comrade, the therapist ought to act on this impulse.

The corollary, equally important in Goodman's communitarian view, was that therapy should not be regarded as a last-minute intervention in the desperate lives of individuals, but rather an ordinary and expected passage at many stages of social development. By the same token Goodman did not envision the end of therapy as a cure in the way that conventional psychoanalysis did. Here is another way in which psychology can be at one with a communitarian politics. The remedy for the abuses of the organized system is not to wrest the reins from one set of leaders and put them in the hands of another, or to reorganize society according to a new ideology of perfection, equally out of touch with how people actually live and work. What is crucial to human welfare is not some standard of living or level of education, industrial base or bureaucratic infrastructure, but simply a citizenry that can rely on its own initiative and resourcefulness, that is not at the mercy of a system outside its real experience but knows itself and its world and can act for its own good, like any other community of creatures on this planet.

This is all straightforward anarchist thinking in the tradition of Peter Kropotkin, Goodman's favorite communitarian philosopher, or alternatively the Jeffersonian heritage of agrarian democracy, applied to the situation at the middle of the twentieth century. Translated into terms relevant to psychotherapy, these anarchist principles are precisely the rationale and aims of Gestalt therapy. Just as the communitarian anarchist has no faith in political rebellion that merely overturns the present regime in order to supplant it with another, so the Gestalt therapist has no expectation that there could be some sort of psychic coup d'état or revolutionary victory that would put the right set of feelings and behaviors in charge of a person's life, somehow liquidating any recalcitrant neurotic tendencies.

Most readers outside the psychotherapeutic profession who have heard of Gestalt therapy will think of Frederick S. Perls as the founder of the movement—Fritz, who gathered disciples wherever he went and was known for his bold, confrontational style in making contact with patients. The same pigeonhole method of history that labels Perls as the founder of Gestalt therapy also has a place for Goodman, the social critic who was making speeches to rebellious students while Perls was performing his theatrical demonstrations at Esalen. Although these identifications are not entirely wrong, they obscure the actual careers of Perls and Goodman, trimming them down to pasteboard celebrities. Even as a simple matter of setting the historical record straight, it is worth challenging these clichés of sixties' nostalgia.

The distinct contributions of Perls and Goodman to Gestalt therapy have been a matter of debate within the movement ever since the beginning. Theirs was a coming together of two very different spirits, and although a true collaboration their work inevitably appealed to different attitudes and traits in their followers. Like most of the great innovators in psychoanalytic history Goodman and Perls were extremely combative geniuses, and it was an extraordinary forbearance that allowed them to work together even for the short time, less than a year, it took to write *Gestalt Therapy*. Probably it was easiest on Goodman, who, for all his egotism and love of polemics, always did his best work with others—so long as he had control of the pen. But Gestalt therapy was a movement as well as a theory, and there were many gifted people who helped make and spread its word. As will become clear in the following pages, Fritz Perls certainly deserved the prestige he enjoyed as the founding father—so long as we are clear about exactly what that entailed. Other figures of the early, formative period—Laura Perls, Paul Weisz, and Elliott Shapiro, to name only the most prominent—also left recognizable marks on the developing body of therapeutic knowledge. But it was Goodman who thought it all through and wrote it down. He was the only one equipped with the learning, the analytic power, and the literary skill to do so.

There were few areas of humanistic concern that Goodman failed to address in his books. His commentaries on the social and political issues of the sixties constituted an extraordinary achievement, but it did not come out of nowhere. It was built on studies in the half-a-dozen separate disciplines of philosophy, aesthetics, psychology, education, politics, and community planning in which he had been working for thirty years. Goodman was a kind of Renaissance man. Late in life he even compared himself to the great sixteenth-century humanist Erasmus—needless to say, an unusual self-image for a social critic in the middle of the twentieth century. It was hard for other scholars to understand why Goodman spread himself so thin rather than settling down to a single specialty, with the reward of a permanent job in a university. And it was equally hard for other social critics to comprehend the exhortations he directed at students, never content with urging them to action but continually bemoaning their lack of regard for their heritage, the Western tradition he had claimed for himself. Indeed, Goodman's life was full of contradictions and unlikely mixtures which, from the right distance, can seem whole and of a piece. When they did not know how to label him at *Time* magazine—"psychologist Goodman"? "author Goodman"?— he suggested "man of letters," an old-fashioned name for an intellectual but one that conveyed precisely what he was.

Paul Goodman was born in 1911, another poor Jewish boy growing up in Manhattan. But his family was not part of the great wave of immigration that made New York City a center of Jewish culture in the early part of this century; on his mother's side the family had been in America for a hundred years. Moreover, the poverty in his family was quite recent. His father had been a successful auctioneer and antique dealer, and the first three children had been raised in style. But by the time Paul was born, his father had run off with his mistress to Buenos

Aires, leaving his wife with nothing but a few pieces of expensive furniture to pawn. She went to work, and her three sisters took turns looking after the children.

To have been "born fatherless" was for Goodman the great shaping circumstance of his life. Because he was a poet and a psychologist, he probably made more of this bad luck than it deserved, but on the whole he did not pity himself. In many ways it was an advantage to grow up without a rival male who at any moment could exert his authority without possibility of appeal. Even the necessity of learning all the rules for himself had its value, as he explained in his journal: "I think back to how, as an adolescent, the others learned to play tennis with correct form, often losing to me, but I could never improve my game, and they did improve. And I am still restive, stubborn, indocile. I am a fatherless boy who cannot go through the regular channels; I am touchy about the regular channels. But I do greedily absorb scraps of information that are dropped, and I use them my own way. Sometimes I end up well-trained; yes, and I even act with the confidence of being trained!"[8] It is tempting to believe that Goodman's peculiar mix of respect for tradition and passion for the here and now grew out of this fatherless childhood, always looking for a patrimony he could claim yet unwilling to waive a particle of his autonomy. It made him especially sensitive to the crisis our society would face at midcentury.

From the very first moments of infancy he was surrounded by older women who pampered and indulged him but among whom his father was a forbidden topic, not just absent but banished, blotted out. And his siblings obviously knew some secret that they did not want to talk about. The past was a blank full of mystery and shame, as irresistible as the facts of life, which the adults also seemed to want to hide from him.

Moreover, although he was certainly well mothered by many loving hands, there were enough disruptions and dislodgings to keep him sharply alert to his world and anxious whenever signs of change appeared. His mother came and went, the cycle of aunts into whose arms he would be handed was not without its slippage, and the family abode itself was shifted once, twice, three times a year until he was ten. This made him happy and bright-eyed but also watchful and not completely trusting.

By the time he entered school Goodman had, in effect, become an only child. One of his brothers had died, and his other siblings, seven and ten years older, had already entered the adult world. Though they were both remarkably intelligent, neither Alice nor Percival attended high school, whereas little Paul, a smiling, confident child, was encouraged to make the most of his braininess. As he grew older and showed how clever he was, it was not just a matter of pleasing his teachers. He pleased himself and delighted in the world he found at his disposal, people and ideas and art. By the time he was seven his big sister was already saving his poems. He always led his class, accumulating medals for his proficiency in languages. He had the best free public education available anywhere in the world, first in the "model" elementary school attached to the municipal teacher's college, then in Manhattan's public prep school, Townsend Harris Hall, and finally in the City College of New York.

This was the route to success for the poor but bright boys of the city, especially the Jews whose parents spoke Yiddish and lived on the lower East Side. Most of these youngsters wanted to be professionals—doctors, lawyers, teachers—but Goodman was different. Although his family was also poor and Jewish, it was not marked by ghetto values or ambitions. True, his mother hoped he might become a rabbi, and like every Jewish boy of twelve, he studied Hebrew for his bar mitzvah, but his exposure to the cosmopolitan culture of the "Empire City" kept him out of any narrow scholarly tunnel, Talmudic or academic. For a while he imagined himself a philologist because of his love of Latin, then he switched to philosophy in admiration of City College's most famous teacher Morris Raphael Cohen. But his classmates were right when they voted him "best poet." Through it all he took for granted that he was a true heir to the Western tradition of Europe and the ancient civilizations of the Mediterranean, as well as a native-born American whose great grandparents had settled here when Thomas Jefferson and John Adams were still alive.

By the time he graduated from college, Goodman had simply fallen in love with life and learning. His friends remembered him at twenty as a pink-cheeked, beaming comrade, always at their disposal for a long walk, happily discoursing in the sunshine about Aristotle and Augustine, Cocteau and Tu Fu, Trotsky and Freud. Every Saturday night a half-dozen of his closest friends gathered at his apartment, where his sister Alice played Wendy to his Peter Pan, serving "the boys" coffee and cake at midnight—and cleaning up the next morning. There were sometimes young women too—"dates"—but fundamentally it was a male world. They called themselves jocularly the Wadsworth Terrace Social and Literary Society, and several of them wrote short stories which they read aloud to one another. But they also played bridge, went to concerts, talked baseball and politics. They were precocious, irreverent kibitzers on all the world. Not quite left-wingers in the usual sense—indeed, one of them claimed to be a monarchist— they nonetheless argued about Communism as all young intellectuals did in the thirties, and some of them had friends who were to fight in the Spanish Civil War. They watched the rise of Fascism apprehensively, but considered themselves internationalists rather than patriots of any cause or country. It was still possible to believe in Western civilization.

Although they all regarded Goodman as their genius, none of them became disciples—that sort of thing came at a later phase of his life. It redounded to their credit that he was already publishing in one of the grander "little magazines," *Symposium.* He had barely graduated when the editors accepted two essays he had written—on Frank Lloyd Wright and Le Corbusier— with coaching from his brother Percy, who was just back from Paris and beginning his own career as an architect. A story was accepted too, and it won an honorable mention in one of the short-story annuals. Clearly he was going to be an important writer. Of course these publications paid next to nothing. It was a good thing Alice had a job, for this was 1931, and the country was already deep in economic depression. Their mother had moved on—they called her "the bourgeois gypsy" now—and Alice was the breadwinner. Through her job in the New York story department of one of the Hollywood studios, she got her little brother piecework as an out-reader, providing little synopses of French novels that might serve as film scenarios, at $5 a novel. A couple of these would pay the phone and light bills, his share of household expenses. After graduating he had cheerfully decided not to try for work as a teacher in the public schools as many of his classmates did. Although he had a strong pedagogic impulse and had himself been a model pupil, he recoiled from the institutional regimen.

More regretfully he faced the fact that he could not go on to graduate school, as some of his friends had done, on fellowships or with family support. And when his chum Benjamin Nelson, now studying medieval history at Columbia University, told him of a philosophy instructor who was "doing great things" with Spinoza, Goodman could not resist. Soon he was auditing Richard McKeon's courses, openly a nonpaying student who nonetheless spoke up in class and even wrote papers for his new mentor. He expanded his studies to include other professors, who were equally welcoming to a bright young fellow obviously there for the sheer love of learning. From now on this would be the way he approached most institutions, ignoring the red tape and regular channels and trying to make immediate contact with the people actually at work there.

Meanwhile his brother had been invited to contribute to *Trend*, "a magazine of the arts," and soon both Goodmans were on the staff, Percy as architecture editor and Paul in charge of cinema, writing a series of essays on film theory. Goodman continued to turn out a new story every month, great quantities of poetry, and some plays, including an imitation of Japanese Noh drama, which *Trend* published in 1934. That same year one of his friends got him a summer job as dramatics counselor in a Zionist boys camp in Vermont; it did not pay much, but he enjoyed adapting Shakespeare and Molière for this audience, staging them alongside his own plays for children.

The camp job lasted several summers and was significant for him in many ways. The novel he wrote about it, *The Break-Up of Our Camp*, shows him struggling with his increasing sense of being an outsider after all in the world he had earlier taken for granted. One aspect of this alienation, though he barely touched on it in his novel, had to do with his homosexuality. As a teenager Goodman had discovered that he was attracted to both boys and girls, but he was very anxious with the opposite sex. If we look for reasons, his having been raised entirely by women probably had a lot to do with it, and especially his closeness to his sister, who acted so many roles in his life. That was his own view of the matter at any rate. Although he had not quite come to the point of open talk about these feelings he was writing love poems to young men and showing them to some of his friends.

Several of his fellow counselors at camp were aware that he was bisexual, and he seems to have discussed his "Greek" attitude with at least one of them, urging the view that the pedagogic impulse was naturally grounded in eros, whether or not it surfaced in particular cases.[9] Why else would a teacher devote his life to his students if he did not love them? Twenty years later, when he asked himself similar questions, he added another level of interpretation for his own case: the young toughs he liked best seemed to him "cast off" or "orphaned," and he wanted to guide and champion them as a way of denying or repairing "my own fatherless state," as he put it in his journal.[10]

Whatever his motives, Goodman was now thinking through his philosophy of education, ideas that would also appear later in his practice of psychotherapy. Despite his own lucky history as a bookish youngster, Goodman felt that schooling more often smothered than encouraged curiosity and learning. He preferred a peripatetic model of education, using the actual city or countryside as subject matter, in the style of Socrates—or the Boy Scouts. It was in the nature of the species that the young were adventurous and inquiring, and except in dangerous or emergency situations, the best thing adults could do was to stay out of the way. "What I envisage," says his spokesman in *The Empire City*, "is groups of half a dozen, starting out at nine or ten years old, roving the Empire City with a shepherd empowered to protect them, and accumulating experiences tempered to their powers."[11] In the sixties these notions would evolve into the storefront mini-school, and the free university *studium generale* organized outside the campus walls by students themselves.

In 1936 Goodman's own teaching career took an academic turn when he was invited by Richard McKeon, who had left Columbia and become a Dean at the University of Chicago, to come and work in the "great books" program at Chicago. While teaching he could also take a few courses and write a dissertation for his doctorate. This was a fateful move, less for its career implications than for its domestic consequences, leaving the home his mother and then his sister had made for him for twenty-five years. Goodman seems always to have felt a bit desperate without some matriarchal base. During his first year in Chicago he alternated between bouts of homesickness and increasingly Ishmaelitish behavior, as if he were testing the limits. Then he met and fell in love with his first wife, a new center to whirl around. By the end of his three years in the Midwest he had an infant daughter as well, reconstituting his family but himself now the father rather than the youngest child. These new and deep attachments did not put an end to his promiscuous homosexual life. He settled once again into the pattern that went back to his childhood: a domestic hearth that was female dominated, stable, and monogamous, balanced against boyish exploits and homosexual adventuring away from home, sometimes comradely but more often casual and anonymous. This depth of commitment satisfied his bohemian wife, as did the common-law marriage bonds they entered simply by speaking of one another as husband and wife.

The university was not so accommodating however. At the beginning of the fall semester of 1939 Goodman was told to keep his sexual cruising off the campus. When he refused, he was fired, though his mentor arranged a small grant on which he could support his family while writing his dissertation. Goodman was now free to return to Manhattan, for which he was still quite homesick. He took the occasion as an opportunity and began once again to think of himself as an artist more than a scholar. He had never stopped writing poems, stories, and plays while turning out seminar papers and learned treatises; now, while cranking out his thesis, he began a new novel—the first volume of *The Empire City*, a kind of homecoming celebration. His wife's mother sent her a little money every month, and they managed to stretch the $1,000 from his grant for a couple of years. Goodman tried for a teaching job, but his credentials never outweighed the personal impression he always seemed to make on the authorities, whether or not he combed his hair and wore his tie. But no matter, he had at last been "discovered" by the avant-garde. James Laughlin, the youthful publisher of William Carlos Williams and Ezra Pound, began to include him in the New Directions annuals, and the liveliest of the little magazines at that time, *Partisan Review*, also opened its doors to him.

Although his literary career looked promising, with his new novel and a book of Noh plays due out early in 1942, the bombing of Pearl Harbor and the U.S. entry into the Second World

War guaranteed there would be few buyers for imitations of Japanese drama or novels prophesying disaster for the capitalist state. The patriotic fervor soon reached even the avant-garde, and since he would not muffle his pacifism, Goodman suddenly found himself blacklisted at the *Partisan Review*, whose editors led the way in what looked like a general Goodman boycott. He was broke, could not even get hack work, and to top it off his marriage was breaking up. For a while he was literally homeless, till he finally found a job in a progressive boarding school outside New York City, where he could live free and have his daughter Susan, now four years old, with him. But this did not last either. By the end of the year he had been fired for seducing his students.

Despite such disasters, so often his own fault, Goodman maintained his cheerful spirits, and although some people found his principles mere self-indulgence and his behavior disgusting, his friends stuck by him. He was beginning to attract disciples now, young people who regarded his troubles with conventional authority as part of his appeal. But for Goodman the previous few years had been unnerving. As usual when there was no domestic shore in his life, he had been swimming out of his depth. It was not surprising, therefore, when he set up house-keeping again, with a young woman he had been courting in the midst of his hectic amours with the "lads" of the senior class he was teaching. Sally Ducksten was a secretary at the school, in her early twenties, herself fatherless and raised in Catholic boarding schools. Although not the bohemian type his first wife had been, Sally was at least as ready for the kind of life Goodman had to offer, a woman of independent spirit and a fierce sense of morality and justice. They moved into a Manhattan apartment, along with Susan, in March 1945.

At this point the long-awaited arm of the state fell on Goodman's shoulder. That spring the military requirements of the gigantic U.S. offensives in both Europe and the Pacific had pushed the Selective Service System to begin drafting fathers. Goodman got his notice. He expected to be thrown in jail, where many of his anarchist friends already were. Even though the war was obviously drawing to a close the organized system could not allow anyone to fall through the holes. As Goodman put it in *The Empire City*, the authorities did not approve of people who were "alive without a registered footprint, learned without a school record, well and fed without a security number, working without papers, natively pious without the oath, scheduled for death not in the army."[12] He made trouble at the interview, lighting up his pipe in the forbidden area, talking when he was supposed to keep quiet, haranguing the doctors and psychiatrists about pacifism and militarism—blatantly a "stinker case"—but what finally got him off was bad eyes and piles. He was 4F.

This ordeal over, things began to brighten up. He and Sally began thinking of having a baby. It would mean giving up her job for a while, but their rent was only $18 a month, and a bit of money was coming in now from Goodman's writing. He had found a publisher, Vanguard, willing to risk printing a book of his stories, then the following year a new installment of *The Empire City*, and in 1947 a psychoanalytic study of Kafka. Though each new book flopped worse than the last, Vanguard kept trying. It did not help that his enemies at *Partisan Review* took special pains to attack him in nasty reviews and what Goodman called a "whispering campaign," directed as much against his sexual behavior as his politics. But other editors were beginning to accept his work again now that the war was over.

His book on community planning, written with his brother, was finally being published by the University of Chicago, and one way or another he was collecting a following, not just among the anarchists whose weekly meetings he attended but also the poets and theater people of Greenwich Village. When his wife gave birth to a baby boy, Goodman was able to get a job in the night school at New York University, teaching Kafka to veterans on the GI Bill. These promising signs notwithstanding, his friends noticed that Goodman's face was not so happy any more. He looked as utterly boyish as ever, but the frown on his brow resulted from more than nearsightedness, and what had once been a cocky tone in his voice was beginning to sound like arrogance to some ears. A sourness was creeping into his disposition. Was there a way of remedying any of this that did not depend on the world itself changing?

The hard knocks of the war years had shaken Goodman's self-confidence. Now he was having a fresh start, and he needed to think through his own behavior if he did not want to repeat the same round of hopes and disappointments. He began a long and painful exploration of his own psyche, in order to understand just how much in his recent catastrophes was his own doing, not entirely a matter of forces over which he had no control, nor purely a matter of principled action on his own part, but also the result of willful, self-thwarting folly. It took considerable strength as well as a sense of desperation to face questions like this. Goodman was now thirty-five years old, at the height of his creative powers, with a large body of work already behind him. His domestic center was once again established, less confidently perhaps than in his youth or in his first marriage, but as it turned out on the firmest foundations—that were to last for the rest of his life. The birth of his son, Mathew, was a crucial event. It confirmed his ties to Sally, who was now calling herself Sally Goodman, and it also brought him into sudden and surprising confrontation with himself, his own infancy, and especially his own fatherlessness. Here were the earliest sources of his strengths and weaknesses, all now put as questions.

Goodman's interest in psychotherapy had begun with a general appetite for learning in his youth. He read Freud and Freud's followers at the same time he was reading Aristotle and Kant, Peter Kropotkin and John Dewey, and by the time he was thirty his thinking was saturated with psychoanalytic concepts. With his discovery of Wilhelm Reich in 1945 there came a dramatic crystallization of all the reading and thinking that had gone before. As he later put it, psychoanalysis became his religion, as much as he had one.[13] At the moment in time we are now considering, his discovery of Reich was to give Goodman the occasion and methods for the greatest effort of soul-work he had yet made in life.

Surprisingly, Reich had invited Goodman out to his laboratory in Queens, and Goodman hoped that the great man had "some task for me," perhaps some commission to explore the bearing of Reich's work on politics. Reich's actual command was just the opposite—to stop coupling Reich's name with the anarchists, as Goodman had done in his article in *Politics*—but this only confirmed Goodman's opinion that there was something worth doing here.[14] As usual he found himself going against the grain. Soon he had arranged weekly sessions with one of Reich's current disciples, Alexander Lowen, from whom he could learn Reich's basic vegetotherapeutic techniques. Whatever the real significance of this decision Goodman preferred not to consider himself in treatment with Lowen, and he refused to cooperate with him in going through properly sequenced work on the muscular armor. Instead he regarded the Reichian approach as an interchangeable calisthenics, a set of exercises which could be learned and applied separately to particular problems of character. He thought of them as analogous to Yoga exercises, and he practiced them according to his own regimen, coupled with traditional psychoanalytic methods such as free association, dream analysis, and the interpretation of early childhood memories. His aim was to put himself through a "self-analysis," in imitation of Freud himself.[15]

It was no humble gesture of discipleship thus to venture in the footsteps of the master. Goodman was seeking his place in the lineage, "Charcot to Freud, Freud to Reich, and so forth." Goodman wanted to be the "so forth." But that ambitious formulation was written in his journal ten years later when in fact he had some claim to a place on the ladder.[16] Although he may have had some notion of becoming a therapist after the call from Reich, the notes he kept during his self-analysis give no hint of any such motive nor do they betray an ambition to master his masters and assume the theoretic mantle. When he began his self-analysis in 1946 it was with much fear and trembling, and in search of solutions to his own dilemmas, though he may have told himself he was seeking his patrimony. He was acting on a murky but persistent intuition that unless he made some great effort to change his character, he would never be happy or find his true calling.

After a period of about half a year Goodman thought he knew enough of the Reichian techniques to discontinue his sessions with Lowen. The self-analysis went forward without any apparent change in direction for another four or five months, and then he added a new component to the routine of exercises, free association, and analysis of dreams and memories. He began a novel based on the events at the progressive school that had led to his being fired. This was *Parents' Day*, a first-person narrative only thinly disguised as fiction, in which Goodman asks himself what exactly in his character and behavior was healthy and justified, what was neurotic and sociopathic. The book slowly took over the energies of the self-analysis, and he only intermittently returned to the Reichian regimen he had followed so many months. Probably the shift made therapeutic sense simply as a way of breaking out of various psychic stalemates that were developing in the self-analysis. It also showed how thoroughly Goodman's art had come to be his way of dealing with every crisis in life. A half dozen years earlier, when his first marriage had begun to show signs of strain, he had written another novel, *Don Juan; or, The Continuum of the Libido*, in which he had attempted to examine his situation in symbolic and even mythological forms, and this novel, too, had become a kind of self-analysis, dependent on conceptions he found in Otto Rank rather than in Freud or Reich, but no less a blend of art and psychotherapy than that we see in *Parents' Day*. No matter how intrigued and convinced by the insights of psychoanalysis, Goodman was before all else an artist, and especially in analyzing his own case he felt more at home with the techniques of fiction. Ironically this was a bias that fate would soon challenge.

Goodman's revived hopes for acceptance of his literary works were ill-founded. Either he was still doing something that readers would not tolerate, or public taste had been so completely captured by the popular formulas of Madison Avenue and Hollywood that there was no longer any room for serious art, even in the so-called avant-garde world. No doubt these were aspects of a single cultural impasse. However it was to be accounted for, Goodman's books would not sell. Vanguard gave up, and the publisher wrote him a sorrowful letter rejecting *The Dead of Spring*, the third volume of his ongoing epic of *The Empire City*, to which he had returned after finishing *Parents' Day*. Although he could still place his shorter pieces, no one wanted his full-length works. New Directions had been promising to do a collection of his stories for almost a decade, and now Laughlin decided to honor the commitment, bringing out *The Break-Up of Our Camp* in a little edition of 2,200 copies in 1949. But Goodman was reduced to self-publication for *The Dead of Spring*, which he considered his single best book up to that time. He sent 200 postcards to his friends, asking for a $5 subscription for two copies of the book, which was then printed on the job press at David Dellinger's pacifist commune in New Jersey.

As for *Parents' Day*, one of Goodman's old friends from the thirties also had a job press, and he offered to print it at his own risk. This openly homosexual book became a kind of underground classic in the gay community, but since there were only 500 copies published, and most of those unsold, its reputation was a good deal wider than its actual circulation. Something like the same situation was becoming the story of Goodman's entire career. As he put it a few years later in his journal, "I am the most widely unknown writer who is yet so intensely known and respected by a few."[17]

Discouraged by such facts, Goodman wrote the long essay "On Being a Writer" for his fortieth birthday, in 1951, once again asking why he was such a failure and concluding with the following ominous sentences: "I have begun to invade the area of writing with my guilt, fear of consequences because it is *my* action. Therefore, just in order to be safe, I must write more effectually or not at all." He also said, "I have the feeling that I am inhibiting myself from writing a major work. . . . I have been telling myself that I am waiting for others to commission me, to mobilize me to action; but this craving for 'external' authorization has in fact lapsed along with 'my own' wants. . . . I am at a loss, in our great city, how to do anything at all that could make an immediate difference in our feeling and practice (and so in my own feeling and practice). Therefore I have ceased to want anything, I do not know what we want."[18]

It took ten years for Goodman to find the answer to his questions about what would make a difference in his own situation and in the larger society. But when it finally came, in the form of *Growing Up Absurd*, the book that made him famous, he had his audience at last, not as an artist but as a social critic. After 1960 Goodman found that his hectoring tone and rebellious thoughts were no longer intolerable to editors and readers. During the next dozen years he could barely keep up with the demand, more than a book a year, and scores of shorter pieces. Goodman had gone from pariah to cynosure overnight.

This transformation was in large part a function of the times. The sixties brought new issues forward and a new generation of readers. Suddenly people seemed to think it was possible to *do* something about poverty and injustice, racism and urban blight, imperialism and militarism. When Goodman pointed to the organized system as the cause of so much of this, the young immediately understood what he was talking about.

Most of the intellectuals of Goodman's generation had abandoned any such ideas or hopes at the beginning of the Second World War and were now merely molting bohemians, radicals with clipped wings flocking to perches in the universities. It was not so surprising if the young ignored their chirps in favor of Goodman's cawing and caviling.

But Goodman's new influence was not entirely a result of the changing mood of the country. He too had changed and had paid a price. Although he continued to write poems, after 1960 he essentially gave up fiction except for one last novel of self-analysis, *Making Do*, which was as much social criticism as it was anything else. To a large extent the abandonment of fiction (and drama) had started long before, at the time he wrote his gloomy essay "On Being a Writer," but it was not really a matter of conscious decision so much as a shift of the imaginative balance in his character, brought on by self-analysis. All through the fifties a gradual realignment was taking shape. In the terms set by his 1951 essay, one could say that he was devoting more and more of his attention to "what we want," and less and less to his own fantasies of desire, "what I want."

Another way of putting this alteration would be to say that Goodman had learned patience and compassion, and could now address his readers in ways they found inspiriting rather than insulting, because he had practiced psychotherapy for ten years among groups of young people, precisely the constituency that would buy his books and take fire from his ideas. His efforts to hear and help others did not allay his bitterness and carping but made it less personal and self-pitying. For a long time Goodman had had his little band of disciples, who recognized his irk as theirs, and whose champion he was. Next his patients joined this cohort, more numerous and less like a coterie. Finally, in the sixties, the young in general were drawn to his banner, along with many others. His angry diatribes, like the famous "Causerie at the Military-Industrial" delivered to the bigwigs in Washington, were no longer directed *at* his fellow citizens but spoke *for* them. Meanwhile he more and more adopted another stance, sweetly reasonable, when he addressed the anonymous public in his books and articles. But there were no more stories.

Here then is Paul Goodman at midcareer, or more exactly at midlife, facing the choice between careers—and here is his world also come to a crisis point at midcentury. It was a moment of darkness rather than light, and the paths chosen were not entirely what they seemed. But they led to the present, and their lessons are for us, so let us now look more closely and try to understand them.

CHAPTER TWO

Fritz and Lore Perls

ONE DAY IN THE SPRING of 1946 Holley Cantine and Dachine Rainer, editors of the anarchist magazine *Retort*, were sitting in a cafeteria near Pennsylvania Station, deep in a discussion of world politics with Holley's friend Harry Paxton Howard, a veteran China hand, whose Shanghai-dated byline was familiar in the Western press.[1] A man at a nearby table, pudgy, balding, with round-rimmed glasses that gave him an owlish look, was eavesdropping. Finally he stepped over and asked in a faintly belligerent German accent if he might join them. He had recently arrived from South Africa, where issues of colonialism and revolution were of great moment. Precisely what the little group now talked about is lost to memory. It must have been apparent that apart from his personal experiences in Germany and South Africa, the stranger was not so interested in politics after all. Indeed, the contrast between him and his new acquaintances was striking in every way. His aspect was dignified and his manners courtly, whether compared with the New York chatter of Dachine Rainer or the bearded taciturnity of Holley Cantine. His coat and tie were thoroughly conventional, whereas Cantine and Rainer were dressed as bohemians. A faded pair of farmer's bib overalls covered Holley's solemn skinniness wherever he went, whether visiting his anarchist friends in the city or pumping his foot-powered printing press in the woods.

Today, as it happened, Cantine was in Manhattan not for conviviality but to go to court. Rainer's ex-boyfriend Moheep, a Muslim revolutionary from India, had planted a gun in her apartment after discovering that she was going off to live in the Catskills with Holley. They were on trial for violating the Sullivan Act. Perhaps they mentioned that Dwight Macdonald had gone bail for them, and the stranger had remarked that copies of *Politics*, Macdonald's magazine, could be purchased in Johannesburg. However it happened, the train of conversation led to a question about one of the regular contributors to *Politics* whom the stranger had hoped to meet in New York, but whose name was not in the phone book. Did they know anything about the author of a recent article on Wilhelm Reich, one Paul Goodman?

Of course they knew him, and they immediately led Perls over to Goodman's apartment on Ninth Avenue, just a few blocks away. Goodman was not at home that day, but soon afterwards the stranger knocked at his door again—and so he met Fritz Perls, with whom he was to collaborate on the chief theoretical work of a new kind of psychotherapy, *Gestalt Therapy*.

Frederick S. Perls was already in his fifties when he came to New York. A German Jew who had known or studied with the first generation of Freudians, Perls and his wife Lore Posner had spent the Hitler years in South Africa, where they had formed an institute of psychoanalysis and developed an increasingly unconventional therapeutic practice. When Jan Christian Smuts

41

announced his retirement as prime minister, the Perls could see a right-wing regime in the offing, with unpredictable consequences, and so after a dozen years trying to make themselves at home in exile they decided that they must find a new sanctuary. This time, however, they could make their move more methodically—no need to slip across the border with 100 marks hidden in a cigarette lighter, as Fritz had done in April 1933.[2]

When he joined the interesting conversation at the next table in the spring of 1946 Fritz was reconnoitering the American possibilities at leisure while Lore waited with the children in Johannesburg. Looking up Goodman was part of this reconnoitering. A South African bookstore happened to carry *Politics*, and Perls had read Goodman's piece on Reich and the neo-Freudians with great interest. Since he himself was more or less in the Reichian camp, he put Goodman high on his list of likely friends and allies in his newly adopted country. What they discussed at this early stage can only be surmised. Two more cocksure personalities never existed, not even during the wars of psychoanalytic succession, and neither of them ever quite trusted or warmed to the other. Even so they must have quickly realized how much they could learn from their exchanges.

Perls had actually spent several years in therapy with Wilhelm Reich, just before they both fled the Nazis, and this was during the period when Reich was first devising the system of exercises aimed at breaking through what he would later call the "motor armor," patterns of neurotic tension and constraint embedded in the musculature itself.[3] Of all Freud's disciples Reich was probably the most ingenious in the realm of practical methodology, which was why he was put in charge of the technical seminar of the Vienna Psychoanalytic Society, before the break with his mentor over politics, and Perls too had a flair for technique that would be his trademark in days to come. In 1932 Reich was still speaking of his overall method as "character analysis." The "exercises" he was trying out on Perls and other patients were designed to be integrated in that method, though in fact they looked forward to the period when Reich would develop a more directly and exclusively biological means of freeing biological energy. At this moment of transition in the early thirties, vegetotherapy was a term not yet invented, nor were the exercises yet part of a systematic approach. "Concentration therapy" was one name Reich considered, and Perls borrowed it for his own technique during the following decade. Perls had already begun to write about the "concentration exercises" he was experimenting with, and when he came knocking on Goodman's door, he probably had a copy of the 1942 Durban edition of *Ego, Hunger and Aggression* under his arm, the first extension of Reich's ideas to be published since Reich himself had abandoned psychoanalysis for the orgone and orgonomy.

Like Goodman the preceding year, Perls now had *his* encounter in the laboratory on Long Island, where he was shocked by the changes in the fiery crusader for sexual freedom he had known in Berlin. Exile had been hard on Reich. "He was blown up like an immense bullfrog, his facial eczema had become more intense. His voice boomed at me pompously, asking me incredulously: 'You have not heard of my discovery, the orgone?'"[4] Apparently that avant-garde bookstore in Johannesburg did not carry the *International Journal for Sex-Economy and Orgone-Research*.

Neither Perls nor Goodman had any interest in the orgone. For them Reich's crucial work had been his critique of Freud, developed in an avalanche of books and monographs in the thirties, that shifted the therapeutic ground away from the repressed desires and traumas of childhood and toward ongoing habits and mores instead, toward the persistent rigidities in the patient and his body, and also in society, with emphasis on the *actual*-neuroses rather than the *psycho*-neuroses. Goodman was particularly admiring of Reich's "Sex-Pol" activism, at its height when Perls was in therapy with Reich, and Goodman would have been eager for anecdotes of that extraordinary experiment in mass sex education among the working-class youth of industrial Germany. For his part, Perls was more interested in Reich's technical innovations, the "practical yoga" that Goodman had been learning from Reich's trainee Alexander Lowen, and he would have wanted to hear all about the "orgasm reflex" and the dramatic "breakthrough" phenomena of vegetotherapy.

Goodman and Perls had much to tell each other, then, from their different vantage points on the Reichian trajectory. Perhaps most important to them both was Reich's axiom of "organismic self-regulation," the notion, as they explained in *Gestalt Therapy*, "that it is not necessary deliberately to schedule, to encourage or inhibit, the promptings of appetite, sexuality, and so forth, in the interests of health or morals. If these things are let be, they will spontaneously regulate themselves, and if they have been deranged, they will tend to right themselves."[5] Taken seriously, such a principle would have enormous consequences for every aspect of psychotherapeutic theory and practice, especially if extended, as Goodman insisted it must be, to "all the functions of the soul, including its culture and learning, its aggression and doing the work that is attractive"—that is, the engagement in life and the world that gives self-regulation its scope and meaning.

Perls and Goodman agreed too on Reich's deficiencies. His current passion for the orgone was a disappointment to them, though they could not take it seriously enough to criticize. Goodman had dinner with Reich's disciple and translator Theodore Wolfe at Percy Goodman's apartment, but how was one to answer when "solemnly assured . . . that the Orgone is what people have meant by God"?[6] Some years later he would write agnostically of Reich's "dumb-bunny" experiments, comparing him to Volta: "I hope he did discover a new form of cosmic energy accumulable in his boxes!"[7]

In effect Reich had left the field to them, and it was only necessary to clear the way to their own higher ground. In *Ego, Hunger and Aggression* Perls had already proposed "trying to develop systematically" the legacy of concentration therapy while at the same time he castigated Reich for using the technique in a "bullying" fashion, "making the patient swallow ideas which he cannot digest, artificial attitudes and actions are induced instead of an organic development of the personality." Yet it was better than orthodox psychoanalysis, which "pretends to demand nothing from the patient, but actually demands the impossible—namely, the compliance with the basic rule [of no censoring] and the acceptance of [the analyst's] interpretations. My advice," Perls concluded, "is to deal not with the Unconscious but, as far as possible, with the Ego."[8] It was these two aims, to refine Reich's early technical ideas and to provide a new account of the ego, unencumbered by the unconscious, that developed over the next four years into Gestalt therapy.

It may be well to say immediately that Perls's accusation of therapeutic bullying was just as applicable to his own practice as to Reich's, especially in his old age when he developed a demonstration technique for training groups and weekend workshops that came to be called guerilla therapy. Among his peers he was considered a brilliant improviser and technician but too much enamored of the instant cure and without patience for the long haul of self-discovery that is at the heart of Gestalt therapy. Even in his first years in New York Perls's therapeutic rough-and-tumble kept his patients on their toes. One of his earliest patients was Isadore From, who would afterwards become a therapist himself and who trained many others in a long career. From reported two such lively exchanges from their first work together: "Once he asked me did I ever have sexual fantasies about him, which kind of startled me. I got up from the couch, turned around and looked at him and said, 'No, you are much too old and far too ugly.' And he said, 'Good, good.' The second was, I had been telling him what I thought would shock anybody. He said nothing. That made me angry. I gave him more shocking details, and he said nothing. Then I angrily threw an ash tray at him and missed him. And he said, 'Good, good, good.' I've thought about that. I think he may have said 'Good' because I missed him."[9]

Another early patient was Jerry Raphel, a gifted young man who later acted in a number of Living Theatre productions, including Goodman's plays. When he came to Perls in the late forties and explained his symptoms, Perls said, "*Ja, Ja,* we can get rid of that in a couple of months. But," he wagged his finger at Raphel, "this is only a symptom. I think what you want is a character analysis. *That* will take six months"—precisely the Reichian attitude, terminology, and timetable.[10]

Perls himself loved to tell stories of his "miracle cures," like the case in South Africa that resulted in his "first recognition" as a therapist:

A soldier suffered from big welts all over his body. As
a last resort he was sent to me. . . . This soldier had a
deep despair in his eyes and was somewhat dazed. In the
army, of course, we had no time to fool with psychoanalysis or any other extensive form of psychotherapy. I
put him under pentothal and learned that he had been
in a concentration camp. I spoke German to him and
led him back to his moments of despair and removed the
crying block. He really cried his heart out, or shall we
say he cried his skin out. He woke up in a state of confusion, and then he really woke up and had a typical *satori*
experience of being completely and freely in the world.
At last he had left the concentration camp behind and
was with us. The welts disappeared.[11]

Of course Perls knew that such cures were common enough
among hysterics—Freud used to dissolve a conversion symptom
of this sort every time he saw Frau Cäcilie M—and Perls also
understood the importance of dealing with material brought to
the surface by means of his technical feats. But his fascination
with technique, including drugs (sodium pentothal, nitrous
oxide, and later LSD), combined with his own restless showmanship and audience-hunger, was always greater than his
interest in his patients themselves.

The psychoanalytic community regarded him as either a
charlatan or a wizard. He was cold-shouldered by orthodox
practitioners from the moment he arrived—his admiration for
Reich would have been enough to guarantee this even without
the criticisms he had made of Freud in *Ego, Hunger and Aggression*—but he had an entrée to the circles of Freudian revisionists through his former contacts in Frankfurt and Berlin. In

particular, the followers of psychiatrist Harry Stack Sullivan sent him patients and even wanted him as a training analyst at the William Alanson White Institute; his foreign medical degree was not valid in the United States, however, and they urged him to go back to school for an American diploma, the farthest thing from his intentions.

Perls had been led to believe that the psychoanalytic profession was crowded in New York, and he spent some months trying to begin a practice in New Haven, Connecticut, instead; but he belonged in Manhattan, and Erich Fromm finally convinced him to give it a try. In three weeks he was established, albeit with several patients like From and Raphel who were penniless students. "He told me that he couldn't take me on," From recalled, "as he needed full-paying patients at that time. He told me I might come back later. I remember that I said, with more courage than I might have had at that moment—'I CAN'T WAIT!' He told me that I would have to wait. Then, somehow, he asked me what I was studying. Out of my bag of studies I mentioned phenomenology. Whereupon he said, 'Lie down on the couch.'"[12]

As From's German was minimal he had read very little of the phenomenologist philosopher Edmund Husserl, but he had taken a course in phenomenology at the New School and realized that he "knew more than Perls about him." And for his part Perls understood that he needed phenomenology more than he needed an American M.D. degree.

Perls was looking for ways of supplying concentration therapy with the philosophical dimension that would give it theoretical power. Too impatient for either scholarship or writing, he had agonized over *Ego, Hunger and Aggression*, and without his wife's stiffening influence he might never have finished it. (Two chapters were primarily her work, and the whole was informed by her familiarity with the existentialist and Gestalt movements.) Perls had the rudiments of a new book in his suitcase when he came to the States, but it was clear that he must find an editor—really, a ghost writer. Fate was offering Goodman.[13]

Isadore From already knew Goodman through their mutual friend David Sachs, a young Ph.D. candidate at Princeton who had met Goodman in Chicago in the thirties. It was a case of many paths to the same door. While From found his way to Perls on his own, Sachs passed the word along to other friends—for instance, Rutgers student Jerry Raphel and Sachs's fellow graduate student at Princeton Rogers Albritton, both of whom were also likely to speak of Goodman in their sessions with Perls. Thus it was not merely the impression Goodman made in person but also his reputation among a group of bright young men that slowly brought him into focus as the collaborator Perls was looking for.

In the meantime, while Perls was seeing patients in a cold-water flat in the East Eighties, across the street from a brewery, Goodman continued his visits to Alexander Lowen's consulting room in a cheap downtown hotel. There was never any question of switching therapists—neither Perls nor Goodman would have been able to endure that sort of collaboration for a minute—but in 1947, when Lore Perls brought the children to join Fritz and to establish her own practice among the refugee psychotherapists in Manhattan, another piece of the mosaic that was to become Gestalt therapy dropped into place. Perls immediately turned over his more impecunious patients to his wife, including everyone in the Goodman circle. Within a year

49

Goodman himself was going to her—for a training analysis, as it eventuated once Gestalt therapy was established.

Lore Perls had always been an independent woman. After seventeen years of marriage to a man who was "a mixture of prophet and bum," she had learned to take care of herself—since no one else would.[14] Neither of the Perlses had suffered greatly from their long separation; he had his life and she had hers. "We lived essentially parallel to each other," said Fritz, "with relatively few peak experiences of violent fights and love." She did not disagree.[15]

It was to Fritz that the basic insights of concentration therapy had come, often as hostile reactions to his mentors. Lore's contribution consisted chiefly in supplying the underpinning, both domestic and cultural. Although not an M.D., she was much more cultivated than Fritz, having studied the classics in a *Gymnasium*, and modern philosophy (Husserl and Martin Heidegger) with Paul Tillich at the University of Frankfurt, in addition to her training in psychology and psychoanalysis. She read Greek and Latin, knew literature and music, was a dancer—and she was a mother.

Fritz and Lore Perls arrived at many of the same ideas by very different routes. Fritz got his emphasis on the body armor from his work with Reich; Lore got hers from the Dalcroze and Loheland approaches to movement and modern dance. Fritz's conception of "oral resistances" was formulated as a critique of the traditional Freudian view, whereas Lore's understanding of sucking, biting, and chewing came from suckling and weaning her own children. At this time Fritz was still using the analytic couch, sitting like Freud out of sight behind the patient; Lore worked face to face, and if she wanted someone to lie down she pointed to the floor, "because that was much more even support and we could do certain experiments with co-ordination and alignment."[16] One of the patients who moved from therapy with Fritz to therapy with Lore explained the difference between them this way: Fritz would demand, "Why are you so *rigid?*" or he would complain in his thick accent, "You're *boring* me!" But Lore would say, "Why are we not friends? Of all my patients, I feel only you are not my friend."[17] When Fritz published a paper in Goodman's little psychoanalytic journal *Complex*, it was called "Morality, Ego-Boundary and Aggression"; in the same issue Lore contributed her "Notes on the Psychology of Give and Take."[18]

These were differences of both character and training. When they met in 1926, Fritz had already been in analysis for some time, first with Karen Horney in Berlin, who had advised him to go to her pupil Clara Happel in Frankfurt. It was there he met Lore, who was studying with the well-known Gestalt psychologists Kurt Goldstein and Adhemar Gelb. By the time they married in 1930 Lore had completed her dissertation on visual perception and had her doctorate. She was now in training for psychoanalysis with Frieda Fromm-Reichmann and Karl Landauer. Meanwhile Fritz finished with Happel and spent a restless year in Vienna, where he had some contact with younger analysts like Paul Schilder, Paul Federn, and Helene Deutsch, though he never laid eyes on Freud himself. He too worked for a while as an assistant in Goldstein's famous research institute, but it was Lore who really knew Gestalt psychology from the inside, having done experimental work for several years with Goldstein's brain-damaged veterans of World War I. As she summed it up many years later, "I was first a Gestaltist and then became an analyst. Fritz was an analyst first and then came to Gestalt and never quite got into it."[19]

Ego, Hunger and Aggression was written a dozen years later, by which time Fritz and Lore had shared so many experiences and influenced one another in so many ways that it would be hard to say precisely what was hers and what was his in their thought. Fritz was an impatient genius. His grounding in ideas was never deep, but he knew in an instant what he could use from someone else's theory. He trusted his own intuition to sort things out, rarely bothering to systematize the insights he plucked from other gardens. Lore on the other hand was a genuine intellectual. She was probably even less theoretically inclined than he, but she had more than a nodding acquaintance with the philosophic movements—phenomenology, existentialism, Gestalt psychology, Eastern religion, psychoanalysis—that Fritz raided for his new theory. In the preface to early editions of *Ego, Hunger and Aggression* he gave her vague credit for "discussions" and "contributions" that were in fact his chief access to most of these schools of thought.[20] She had actually written first drafts for several of the chapters. Even so, the insights *were* his, and the energy that made them work in practice was not unrelated to his impatience and volatility.

Goodman was drawn to each of them. In Fritz he saw his own views of Freud and Reich modified and given a powerful reformulation in Gestalt terminology, the ramifications of which were to be worked out in the writing of *Gestalt Therapy* a few years later. But the Gestalt perspective was not yet dominant in Perls's thinking, and Goodman first adopted another, even more characteristically Perlsian notion from the grab bag of *Ego, Hunger and Aggression*—his theory of "dental aggression." Early in 1948 Goodman was already harping on this theme, and tying it to pacifist issues—for example, in the anarchist magazine *Resistance*, where he carried on a running debate with West Coast vegetarian-anarchist Marcus Graham, and in *Politics*, where he contributed to a collection of memorial tributes to Mahatma Gandhi—arguing Perls's position in apocalyptic crescendos that must have amused Fritz: "If we are looking for the ideal condition of spontaneity, fearless creative life and enjoyment," Goodman said, "it is necessary for us to face up to, to admit to ourselves, and to feel whatever nausea and savage-biting is within us. To scrutinize what it is we eat and how we eat it, and let the nausea rise, and the rage." Goodman took particular delight in pointing out the "repressed cannibalism" he saw behind much vegetarianism, including Gandhi's, though he added, approvingly, that "Gandhi apparently thought that in certain political circumstances any food whatever was unpalatable."[21] This last turn of the argument is typical of how Goodman opened up the political dimension of Perls's ideas. Contact between them was often fruitful in this way. Goodman's anarchism made the difference.

From Lore Perls he had other kinds of things to learn, more in the realm of give-and-take. For the most part it was not ideas or intellectual gossip that passed between them, however much Lore knew about Gestalt psychology or Frankfurt existentialism or the first generation of Freudians. Rather Goodman came as a patient, ready to confide in her, and hoping for some relief from his sense of failure as a man and an artist. Unable to find either the community or the audience that would put up with him, he wanted to know, What was he doing wrong? He thought of himself as "misunderstood."[22]

They began where his self-analysis left off. Goodman's initial explorations of his own character armor, guided by the Reichian map he got from Alexander Lowen, had led him into an intricate maze of memory and fantasy, charted in pages and pages of free associations, dream reports, and conjectures about his childhood traumas. These he had dutifully produced in daily stints: first the Reichian exercises, then the stubby pencil and the blank page, in solitary dialogue with his recalcitrant body. This stage had taken up much of 1946 and 1947. After that, as we have seen, he made a second effort of self-discovery, writing up his most recent life crisis as case-history—his expulsion from the progressive school for seducing his students, which he turned into fiction in *Parents' Day*. From each of these undertakings he had learned something, but the result was neither health nor happiness. Perhaps the problem was that there was no one he trusted and respected, no peer to tell his story to. As he struggled with the truth about himself and the world, he fell into deeper and deeper gloom. His body complained, his spirit sank. The very spring that he challenged vegetarians to bite and chew with more gusto he was himself suffering from what he called, in a letter to his friend Benjamin Nelson, "petty degenerative physical ailments—a brake on rapture & despair. (By such means we live on to tell the tale.) So fearfully & wonderfully made—I repress my wonted irony, so I can't even get a smile from it."[23] His ailments were the classic psychosomatic maladies of the senses and appetites, toothache, sinusitis, myopia, chronic hemorrhoids. Not that they were not real medical problems. Soon he was having two of his rotten teeth pulled—"jaw like a balloon," he wrote Ben in another letter, posted on a day when Fritz and Lore were coming to dinner.[24]

There were concentration exercises for some of these complaints in *Ego, Hunger and Aggression*—Goodman recommended them to his vegetarian readers—but it was Lore and not Fritz he turned to for help in his own case. As with Alexander Lowen, he spent much of his hour on the floor breathing and sighing deeply, but this time he went into therapy acknowledging that it was more than technical expertise he was after. It says much for Lore Perls that Goodman was able to put aside his pride. Like many psychotherapists he knew too much for his own good. It was crucial to avoid the battle of wits that conventional analysis often became. But the Reichian strategies for circumventing the intellect had succeeded in stirring up feelings of anxiety and confusion in him without resolving anything. Goodman reported continuous therapeutic skirmishing going on in his body, as his aches and pains fled from one place to another, heightened feeling here resulting in increased tension there.[25] He had not been able to find a next step and had fallen back on interpretation—his notes of self-analysis, his autobiographical novel. In choosing to work with Lore Perls he was not quite returning to the wordless therapy of the Reichians, nor was he continuing to brood over childhood memories, fantasies of rivalry with his peers, sexual obsessions, and the like in the Freudian manner. Instead Goodman and Lore Perls concentrated on the two goals of Gestalt therapy: heightened awareness in the present moment, and a livelier engagement of self and world, action in the realm of possibility. "The therapy for him," Goodman advised for a type like his own, "must be to learn more practical techniques, and there must also be a change in social relations so that his efforts can bear fruit, and biding that, a little philosophy."[26]

Just how much difference Lore Perls actually made in his case is hard to assess. She was widely respected by her colleagues, especially as a leader of training groups, and Goodman himself once said that she was "the best psychotherapist in New York City."[27] When he dedicated *Growing Up Absurd* to her in 1960, he was acknowledging her share in making it possible for him to write such a book. More than anyone else she had helped him face the world less defiantly. What she understood about his case was that he could be healed only if he turned away from himself to others. Ultimately this would be accomplished when he had his own patients to treat, and Lore was his mentor in this as well, his training therapist. Again he seems to have been speaking of his own situation when he wrote in *Gestalt Therapy*: "With the stage of becoming an authority, a teacher, a parent, the field has altered again: for the independent person is now less on his own, since others spontaneously attach themselves to or depend on him simply because he has ability, and they give him in turn occasions for new out-going acts. It is a rare person who grows as mature as this: to advise, guide, and care for without embarrassment, domination, etc., but simply *noblesse oblige*, giving up his 'independent' interests as really less interesting."[28]

Goodman's explorations in psychoanalysis went forward on several fronts at once. Just as his self-analysis prepared the way for his work with Lore Perls, so his article on Reich and the Freudian revisionists led into other projects, concurrent with his self-analysis, that finally culminated in the collaboration on

Gestalt Therapy. The chief items in the early stages were his book-length study of Franz Kafka and the preface he wrote for a little anthology of Freud's essays, *Freud: On War, Sex and Neurosis*, both published in 1947.[29] These works are interesting in their own terms, as examples of how Goodman applied Freudianism to literary and political problems. And for the first time, in *Kafka's Prayer*, he wrestles with the religious implications of psychoanalysis, a theme that persisted in his thought to the very end of his life and that sheds light on the nature of his own therapeutic history, perhaps best understood as a quest for spiritual peace. Orthodox Freudianism could take him only so far on this path. He pushed it as far as he could in analyzing Kafka's major romances, *Amerika*, *The Trial*, and *The Castle*, but the more telling section of *Kafka's Prayer*, and the one most important to Goodman, deals with Kafka's shorter parables and especially the aphorisms, and here Goodman's approach owes more to religious existentialism (primarily Kierkegaard) and to Taoist wisdom than to Freud or any of his followers.

Though taken up separately in his book, the two approaches, Freudian and existentialist-Taoist, are not completely quarantined from one another, and Goodman does not seem to feel them at odds. Nonetheless, the difference between them is enormous and shows clearly that traditional psychoanalysis had become a dead end for him. However ingenious his readings of Kafka's monstrous paranoiac fantasies, after a while it is hard not to resent Goodman's interpretations. They pile up like barnacles on a derelict ship, encrusting every inch of text and finally dragging the romances under.

But in the other half of *Kafka's Prayer* Goodman uses existentialist and Taoist ideas to further a very different psychoanalytic enterprise, as he examines Kafka's aphorisms one by one, holding them to the light, like a Talmudic sage. "Writing is a form of prayer." So Kafka said, and so Goodman ever after would himself affirm. Writing was their way of confronting "the pressing moment"—though sometimes "even too closely for art."[30] Kafka helped Goodman explore the connections between writing and religion in a psychoanalytic context: "By religious truth," Goodman said, "I mean the expression of the relations among the ego, the soul, and the world that can lead to happiness."[31] Although he never found such happiness more than fleetingly, in writing or in life itself, Goodman never gave up this effort to find "the true Way," whether he talked about it in religious or in psychological terms.

One of the themes of *Kafka's Prayer* is the idea of community. Kafka's fixation on bureaucracy as nightmare had its counterpoint in intermittent pastoral visions of the good society, and Goodman found passages in his author that matched and augmented his own conception of the anarchist way of life as well as his critique of the state. The millenarian social ideas he had been articulating for the last few years in *Politics, Retort,* and other anarchist magazines were now reconstituted in a psychoanalytic context. His tone was still prophetic rather than pragmatic—it is not yet the Goodman of the sixties we hear—but there is a growing sense of coherence and certainty as he asks himself: "Is what Kafka says true? What is true for my happiness, and what is false and to be rejected?"[32]

It is significant too that the preface Goodman wrote for Freud's essays was so emphatic about the same issues; he sums up Freud's achievement in a way that throws his own priorities into bold relief: "the reward of hitting on a new subject-matter in universal common experience has been to cast a wonderful light on just those matters of universal common experience that all men have always considered the *most* important and the *most* relevant: man's character, love and the choice of lovers, war and mourning, and the grounds of law and civil obedi-ence."[33] But Goodman also thought that Freud failed to live up to his own insights. "There is a somberness in Freud's writings that comes from the fact that, having diagnosed a social disor-der and having sternly given the aetiology, he rarely goes on to suggest a cure or prophylaxis. . . . Instead he says, 'It cannot be helped' or 'There is no telling what evils another arrangement would entail.'"[34] Freud was unwilling to take such social risks, but Goodman and his anarchist friends thought that there was no other responsible choice.

CHAPTER THREE

Bones to Pick with
Wilhelm Reich and A. S. Neill

GOODMAN'S NOTES for his preface to *Freud: On War, Sex and Neurosis* were scribbled on the back of a page of free association that was part of his self-analysis in the spring of 1947. By this time he had known Fritz Perls for almost a year but was not yet in therapy with Lore. The notion of becoming a therapist himself had probably not yet occurred to him, although in retrospect it is easy to see that he was on the verge of a conversion experience brought on by his self-analysis. Let us pause for a moment at this brink.

Goodman's work on the Freud volume led to further psychoanalytic writing, much of which remained outside the orbit of Gestalt therapy even after his collaboration with Perls and the founding of the Gestalt Institute. Although *Gestalt Therapy* was to be the most elaborate working out of Goodman's psychological ideas, its conceptual reach did not fully encompass them—there was a further horizon. It will be useful therefore to consider the thrust of Goodman's other psychoanalytic writing before examining his contribution to *Gestalt Therapy*, the book he wrote with Perls, in order to better understand how that contribution fit into the larger pattern of his thought.

The publisher-editor of *Freud: On War, Sex and Neurosis* was a red-haired and strong-willed young man named Alexander (Sander, and also Sandy) Katz, who, like Fritz Perls, had first read Goodman in *Politics* magazine. Initially Katz was more interested in Goodman's essay on "Revolution, Sociolatry and War" than in the article on Wilhelm Reich and the Freudians.[1] Katz was a draft resister, and had spent nineteen months in Lewisburg Penitentiary for refusing conscription during the Second World War. After his release he was active in the Committee for Non-Violent Revolution (CNVR) with David Dellinger, Bayard Rustin, and other radical pacifists, a group whose members included not only men who had done time together at Lewisburg but also a number of Goodman's anarchist friends who put out magazines like *Politics* (Dwight Macdonald was a CNVR member), *Why?* and *Retort.*

When Katz decided to start a little publishing company, the Arts and Sciences Press, funded by his businessman father, his aim was to print a wide range of radical thought, not just the literature of the pacifists and anarchists. Having decided on the collection of Freud's out-of-print essays with political relevance as his first venture, Katz asked Goodman to introduce them. *Freud: On War, Sex and Neurosis* did well, and in order to build his list quickly and take advantage of the moment, Katz bought the unsold copies of two other Goodman volumes, *Stop-Light* and *Art and Social Nature*, from *their* one-man publishers, thus establishing himself as Goodman's chief promoter.[2]

The Arts and Sciences Press turned out to be as vulnerable as most of the others that had published Goodman. In 1948 a new draft law was passed by the Congress; Katz refused to register and was sentenced to another year in jail. When he got out in 1949, he went stubbornly back to the barricades. This time he determined on converting his press into a magazine. Dwight Macdonald had apparently lost interest in *Politics*—he was putting out only a single issue each year now—and Katz thought he could pick up at least part of its readership by concentrating on cultural studies with a psychoanalytic slant of the sort that Goodman had recently been writing for Macdonald in a column called "The Social Format." *Complex* was to be "a magazine on psychoanalysis and kindred subjects, something akin to the *Imago* but with somewhat broader appeal and stressing social aspects."[3] It was to be a quarterly, at fifty cents a copy (offering the Freud volume as a premium with two-year subscriptions), and Goodman was to share the editorship with Katz and Gertrude Kurth, a traditional Freudian (who dropped out as soon as she saw the Reichian bias of some of the material her coeditors were accepting). Goodman's pay was $50 per issue, plus free advertising for his books, including those he had piled in his own closet. Work began in the late autumn of 1949, about the same time that Goodman contracted with Fritz Perls to do another job of editing, putting Perls's manuscript on concentration therapy into proper shape for publication. He was not really looking for such work; it simply fell into his lap.

Although Goodman did not seem so very enthusiastic about having a magazine of his own ("my editorial control extends about 3mm.," he wrote Ben Nelson[4]), nonetheless he immediately began to solicit his friends for articles. Nelson sent him an essay already in print and therefore not suitable, but other friends from graduate school days promised to write something for *Complex*—Abraham Kaplan, who had become chair of the philosophy department at the University of California, Los Angeles, would examine the social and ethical responsibilities of psychoanalysts, and Nathan Leites, whose book *The Movies*, written with Martha Wolfenstein, had just come out, undertook a survey of film treatments of psychiatry. Gertrude Kurth also had useful contacts, especially among the émigrés who practiced in New York, and Katz was energetic in approaching prospective contributors. Nonetheless a large share of the first few issues was collected by Goodman—including essays by both Fritz and Lore Perls.[5]

Not every advertised contributor actually appeared. No matter how many times Goodman nudged his friend Ben, the something "you're going to do" for the next issue failed to materialize, nor did the pieces by Abe Kaplan and Isaac Rosenfeld ever arrive. Another case, of considerably more interest, was that of A. S. Neill, the cantankerous Scotsman through whose writings on education Goodman had first heard of Wilhelm Reich. Summerhill, Neill's school in England for "problem children," was not yet famous, but his reputation among radical educators was already made. It was just such a voice that Goodman and Katz wanted in their magazine, where the emphasis was to be on the ways that psychological problems interact with social institutions and on how to change both institutions and ways of living. As Goodman had put it in a little manifesto he wrote for the first issue, "we hope that our writers will carry their analysis also to a point where the concrete details of everyday life and political exercise will have been so clarified that feasible practical action is indicated. . . . It is in principle impossible to deal seriously with the subjects that must be dealt with without giving offense and rousing resistance."[6]

This last remark was enough to rouse resistance in his fellow editor Gertrude Kurth, and Goodman's manifesto never appeared, but its intent was certainly behind the invitation that

Goodman and Katz sent to Neill, whose books had been giving offense for many years. Yet when Neill actually wrote the requested article, the editors found it disappointingly bland and for their readers even rather naïve, a beginner's version of such Reichian dogmas as self-regulation. Although the rejected article cannot be certainly identified, it was no doubt in the same vein as a brief piece Neill published that same month in the *Orgone Energy Bulletin,* "Self-Regulation and the Outside World." Conceivably, this was the very article *Complex* had rejected. The tone is pure Neill, as far from the scientific solemnity of the Reichians ("Is there anything in Orgone study to destroy a guy's sense of humor?" Neill once asked Reich[7]) as it was from the high intransigence of *Complex.* "I see no other way than compromising a little for the child's own sake," Neill wrote. "If we say to a son of 5: 'Tommy, you can play with your wee wee as much as you like at home, but don't do it in school or the street or a store,' we are of course doing something bad, but the alternative is worse, the stiff-stomached disapproval of other parents who won't let their children play with the 'dreadful child.'"[8]

The issue of how much one might trust in the free self-regulation of children was precisely where Goodman and Neill were likely to disagree, but surely Goodman would have subscribed to most of Neill's final words, if not to their salaam to Reich or the pointed omission of homosexual play among the rights of the young:

> When the outside enemy gives [children] fears and complexes, we must always attack with every weapon we have, and, fortunately, the voice of a parent is of greater force than that of the parent over the garden wall. Until

I met Reich I thought that it was enough to give the
child freedom, trusting that freedom alone would save
the child. Reich said: "No, that isn't enough." He was
right. With the enemy at the gate we must be positive,
not only, for example, taking sex-play for granted (as we
would do in a sane society) but positively showing the
child that we are fighting for its natural right to self-sex
and heterosexual play.[9]

Instead of printing it, the editors sent Neill's manuscript
back, along with a copy of the first issue of *Complex* and a
request that he favor them with something more sophisticated.
The exchange that followed is worth quoting at length for it
shows Goodman in dialogue with the older generation of radicals—not just Neill but also, indirectly, with Wilhelm Reich
himself—on issues that Goodman considered crucial to the
social revolution Neill and Reich had begun but that gave
offense and roused resistance even in them. Here is Neill's
response to the rejection of his article:

Dear Mr. Katz,
     Thanks for MS, letter and copy of *Complex*. It puzzles
me why you ever asked me to contribute; it must have
been because you read something I'd written, and therefore must have known my attitude and style.
     Looking over *Complex* I see that I cannot contribute
to it. Trying hard to discount my disappointment at having a MS sent back after being asked for, I may fail to see
your journal objectively. But it seems to me that it is a
magazine for high brows, for intellectuals who love to

skim along the surface and ignore the deep flowing tide. . . . I don't see a line in *Complex* that points to a new orientation to life and psychology. You say my MS isn't up to the level of your readers, but how many are up to my level? How many know a damn thing about self-regulation or for that matter stiff stomachs? . . .

To me the journal is in the past tense. If you haven't realised that Reich has killed psychoanalysis and that the new era is a bio-psychological one, then *Complex* will appeal only to the learned and the American equivalent of the London Bloomsburyites. No, sir, it ain't dynamic.[10]

Yours sincerely,
A. S. Neill

Neill sent a copy of this note to his friend Reich, who confirmed his view of Goodman and Katz as "psychoanalytically spellbound intellectuals who enjoy words more than depth. Briefly, they are hopeless."[11]

For some years now Reich and Neill had been fending off overtures from the anarchists in both London and New York. In 1946, when the Freedom Press expressed interest in Reich's books, Neill warned him, "If they publish you then your public will be limited and the big public will be suspicious. . . . Some anarchists are claiming you as one of them already, so be careful."[12] It was at that same time that Reich asked Goodman to stop linking his name and Neill's with the libertarian movement, protesting, as Goodman reported it, that Neill "had enough trouble with his middle-class parents because of the sexual issue, without bringing in anarchism too."[13] By the spring of

1950, experience had proved them right to worry about their reputations, especially in the United States. There had been several nasty articles on the "cult of sex and anarchy" in liberal periodicals, and the Food and Drug Administration was already pursuing the investigations that ultimately led to Reich's imprisonment and death. That summer the American consul in London denied Neill a visa to attend a conference at Reich's Orgone Institute in Maine—no reason given.[14] In short, Reich and Neill were already feeling hounded and at bay in the ideological swamps, when out of nowhere came these pesky Americans Katz and Goodman, buzzing and stinging.

Goodman wrote a long reply to Neill's letter, spelling out the issues as he saw them.

> Dear A. S. Neil [sic],
>   I assure you that most of our readers, who are largely "progressive" academics (including some Reichian practitioners, by the way), know "about" self-regulation and "approve" of self-regulation of children. Obviously this kind of crude information and preliminary propaganda is not useful. What we hoped (and hope) for from you would be detailed implementation, concrete social invention, drawn from your considerable experience. Consider a simple but difficult debated problem: the witnessing, or not-witnessing (and participation, or nonparticipation, and what degree of participation or censoring), of children in the first years of the sexual intercourse of the adults. This is a pressing issue in most of our homes. Suppose your best evidence dictated privacy: this would occasion a vast and revolutionary

change in the arrangements of our physical environment, and this should then become an immediate major
political issue, to the best of our ability to make it so.
Suppose, on the contrary, the privacy is inessential if the
general education of small children is altered accordingly, then *how* accordingly, and what about the issues of
participation, etc.? We are trying to get a description of
this problem among the Mohave Indians (where privacy
is inessential)—would you say, as you do of Ashley
Montagu's article, that "it does not matter fundamentally"? . . . Or consider the problem of defecation.
Agreed that nothing need be done about it so far as
"training" is concerned—and thousands and thousands
of persons in America agree to this and practice it—a
simple physical contraption that would eliminate dia-
pering at night would be now of more use than re-hash-
ing a general theory. . . . Or tell us something in detail
about when small children will go to bed—when their
rhythms may or may not coincide with the adults' con-
venience, and the adults likewise have needs. I don't
know any of these answers—I should like to be informed
about them.

The bother with you, Neil [*sic*] (let me say it as a
friend), is that you think that, theoretically at least, your
revolution is over; or, to a degree, you are willing to let
Reich do your thinking for you. But it is the essence of a
dynamic theory that it at once, applying itself, gets
involved in new troubles that make the old ones pale
and recede. Nor is it the case that there's no use in going

on to the new points till the old ones are "accepted." For it is just in the new points of concrete detail that the principle becomes inevitable and accepted.

You imagine that you are very practical; but you must know that what is narrowly practical is not practical at all. It is a system of bio-social resistances, avoiding true creativity. I'm damned if I know what is practical in the long run, so I judge by my tact for the interesting and concernful. [Theodore] Reik's paper on [Anatole] France's irony struck me as very inward and interesting, because obviously Reik is attuned to just this kind of attitude himself; now this happens to be a very common attitude among precisely the good heads in our coercive institutions; is it useless to give such persons a clue of what goes on in them? Humane studies are *always* practical, when they have inwardness and vitality in them; you'd be surprised how they come home to one. To put this another way: the best way of getting a new orientation is not necessarily, indeed it is almost never, by "pointing to a new orientation," as you counsel.

The "new era" is not a biopsychological one but a unitary one—unifying the psychosomatic unity and the interpersonal unity and the cultural-anthropological unity and the educational-political unity and the ecological-economic unity, etc. Neglecting any part of this, and singly concentrating on one part, won't make a humanity according to my aspirations. And it seems to me that in its horse-and-buggy way the old analysis of Freud, Jung, Ferenczi, etc. has done more for this unification than anything I can think of in a couple of hundred years. Reich has extracted a marvelous thing from that matrix; and there's still more to be extracted from it.

Lastly, I am annoyed by your references to "high-brows," "Bloomsbury," etc. You presumably do good work in education (I have no first-hand acquaintance with it), and certain uses of words and arts are not your look-out; but the kind of prejudiced contempt you express is simply ignorance and withdrawal grounded in suspicion and fear. Let me assure you that any new spirit will involve a reform in language from the present "common-sense" abuse of speech; and this change will be, is being, worked out in its own context—not by looking thru microscopes or at tense-muscles.[15]

Best wishes,
Paul Goodman

Goodman sent a copy of this prickly letter to Reich, trying to draw him into the controversy, but Reich was not to be provoked so easily. Instead, he wrote Neill, in the scornful vein that was becoming more and more pronounced in his utterances.

My dear Neill:

I just had a letter from *Complex* and from Paul Good-man to you. I suggest you forget Goodman. He is one of those intellectuals who does everything only in the form of words. What he suggests in his letter, for example, the derivation of social requirements from the needs, like separate rooms for young couples, has been done repeatedly by me some 20 years ago. It was the psychoanalytic movement, which he so arduously defends, which choked those demands off wherever it could—Freud among them. He did not understand a thing, and he is fresh to boot. Such a man has no idea whatsoever what it means to build up a school practically to keep it going as you did. I would not bother about them. The forming of the "New Era" will surely not be the work of fellows of this type.

I hope to see you soon no matter what will happen in the world.[16]

Wilhelm Reich

Meanwhile Neill himself had already answered the brash young Americans. He enjoyed a tiff of this sort and was the master of a more agile polemical style than his friend—indeed he clearly has the better of the exchange, if one wants to tally up.

Dear Katz and Goodman,

Thanks for both letters. I'd rather you didn't print my [letter] because you would print your reply, and I'd be 3000 miles away and outside any controversy.

Your letter, Goodman, shows that we are talking different languages. I am not interested in discovering, e.g. whether a kid should see its parents having intercourse. There are too many unknown factors standing in the way. No one has ever seen a healthy child, and if one did see one, what effect would seeing intercourse have on it if the parents were not free? Your question involves the larger one: Is sex intercourse a private thing or is it potentially a communal affair? I don't see how we can know unless and until folks are completely free from sex inhibitions as animals are.

You fire a lot of questions at me, but I have written something like 16 books answering a thousand questions that you or others might think of, answering not in theory but in actual practice. There is this difference between us, that you theorise while I practise. (I know nothing about you and you may be dealing practically all day long; I am only going by your letter and the books mentioned written by you, Goodman.) You say I let Reich do my thinking for me, yet, you know, I started my school in 1921 and didn't hear of Reich until 1937, and knowing Reich hasn't altered my school practice one bit, although he has given me personally a hell of a lot. In him I discovered what I'd been looking for for years . . . the link between the psyche and the soma, and, really, that was what got me annoyed with *Complex* for devoting so much space to the old symbolism Reik era. And in a way it applies to your own very clever article on weeping etc., for it does not touch the somatic and might therefore be called dated. I think of the terrible weepings and angers I had when in 1938–39 I underwent what was then called Vegeto-Therapie with Reich in Oslo. Violent reactions that sprang from Reich's attack on my stiff muscles.

I don't understand your letter, Goodman. You are too learned, too clever for me. I am a very simple person who can't think abstractly. You accuse me of thinking "theoretically at least that (my) revolution is over."

What revolution? If you do as I have done, stood as it were outside children for 30 years observing what children do when not under adult discipline, is that revolution? If I had the power to alter all State schools so that they fitted the child as I have seen the child, that would be revolution, but as I have 60 children out of a few million British children who are all being educated the other way, my "revolution" simply doesn't exist. All I am is a kind of scientist observing and sometimes hating to accept what I observe, e.g. the fact that no kid under 18 ever wants to work in a garden or tidy up a garden path. The fact that the usual conditioned child of "modern" parents is incapable of having a satisfactory love affair.

Call it prejudice on my part; you write of me "the kind of prejudiced contempt you express is simply ignorance and withdrawal grounded in suspicion and fear." Fear of what I dunno; a guy who will be 67 this year shouldn't have any fear of the Reiks of life, but don't let's be personal any more. I put it this way (and it isn't contempt either): I read the Orgone literature, not understanding much of the physics-biology side, but in the main I say to myself: I like this; it touches something deep in me: it fits into my view of my own pre-Reich work. I read *Complex* No. 1 and say to myself: This doesn't catch my interest any more than reading the *Psychoanalytic Review* would. It takes me back to the time I spent with dear old Stekel in Vienna in 1922–24, the days of symbolism and dreams and unconscious slips of the tongue, etc. And now I'll sit down and con your last sentence for the umpteenth time and wonder what it means, and in case you are like me and don't keep carbon copies, here it is. . . . "Let me assure you that any new spirit will involve a reform in language from the present 'common-sense' abuse of speech; and this change will be, is being, worked out in its own context—not by looking thru microscopes or at tense-muscles." Oh, Paul Goodman! What the hell does it mean? When I come back to N. Y. in August to lecture and hold seminars and attend the Orgonon Conference, I may have a chance of hearing from you in person what you do mean.

Yours,

A. S. Neill

p.s. The old brigade Freudian in me asks: Why does Goodman spell my name with one L? Answer (perhaps!): When you give a guy 'ell you first of all take away an L and then compensate. Just about as mad as many a symbolism interpretation though.[17]

Goodman's tone had been hectoring, baiting: "I assure you . . ."; "The bother with you . . ."; "you'd be surprised . . ." "Let me assure you . . ." Neill answered like the canny Scot he was, unwilling to be quoted in *their* columns, modest yet clear about his own accomplishments, devastating on the topic of "cleverness" versus "common sense." And well he might say, "Oh, Paul Goodman! What the hell does it mean?" For both in his letter and in his "clever article" on "The Intellectual Inhibition of Explosive Grief and Anger," Goodman had fallen into the prophetic style—half psychoanalytic jargon, half private rhapsody—that spoiled much of his work during this period. It was just this vice that George Orwell had condemned in his well-known essay "Politics and the English Language," choosing as one of his noxious examples a passage from Goodman's 1945 article on Reich and the Freudian revisionists.[18] Orwell had not named Goodman, but it is hard to believe that his strictures escaped the notice of the *Politics* circle in New York, any one of whom would have delighted in calling Goodman's attention to the issue of *Horizon* in which they appeared. Was Goodman still smarting from that slap on the wrist when he now spoke of "a reform in language from the present 'common-sense' abuse of speech"?

Even so, if we look beyond the rhetoric in these letters, it is Goodman who has the most to say. For all his cleverness, he has real questions he wants answers for. The topics he urges Neill to write about, for instance, come out of his own somewhat baffled experience as a father—when *should* Matty go to bed? It was a problem he and Sally had not solved, and the three-year-old was often to be found playing sleepily but stubbornly in the midst of company after eleven o'clock at night.[19] What is most significant is that Goodman does not automatically assume that an impasse in child rearing must come down sooner or later to coercion, requiring the child to accommodate to its parents' wishes. This was the sticking point for all psychological problems: Goodman took it for granted that solutions would call for new arrangements in the environment, both physical and social, rather than engineering the adjustment of individuals to the status quo.

When Goodman speaks of "humane studies," he means not only psychoanalytic readings of literature, like Reik's essay on

Anatole France, but also the investigations of child rearing he proposes to Neill, or his own treatise on the inhibition of grief and anger by intellectuals. "Humane studies are *always* practical when they have inwardness and vitality in them."

Another emphasis overlaps with the two just mentioned: when Goodman affirms a "new era" of unitary thinking, bringing together the insights of psychoanalysis, anthropology, politics, and so forth, he is speaking of exactly this practice of humane letters that *Complex* had undertaken. The table of contents of the first issue was indicative. Besides Freud on jealousy, paranoia, and homosexuality, there was Reik's piece on the psychology of irony, anthropologist Ashley Montagu on female adolescent sterility, and Goodman on grief and anger.

To the embattled Wilhelm Reich this eclecticism would seem the worst sort of intellectual folly, though it might have been more congenial twenty years earlier, when he himself was deriving "the social requirements" of life from "the needs" of human nature, and Freud had not yet "choked those demands off" in fear of public opinion. Of course this was what Goodman meant when he said that it was "impossible to deal with the subjects that must be dealt with without giving offense and rousing resistance." Reich and Neill had led the way, but now it was necessary to apply their "dynamic theory" and get involved "in new troubles that make the old ones pale." Reich might think that his new science of orgonomy was a great leap forward, but "looking thru microscopes or at tense-muscles" did not seem such an advance to Goodman.

In short, this exchange constitutes Goodman's formal break with Reich, at once an acknowledgment of indebtedness and a charge that his mentor had allowed himself to be sidetracked into scientism. Neill and Reich might accuse Goodman of doing everything "only in the form of words," a mere "Bloomsburyite" of psychoanalysis, but Goodman was never ashamed of the intellect or apologetic for his calling as a man of letters. At that very moment he was deep in the effort of thought and language that did pick up where Reich left off; the "new spirit" was, as he said, "being worked out in its own context," and the writing of *Gestalt Therapy* was part of it.

The second issue of *Complex* confirmed all of this. The traditional was represented with the essay "The Psychology of Pity" by Ludwig Jekels, at eighty-two the oldest pupil of Freud still active, and there was a discussion of hypnotism as a technique for mass psychotherapy, with a paper by Hugo Beigel and commentary by Goodman. They also printed remarks on the question of state-supported therapy from Freud's address before the Fifth International Psychoanalytic Congress in 1918. Lore Perls reviewed two books of literary criticism that made use of psychoanalytic concepts, awarding the palm to Lionel Trilling's *The Liberal Imagination*. Goodman translated a piece on "The Necessity of Evil" by the French Catholic analyst René Laforgue, and he also contributed a review, but his name did not appear in the table of contents as author of any major article. Nonetheless the centerpiece of the issue was in fact his, a chapter from his current collaboration with Fritz Perls, titled "The Anthropology of Neurosis."

This chapter was not an attempt to epitomize Gestalt therapy—indeed, there is no mention of the forthcoming book, a curious omission since the contract was already signed and the manuscript almost finished. Furthermore, the article appeared under Perls's name alone, although it was in fact pure Goodman, a particularly bold statement of the orientation that was his chief contribution to the new theory. In it one sees again, now clearly spelled out, the points he had been arguing in his exchange with Neill and Reich. Thus, for example, he begins by reminding the reader of Freud's insistence "that not medical men but (with medical collaboration) literary men, teachers, lawyers, social-workers, etc. make the best psychoanalysts, for they understand human interests."[20] And he goes on to show, in the perverse vein he was master of, that neurosis is not to be regarded as a breakdown of healthy functioning so much as a lia-bility of a complicated social species, which—he uses the term from Reich and Neill—is "organismically self-regulating." In considering the healthy organism we are struck, he argues,

> not only by the wonderful system of specific adjust-ments, signals, co-ordination, subtle judgement, that go to maintain the general equilibrium, but also by the devices that serve as cushioners and safety-valves to pro-tect the whole. Such are blotting-out and hallucinating and dreaming, and regarding as-if, and accepting instead-of; and such, in traumatic instances, are immo-bilizing, isolating, re-doing, flight, and so forth. This is an organism of great power and efficiency, but also one that can take rough treatment and bad times. The two sides go together: ability leads to adventure and adven-ture to trouble. Man *has* to be malleable. These safety-functions all, of course, play a chief role in mental disorders, but they are themselves healthy.[21]

In less than ten pages Goodman sketched out a psychoso-matic history of our species from the moment of its first upright step. To be sure, this was a literary more than a scientific feat, but no less compelling as background for Goodman's view that, "far from being able to take fitness to social institutions as a rough norm, a doctor has more hope for achieving the self-developing integration of a patient if the patient learns to adjust his environment to himself rather than to *mal*adjust himself to society."[22] This was his contribution to the radical anthropology of the last 150 years, from Rousseau to Engels, and from Darwin to Freud. Goodman put his own characteristic stamp on it in the formula, "ability leads to adventure and adventure to trouble." It was a truth that Reich and Neill understood only too well.

It is obvious enough why Goodman chose not to put his name to this excerpt from the book he and Perls were writing even though it happened to be a section that was almost entirely his, both the ideas and the language. His presence in the magazine was already a little too pervasive, especially in this second issue, where he appeared as editor, translator of two articles, commentator on a third, and one of the book reviewers—over half the issue had his hand in it. None of the three editors was happy about this, though for very different reasons, and by the next issue Goodman had dropped out completely, just as Kurth would do after *Complex* no. 4, in which Katz insisted on printing a long Reichian polemic by sociologist Don Calhoun. From Goodman's point of view, the magazine had failed to attract the kinds of rousing and offensive contributions he had hoped for—he was doing it all himself—whereas Kurth thought it had been only too successful. For his part Katz felt that Goodman had not done his job, which was to fill the magazine with lively voices from among his wide contacts.[23]

Two years later Goodman would be back, as sole editor of *Complex* no. 9, the publication's final gasp. Again it was *his* magazine, filled with his friends. Of the four last essays, one is by him, one by Fritz (that is, really by Fritz), and one by Lore. The fourth was by Kilton Stewart, then practicing psychotherapy in Manhattan, a follow-up on his study of the dream culture of the Senoi in Malaysia (in *Complex* no. 6), which was to become a famous essay, anthologized and widely taught in undergraduate anthropology classes. (That its contentions were themselves largely wish fulfillments was not revealed until 1985, when G. William Domhoff exposed Stewart's exaggerations in *The Mystique of Dreams*.[24] Too bad; it would have been nice to go on thinking that an entire culture practiced dream-therapy.)

CHAPTER FOUR

Writing Gestalt Therapy

THERE WAS STILL another reason in 1950 for not putting Paul Goodman's name to "The Anthropology of Neurosis." At this stage in the history of *Gestalt Therapy* it was not yet clear just whose names would appear on the title page. In the beginning the arrangement had been that Goodman was merely Perls's editor, undertaking to put a short manuscript into shape for publication. The $500 fee for this job—a princely sum for Goodman—suggests the extent of the ghostwriting deemed necessary. Perls was blocked as a writer. As he himself said, only half facetiously, *Ego, Hunger and Aggression* had been the result of deciding to teach himself to type, and his later efforts, *In and Out the Garbage Pail* and *Gestalt Therapy Verbatim* owed a lot to similar new toys he played with, tape recorders and movies.[1] Examples of his unedited writing are few and brief, but they demonstrate what agony it was for him to be alone with himself and the empty page. Perls was full of insights and had a keen nose for what was worth borrowing from other people's work, but his here-and-now mind was bored with anything that demanded perseverance or discipline. *Ego, Hunger and Aggression* was a hodgepodge of shrewd observations and anecdotes, collected with marvelous intuition but hopelessly disordered and fragmentary.

And yet, though the ideas never cohere as theory, their general drift affected some readers profoundly. There were psychoanalysts in New York who upon reading *Ego, Hunger and Aggression* called Perls and asked to be accepted as patients. Goodman himself was impressed—more by the man than his book, but the new manuscript had possibilities, for it was an attempt to bring more order to the same set of ideas.

Ego, Hunger and Aggression was divided into three parts—first, a general critique of psychoanalytic ideas, applying concepts borrowed from Gestalt psychology and other, more esoteric theorists of holism, especially Jan Christian Smuts and Salamo Friedlaender; second, an exposition of Perls's chief contribution to psychoanalytic theory, that is, his elaboration of the biology of hunger and feeding as a model of psychic life, emphasizing the mechanisms of aggression and assimilation; and third, a compendium of concentration therapy exercises somewhat in the Reichian manner, developed to foster awareness of the present moment at the organism/environment boundary. The exercises in "dental aggression" show Perls pushing his most original idea in his favorite medium, therapeutic acting out, and indeed he called them "the quintessence of this book."[2] He buttonholes his reader:

> If you are afraid to hurt people, to attack them, to say
> "No" when the situation demands it, you should attend
> to the following exercise: imagine yourself biting a piece
> of flesh out of someone's body. Can you imagine biting it

clean off or do your teeth only make an impression, as if you were biting on rubber? If, in your imagination, you are able to bite right through, can you experience the proper "feel" of the flesh on your teeth? You might condemn such an exercise as vicious and cruel, but this cruelty is just as much part and parcel of your organism as it is of the animal's in its struggle for life. Your biological aggressiveness has to find outlets somewhere and somehow; even behind the forgiving character, there lurks a latent aggressive nature which must come out in one way or another, as projection or as moralizing or as killing with kindness.

What, if you come to think of it, has mankind gained by repressing the individual biological aggressiveness? Look at the ingenious means of destruction and the amount of suffering in the present war. Is that not proof enough of the fact that just through the vicious circle of pseudo-metabolism aggressiveness has developed to the present paranoiac stage of wholesale destruction?

The more we allow ourselves to expend cruelty and lust for destruction in the biologically correct place— that is, the teeth—the less danger will there be of aggression finding its outlet as a character feature. Those pathological fears we might harbour, too, will greatly diminish; for, the more the aggression is invested in biting and chewing, the less aggression will be left for projection. The result will inevitably be a decrease in the number of fears (phobias).[3]

Let us note Perls's tone here, as he unveils his chief psychotherapeutic idea in its larger cultural context. It is very much the tone of the public lecturer, strongly flavored with showmanship, not to say salesmanship. Like his Central European predecessors of the nineteenth century, the phrenologists and mesmerists and hydropathists, Perls was most at home on the platform, demonstrating his discoveries by their practical application. As one of his followers was to put it, "I've never known a magician, and now I know what a magician can do."[4]

The contributions of *Ego, Hunger and Aggression* that affected readers most powerfully, and brought Perls disciples and collaborators, were these concentration exercises, which several of his first American followers took up not so much as therapeutic tools as pedagogic experiments. Both Elliott Shapiro in classes on abnormal psychology at Brooklyn College, and Ralph Hefferline in classes at Columbia, asked students to perform Perls's exercises and write up the results.[5] This was encouraging to Perls, and he made Hefferline, who was also his patient, into a kind of coinvestigator. Perls supplied a new and more comprehensive series of exercises, which Hefferline put his students through and then worked up as a manuscript. This would be the practical demonstration in Perls's new book, to follow the theoretical presentation of what remained his central interests, ego, hunger, and aggression.

But the theory was yet to be written, though Perls had some of it sketched out. He was ready for a factotum in this area too, someone who could organize his ideas and produce a manuscript under his supervision. He looked around and struck a bargain with Goodman, who understood the psychoanalytic context, was in training with Lore, and could write. Goodman was willing to do the job for the $500 Perls offered.[6] That would pay his rent for almost two years.

A contract for the book had already been signed with Art Ceppos of the Julian Press, an acquaintance of Perls. As publisher, Ceppos was to have an important hand in the final product. Originally, Goodman's section was to constitute the book proper while Hefferline's material would serve as a kind of glorified appendix. After seeing the completed manuscripts Ceppos insisted on reversing their order, so that Hefferline's practical exercises would come first, to ease the reader into the basic concepts—and to capitalize on the fact that "how-to-do-it" and "self-help" books were popular at the time.[7]

Goodman's experience with vegetotherapy had been useful in developing the new series of concentration exercises. But that was nothing compared to the flood of ideas that came once he had committed himself to the project. Goodman had not anticipated how much he would become involved when he began to expound Perls's conceptions. He described the process to his friend Ben Nelson: "I've been writing away on Perls's book—which has now turned into a collaboration. Altho the last thing I want at present is to write a book on the theory of therapy." Then, a few weeks later, he reported, "I've been working myself to death on the book I'm doing with Perls, which is turning out to be astonishing. What I've done is add a lot of *existenz* to the Gestalt-psan. [psychoanalytic] base, and the results (in therapeutic practice) are strange to behold—but Perls insists they're right. I've got the secret it seems."[8] The facetiousness of these communiques was a relic of college days when members of Goodman's circle rarely spoke to one another in any other tone. Perhaps there was an ironic edge to it in Nelson's ear, since he himself had been sounded out by Perls as a possible editor of his manuscript.[9] Like others who knew them both, Nelson thought Goodman was the man for Perls, and had told him so. His opinion was worth taking seriously, for he himself had recently collaborated with Goodman on an article for *Commentary* magazine.[10] He was well aware of the division of labor that his friend would take for granted, for he had seen it from the inside as well as observing it for twenty years in the frequent collaborations of Goodman with his brother Percy. The pattern was always the same. The original impetus would come from someone else, not Goodman. His collaborator was expected to provide facts and figures and a sense of the issues and their ramifications—expertise and a sounding board—but the shaping imagination was Goodman's. It galled Nelson a bit to relinquish so much of the conceptual say-so, and he and Goodman did not repeat the experiment, but the same sharing of responsibilities had always worked beautifully with Goodman's architect brother, with whom he wrote many works, beginning with his very first publications in 1931, when he was only twenty years old, and including their influential book on planning, *Communitas*. Typically, Percy had proposed this latter project, offering a scheme for "the city of tomorrow" that he had conceived as a promotional exhibit (but Otis Elevator didn't buy it) for the World's Fair of 1939. Paul quickly transformed it into parody, a satiric portrait of the consumer society. Percy saw the point and took no offense; soon a book had grown around his germ. He was not insecure in his own calling, for he had practical and historical mastery of it and had never lacked for success and admiration. As the elder brother he was proud of Paul's analytic powers and philosophic imagination. And Paul looked up to him as a designer and plastic artist. They were able to collaborate without rivalry.[11]

In the present case, although Perls was hardly a big brother to Goodman, neither was he much concerned about property rights in ideas, whether his own or other people's, and he had no ambitions of the sort that Nelson, for instance, cherished to master his discipline and be known as an authority. As for Goodman, although it seemed to him that he had no special call to write such a book as *Gestalt Therapy*—and Perls had engaged him merely to put his own ideas in order—the work became a collaboration almost immediately. Characteristically, it was Goodman who was creating the theory as well as the prose in which it was couched, and Perls settled comfortably enough into the role of the expert who approved the results.

To distinguish their separate contributions, one might begin by comparing the two parts, or "volumes," of the book as it finally emerged. Many Gestalt therapists using the book since 1951, as training tool or sacred text, have made light of the first, do-it-yourself section, where the major concepts are presented in popular language originally designed to help orient the psychology students in Hefferline's classes who were performing the experiments as a series of assignments.[12] Aside from the orderliness imposed by its format—the sequence of exercises one by one—the approach of this part of the book is not very different from that of *Ego, Hunger and Aggression*, where a similar mix of hypothesis, experiment, and commentary may be seen. The centrality of the exercises reflects Perls's bias toward the side of the psychoanalytic tradition that came to him through Reich, his penchant for technique. There is a tendency in this half of the book to treat the Reichian idea of organismic self-regulation as if it were simply a matter of conjuring away "conscience" and "self-control," and trusting to one's appetites and impulses to negotiate the world.[13] Both Reich and Perls sometimes seem to envision a heroic Self bursting its chains and laying claim to a long-withheld patrimony of animal life. For all his own romanticism, Goodman had a conception of both self and world more subtle than that, based on a cultural rather than a biological symbiosis. Self-regulation for him was, accordingly, a more complicated matter of continual creative adjustment, involving considerable social and political risk taking. In his half of the book he speaks explicitly of "the more total self-regulation, of all the functions of the soul, including its culture and learning, its aggression and doing the work that is attractive, along with the free play of hallucination."[14]

Goodman's emphasis actually went back to the early concerns of Wilhelm Reich, whose crusade for sex education and work democracy, long since abandoned (though never abjured) in his pursuit of the orgone, happened not to interest Perls as much as it did his collaborator. Perls certainly agreed with the notion developed in "The Anthropology of Neurosis" that society suffered from "chronic low-tension disequilibrium," a continuous state of anxiety induced by the evolution of modern civilization. But his interest lay in developing techniques for breaking through the omnipresent rigidities and inhibitions in the therapist's office, rather than in taking psychoanalysis "into the streets," as Reich had once demanded and as Goodman and some of his young anarchist friends were ready to proclaim.

Just how far Goodman was willing to press this more public goal can be seen in his notes for lectures he gave to Gestalt trainees a few years later.

Our slogan of "adjust the social reality to our needs"
makes sense when the social reality offers real possibilities; but the situation is that in many important spheres
the possibility itself must be created: E.g. marriage, education, dwelling, jobs, political initiative, social identification; what is the meaning here of "adjusting the social
reality to our needs"? Now the usual view is that given
more individual competence & contact, these other
things may be tackled better. Yes; but not if at the same
time a freezing occurs, i.e., if at the same time there is
not a growing unrest, dissatisfaction, compassion, vocation, frustration, psychotic fancies such as religion, art.
The theory is that it is fundamentally these latter things
that were inhibited.[15]

In short, one might say that for Perls it was the technical
side of Reichianism that was interesting and for Goodman the
political side. But this is a crude dichotomy, as both of them
would immediately have objected, leaving out of account their
effort to integrate precisely these concerns in *Gestalt Therapy*
by means of concepts borrowed from other thinkers than those
in the psychoanalytic tradition, especially the Gestalt psychologists whose influence on both Fritz and Lore Perls had been
powerful and direct during their training years in Frankfurt and
Berlin. Gestalt ideas of the dynamic relation of figure and
ground and of the holistic approach to experience allowed a formulation of the subject matter of psychotherapy that brought
technical and political issues together—as, for example, on the
second page of Perls and Goodman's theoretical argument:
"Our approach in this book is 'unitary' in the sense that we try

in a detailed way to consider *every* problem as occurring in a social-animal-physical field. From this point of view, for instance, historical and cultural factors cannot be considered as complicating or modifying conditions of a simpler biophysical situation, but are intrinsic in the way any problem is presented to us."[16] The Gestalt underpinnings of this approach are spelled out on the next page: "[P]sychology studies the operation of the contact-boundary in the organism/environment field. . . . [T]he contact-boundary, where experience occurs, does not *separate* the organism and its environment; rather it limits the organism, contains and protects it, and *at the same time* it touches the environment. . . . Let us understand contacting, awareness and motor response, in the broadest sense, to include appetite and rejection, approaching and avoiding, sensing, feeling, manipulating, estimating, communicating, fighting, etc.—every kind of living relation that occurs at the boundary in the interaction of the organism and environment."[17]

The application of Gestalt concepts and terminology to psychoanalytic topics had begun in *Ego, Hunger and Aggression,* where Perls modified what he had learned from Kurt Goldstein and the Gestalt psychologists with notions he found in Jan Christian Smuts ("evolutionary holism"), Salamo Friedlaender ("differential thinking"), and Paul Federn ("ego boundary"). The crucial idea, that the ego is not a substance or part but rather a *function* of the organism in contact with its environment and that neurosis is largely a matter of loss of contact, that is, an ego-disturbance—all this is to be found in *Ego, Hunger and Aggression,* though only a few pages are devoted there to what fills whole chapters in *Gestalt Therapy.*[18]

Interestingly enough, Perls seems to have taken his Gestalt orientation primarily from Goldstein, a neurophysiologist and not one of the inner circle of Max Wertheimer, Wolfgang Köhler, Kurt Koffka, and Kurt Lewin. Perls was familiar with the work of these four through Lore, who had studied with Wertheimer as well as Goldstein, and had read through the whole Gestalt corpus, but it is not clear that Fritz had actually perused even Goldstein's books. That was not the way his mind worked. To say that Goldstein was the most important to him is merely to register that it was his name Perls dropped when he wanted to lay claim to Gestalt ideas—since Perls had served in Goldstein's lab, however briefly, and felt a connection there. The fact that Goldstein and Kurt Lewin, for instance, had pressed Gestalt conceptions into service for personality theory seems not to have meant a thing to Perls, though it would have been a better reason for taking Goldstein as his main Gestalt reference point. Perls had grasped what was essential to his own theorizing, and if his sense of the Gestalt movement was shaky, that did not prevent him from using its concepts to elaborate what he called mental metabolism.[19]

Perls's four main categories of impaired ego-functions—introjection, projection, retroflection, and confluence—were all based on his alimentary model of organism/environment relations, various ways in which the identification/alienation function at the contact-boundary could go wrong. In *Ego, Hunger and Aggression* these ideas were presented almost allegorically, with no phenomenological texture and little sense of their ideological ramifications. Perls was given to anecdote and spur-of-the-moment illustrations, but this is not the same as looking closely at experience. When Goodman said in his letter to Ben Nelson that he had added "a lot of *existenz* to the Gestalt-psan. base," one thing he meant was that he had filled out the theory by merely describing various psychic conditions and experiences in the here-and-now language of ordinary life. There is more to be said about the influence of existentialism on *Gestalt Therapy*, but perhaps the most important contribution that Goodman made to Perls's set of insights was simply to flesh them out in phenomenological language so that readers can bring their own experiences to bear. What Perls was trying to draw into awareness through the concentration exercises worked out with Hefferline, Goodman was finding a language to explore in an account of the psyche itself. Perls tended to fall into a tone of hectoring demonstration while Goodman adopted a quieter voice of explication—teacherly, even a bit magisterial, but unfailingly patient as he unpeels his onion: "We say it in this odd way . . . ," or, "The verbal embarrassments here are deep in our language."[20]

Oddly enough, given this emphasis on clarity and precision, many readers find Goodman's style difficult, and some Gestalt therapists using the book as a training tool have even argued that it is purposely so, to prevent readers from avoiding its lessons by an easy introjection.[21] Perhaps this notion had its source in Perls's gambit at the opening of *Ego, Hunger and Aggression*, where he quoted Bacon's famous dictum that some books require much chewing to be properly digested. Be that as it may, Goodman certainly did alter his usual manner in writing this book. His rhetoric is under restraint, and nothing is left to the imagination. The Gestalt terminology of Frankfurt was itself a kind of weight on the prose, especially since it originated in the very different context of academic laboratory experiments, and its application to psychoanalytic ideas required an elaborate effort of definition and reconstruction. The phenomenological method, which grounded these ideas in close descriptions of ordinary experience, added further ballast to the work of definition, as did the careful specifying of implications, peering as it were into every corner of the Freudian account and asking the reader to reconsider its significance. No wonder Goodman's style moved at a deliberate pace with all these drags on narrative flow.

Another kind of hindrance to easy assimilation has to do less with style than with Goodman's theoretical approach. He refuses to be systematic in the mode of the physical sciences, and this results in momentary snags of apparent inconsistency where a watchful reader is likely to exclaim, "Ah! but ten pages ago you said . . ." At such junctures a sympathetic, and determined, reader will usually be able to work through the redefinitions and conceptual adjustments that bring the theory back into line with itself. Sometimes the problem is merely in the new terminology fighting with the old, sometimes it goes deeper into cruxes of the theory itself.

That Goodman did not seem to realize how thin the ice was as he skated along, or did not care, is something to be explained by his own philosophical and scientific biases. He was a pragmatist in his social thought, including both his psychology and his politics. As he repeatedly pointed out during the sixties, the anarchism he advocated was not a systematic dogma but an "attitude," a stance in the world.[22] So too his version of the Gestalt movement. He was not laying down course after course of theoretical bricks, building an airtight fortress of belief. The point of the phenomenological treatment of concepts was precisely to inculcate a new attitude, to accustom readers to a different angle of vision. This was important for both patients and practitioners, neither of whom have any real stake in the theoretical wars among psychotherapeutic camps but must deal with the here and now of life itself. Gestalt therapy was the psychological mode of Goodman's anarchism, just as decentralist principles, libertarian values, and the autonomy of citizens made up its political mode. I will speak further about this aspect of Goodman's thought in discussing the debt Gestalt therapy owes to William James. For the moment, let me simply suggest that a reader looking for tight logic and systematic interdefinition of concepts in Goodman's half of *Gestalt Therapy* will be frustrated.

A good example of how Gestalt ideas can transform the psychoanalytic perspective may be seen in the development of the notion of the "unfinished situation." Based on the Gestalt concept of "closure," and part of the general theory of figure/ground wholes, the unfinished situation provided a new account of what traditional Freudianism treated as repression. In *Ego, Hunger and Aggression* the concept has no active role to play, though the phrase is used a few times; in *Gestalt Therapy* however, the unfinished situation becomes a major concern.[23] In Goodman's account of repression, the focus is on the present moment, not the buried past: "one swallows one's anger, hardens oneself, pushes the urge out of mind. Yet in the new situation, the painful suppressed excitation persists as part of the ground. The self turns to cope with the new figure, but it cannot draw on the powers engaged in keeping down the suppressed excitation. Thus the ground of contacting the new figure is disturbed by the existence of the painful suppression, which is immobilizing certain of the ego-functions. . . . This persisting disturbance prevents final contact in the new adjustment, for all concern is not given to the figure."[24]

Of course all terms like unfinished situation or repression are metaphors, not a precise calculus of psychic states or events. They encourage different ways of understanding behavior. The Freudian model put a powerful emphasis on temporality, ascribing to past experience a fateful influence on present feeling and act. Such temporal relations were also conceived as a kind of geological stratification, one layer upon another, hiding original sources of dysfunction deep below the surface. Whether spatial or temporal, the Freudian metaphors point away from the present moment and awareness of the here and now, with well-known implications for therapy. The psychological model developed by the Gestalt school of Wertheimer and his colleagues, based as it was on experiments in perception, tended to emphasize immediate experience and its organization in an active present. Its metaphors, like figure/ground, focus attention and suggest attitudes toward behavior very different from those of Freud.

The term unfinished situation is perhaps especially useful because it is not tightly bound to either of these metaphor systems. Although some of the Gestalt psychologists, especially Kurt Lewin and his students, had theorized about the "demand" character of a field in which equilibrium was prevented by incomplete tasks, it never occurred to them to apply such conceptions to psychoanalytic concerns. Even within the confines of their experimental approach the unfinished situation is little more than a variable introduced to measure the drive for closure. Goodman's handling of the term was never so technical as to suggest that the unfinished situation was a precisely understood category. It served his purposes well because its tie to Gestalt notions was not hard and fast, and its meanings in common speech allowed him to move easily into a phenomenological account of experience that could also reach out to the Freudian model, which had its own unfinishedness to be resolved.

The same orientation gave rise to a reconsideration of the concept of "sublimation," which Goodman regarded as an artifact of Freud's locating the unfinished situation in the past, buried under layers of repression. "Strictly speaking, there is no special process as 'sublimation' at all," Goodman claimed. "What is called 'sublimation' is a direct but imperfect satisfaction of the same need." He offered the example of Gandhi, whose power

> to move millions by his famously childlike personality had as one of its important aspects his peculiar attitude toward food: when Gandhi refused to eat or agreed to eat, it was politically momentous. Now shall we interpret this as an infantile petulance? Then how was it so effective? But on the contrary, it was an extraordinarily direct keeping alive of the child's *true* feeling that it makes all the difference in the world under what conditions of love and hate one eats. Gandhi probably fasted not primarily as a calculated threat, but because under certain conditions food was nauseating to him. This spontaneous physiological judgment and consequent considered act, in a context not of the nursery but of the adult world where it is equally relevant but universally disregarded, touched every heart. It was effective not because it was symbolic or a substitute, but because it was a spontaneous response to an actuality.

The Freudian theory of "sublimation," however, was again the result of his too closely associating the persistent drives with their past situations and thoughts.[25]

I have chosen the term unfinished situation to illustrate Goodman's psychoanalytic application of the Gestalt framework because the phrase has come into common use among clinicians, even those outside the circle of Gestalt therapists, and is, like much of Goodman's theorizing, readily taken into common parlance. Goodman was perhaps more at home in the vocabulary and conceptual field of the Gestalt psychologists than his collaborator, even though it was Perls who had worked with Goldstein and who made the first attempts to apply Gestalt terminology to psychoanalytic concerns. Yet it must be said that neither Perls nor Goodman felt any need to master the tradition they were borrowing from. Goodman had read Goldstein's major book, *The Organism*, and the classics of Koffka and Köhler, but it is not likely that he knew much of Lewin's work or had any familiarity at all with the literature published in research periodicals, for which his German would have been barely adequate. His usual method of working up a field was to read the standard texts while relying on experts like his brother or Ben Nelson for a sense of the larger picture. He could not afford a large library, and he borrowed books from his friends when he needed them. He rarely took notes and often quoted from memory or made casual reference to texts rather than careful citations. It was Willis D. Ellis's *Source Book of Gestalt Psychology* (1938) that he used when he wanted to argue from authority.

But as Goodman admitted in his journal at the time he was writing *Growing Up Absurd*, quoting the authorities was often "only a stylistic device" with him.[26] It would be a mistake to argue, for example, that he got his notion of the unfinished situation from the study "On Finished and Unfinished Tasks" (1927) by Lewin's student Bluma Zeigarnik, even though Ellis considered it exemplary enough to be included in the *Source Book*. It is more likely that Perls put the idea into Goodman's head. Perls too had used Ellis's compendium when writing *Ego, Hunger and Aggression*, and had even cited Zeigarnik's experiment—attributing it to Lewin himself—while making an argument of his own about the etiology of Freud's "compulsion to repeat."[27] As so often in Perls's first applications of insights borrowed from others, the Gestalt notion of the unfinished task appears here merely as a bit of ammunition in a scattershot attack on Freud's theory of the return of the repressed. There is little focus and no persistence in the analysis. After a quick page of anecdotal examples invented on the spot, without reference to Gestalt principles or research, Perls moves on to a diatribe against Freud's positing of a "death instinct," and proposes the "tendency to equilibrium" as an alternative to all talk about "instincts." Nonetheless, Perls's view that Freud's theory of repression put too much emphasis on the past, and his intuition that Gestalt ideas about the drive for closure could bring phenomena into the present and explain them as part of ongoing needs and unfinished tasks, all this, however sketchily developed, was surely somewhere in the background of Goodman's elaboration of the concept of the unfinished situation in his and Perls's collaborative theory.

CHAPTER FIVE

The Intellectual Tradition

GOODMAN'S OWN FAMILIARITY with Gestalt psychology went back to his postgraduate days, just as Perls's primary exposure had come soon after his medical training. Moreover, the circumstances of Goodman's early contacts with Gestalt theory made it natural for him to integrate it with the thought of other schools and traditions. His first contacts were in the fall of 1934, when he was living a bohemian life at the center of his little clique of young intellectuals, trying to publish his stories and poems in the literary magazines and auditing classes on Aristotle at Columbia. His older sister paid the bills, but Goodman earned his own spending money, as a reader for Hollywood scenario hunters and as a tutor for college students. These were irregular and infrequent sources of income, but his needs were minimal. That October Goodman picked up a few extra dollars by tutoring a recent refugee from the Nazis in English. His client was Kurt Goldstein.

The association was brief and only the barest record of it survives, in a letter his sister wrote to a mutual friend.[1] Nonetheless it was the beginning of Goodman's interest in Gestalt psychology, which might be said to have arrived in America in

1934. That same autumn Wolfgang Köhler was giving the William James lectures at Harvard, lectures that became the basis of the most philosophical of his books, *The Place of Value in a World of Fact,* and he too would soon be emigrating (a job was found for him at Swarthmore College) along with Kurt Koffka (who went to Smith College), Kurt Lewin (the University of Iowa took him in), and Max Wertheimer (who ended up at the New School). The basic Gestalt texts written by these distinguished figures were coming into print in English during the thirties, and Goodman read a number of them.

If we can judge simply by the frequency with which Goodman quoted him, Goldstein was the one whose work Goodman most admired. He read *The Organism* carefully at some point—probably as part of his reconnoitering the field before writing *Gestalt Therapy*—and he was particularly interested in Goldstein's *Language and Language Disturbances,* which appeared only a few years before Goodman's collaboration with Perls. He was still referring to Goldstein's work on aphasia twenty years later—it was a touchstone for him.[2] Curiously enough, Goodman never told the story of tutoring the exile during his first weeks in America, nor did he, any more than Perls, presume on old acquaintance to bring Goldstein into their camp.

The heavy borrowing of language and approach from the Gestalt psychologists was what led Perls, Hefferline, and Goodman to give their book its name. However, this decision was not easily made, nor did it sit well with every interested party. Among those who objected was Wolfgang Köhler himself, who had been sent a copy of the proof sheets in hopes of an endorsement. There was apparently some delay in transmission, so that Köhler had the proofs in hand only two days before he had to make up his mind about its value. To Gestalt theory's chief surviving spokesman (Koffka had died in 1941, Wertheimer in 1943), this new application of the theory seemed "rather harmless, but also almost cheap," and he urged that the title at least be changed. Even granting the book its cogency, it was misnamed: "the Gestalt psychologists are being criticized in the text precisely because they have *not* done what the authors feel must be done. Why then borrow the name of a psychology which, according to them, has missed the main issues?"[3]

As one might expect, it was Goodman rather than Perls who responded to these criticisms. He leapt at the chance to engage the author of *The Mentality of Apes* in dialogue:

Dear Wolfgang Koehler,

Dr. [Molly] Harrower has forwarded your note about our *Gestalt Therapy*. May I make a few comments, to avoid misunderstanding. Likely you had time to read only the first sections—if you had gotten to the more systematic part (Theory of the Self at the end of Vol. 2), your remarks would be less relevant. The strategy of arrangement of the book was to begin on a more "popular" level—more available in conception, American reading habits, etc.—and to work toward the more difficult and original. This resulted in a language and treatment of concepts which, to my personal taste, is often just about tolerable; your expression "almost cheap" is harsh but not unfair.

To get on to more important matters: our proposition is not that Gestaltists have "missed the main issues," as you say, but have achieved them and not pressed them.

Our method in clinical work is in principle simple: to concentrate on the unity of the behavior, for example, the coherence of the image that is being described, the expression on the face during the description, and the tone of voice employed. When the distortions (non-simplicity) of this unity become aware, at once disturbances in the *conditions* of the concentration begin to become foreground, for example, something avoided in contact between the patient and therapist, unaware muscular tensions, and so forth. We try, that is, to carry on an *open* experiment rather than a controlled one: the question is not, Under what conditions do we get a coherent behavior? but rather, As the behavior tries to achieve simplicity, what conditions must be changed? This leads us then to formulations in theory concerning the *dynamic* relation and sequence of figures and grounds. Vol. 2 of our book tries to sketch such a theory, and I may say that it seems to me to be not irrelevant to Gestalt Psychology but a contribution *in* that psychology.

To put it another way, we are taking up Goldstein's therapeutic indication that in any malfunction (for example, a disabled and retracted limb) we must alternately regard the protected part as the figure or the ground. The bother with Goldstein's position—if I may go off on a tangent—is that he continually tends to defeat himself with his remarkable prejudice that extensor behavior is less "dignified" and less "human" than indrawing behavior (I would cite you a passage or two from his *Organism* but I don't have the text to hand). The result of this is that the environment is effectually ruled out as a source of *curative* energy—despite the fact

that he occasionally mentions, generally in a parenthesis, that the environment *does* lend energy to forming
the figure. That is, he condemns himself to a *mere* physi-
ology, just as most other g[estalt]-psychologists restrict
themselves to a perceptual or interpersonal psychology.
In our book we try to redintegrate [*sic*] these divisions.
This leads to considerable metaphysical adventuring,
very much at variance with popular conceptions—and
all of this is the subject matter of Vol. 2.

Finally, let me make a remark on the title of our
book. It is hard to find a title to satisfy 3 authors. Prof.
Hefferline and Dr. Perls have connections of piety with
Gestalt. (Dr. L. Perls—Dr. F.'s wife and co-worker for 20
years—was, for instance, a loving disciple of Wertheimer's.) As for me, my affiliation in the way of expressing
these ideas is modernly from, say, Husserl's *Ideen* or, on
the converse side, from Dewey. But ultimately, both for
you and for us, the most intrinsic—and in many ways
still the best—expression of our position is that of Aristotle and Kant. What then? Allow me to say that my
guess is that, from the point of view of public appreciation, the traditional Gestalt Psychology will get more
profit from our use of that language than our book will
get from being called *Gestalt Therapy*.

Personally, let me thank you for the formative influence of your books on me when I was a young man.[4]

Sincerely,
Paul Goodman

Goodman succeeded no better in drawing Köhler into
debate than he had with Reich. After publication a copy of the

book was sent to Kurt Goldstein as well.[5] Although he was always cordial to his former pupils and was himself practicing his own brand of Gestalt psychotherapy in Manhattan, Goldstein made no move to connect with the new group forming around Perls. Perhaps an anecdote about one of their encounters will suggest why. Soon after *Gestalt Therapy* came out, Perls, whose impulses were always entrepreneurial, appeared at a conference of psychoanalysts in Atlantic City with a copy of the book under his arm, the dust jacket prominently displayed, but without an official namecard on his own lapel. He had no invitation and was condemned to pace the hotel lobby like a sandwich-board huckster while the meetings went on above him. As luck would have it, he happened to spy Goldstein, who was to address the conference that day, approaching the elevators. Perls was at his side in a flash, embracing his white-haired mentor with unfeigned joy, offering to carry his papers for him, and crowding into the elevator full of his psychiatric confreres. Goldstein affably allowed Perls to take the papers under his arm and join the entourage . . . but the book with the bright new dust jacket went unnoticed.[6]

In Goodman's letter to Köhler he had offered Goldstein's work as an example of the way he and Perls had borrowed from, and improved on, the Gestalt school, and he had spoken of the "connections of piety" both Fritz and Lore had with the founders; when he came to his own part, not as theorist but "in the way of expressing these ideas," he had claimed an "affiliation" with Husserl's *Ideen*. By this he meant to suggest a parallel rather than an influence, as he hastened to add that "on the converse side"—the phrasing is equally evasive—his kinship was with Dewey. In dropping these names Goodman was announcing the phenomenological and pragmatic biases in his way of handling and modifying the Gestalt inheritance. Let us also once again recall the characterization of *Gestalt Therapy* he offered Ben Nelson: "What I've done is add a lot of *existenz* to the Gestalt-psan. base." In both these accounts Goodman is identifying his own contribution to the new theory. Perls, and to some extent his wife, supplied the Gestalt framework, while Goodman drew on existentialism, phenomenology, and their American "converse," pragmatism, in formulating his and Perls's joint critique and reconstruction of psychoanalysis.

With so many strands of influence it is not surprising that there had been argument over the name of their new therapy not only with Köhler but among the namers themselves. Other possibilities had included the old phrase Perls had gotten from Reich, concentration therapy, and two new labels suggesting a more philosophic bias, "actuality therapy" and "existential therapy." Lore Perls, who had the closest ties with both traditions, *Gestalt* and *Existenz*, thought they "could get into difficulties" by calling it Gestalt therapy, but she also agreed that using the term existentialism would lead people to associate them with Jean-Paul Sartre's "nihilistic approach."[7] The book itself did not confront the problem directly, but a few years later, when Goodman discussed existentialism in his training seminars, he spoke of "Existential subjective individualism" as "a neurotic character defense: too much active ego. The existent as it comes to be is *neither* objective nor subjective. Contact is prior to organism/environment."[8] He had Sartre in mind here and was distinguishing the fashionable French stance from earlier, more phenomenologically oriented positions, not so much from Husserl as from literary and religious figures—Kierkegaard,

Kafka, Buber, and the Taoist sages Lao-tzu and Chuang-tzu, all of whom were in his existentialist pantheon.

In sorting out these various strands, it is important to remember that both Fritz and Lore Perls had lived for a time at a major crossroads of *Gestalt* and *Existenz*, and that the amalgamation had been subsequently worked out in twenty years of psychoanalytic practice. *Ego, Hunger and Aggression* never mentions existentialism, but a short chapter called "The Sense of Actuality" shows that Perls already had his here-and-now orientation when he wrote that book: "Self-realization is only possible if 'time-space awareness' penetrates every corner of our existence; fundamentally it is the sense of actuality, the appreciation of the identity of reality and present."[9] In a preview of passages in *Gestalt Therapy*, he goes on to argue that Freud's concept of regression tends to foster a kind of "indulging in the past" at the expense of present awareness and acceptance of responsibility for oneself: "What happens, in my opinion, is rarely an historical repression; it is the mere fact that the patient's true self, his 'weaknesses,' become more clearly visible. . . . He does not regress to the state of his childhood anxiety. His nucleus, his true self, was never anything but excitable; his under-development has never ceased to exist. He has fallen back to his true self, perhaps to his constitutional nature, but not to his childhood."[10]

Compare the following paragraph from the second volume of *Gestalt Therapy*, which adds the concept of the unfinished situation to the analysis and which, in its example, shows Goodman's characteristic use of material from his own experience:

In therapy, the so-called "regressions" are aware loyalties, and it is pointless to deny or denigrate what the patient has really felt as his own; the task is to find out the unaware unfinished situations that are taking energy from the possibilities of the present. The classical instance is the impossibility of "changing" homosexuals who have once gotten important sexual satisfaction, especially since they have creatively overcome many social obstacles in order to get it. The method is clearly not to attack the homosexual adjustment, for that has been the result of the self's integrative power, it is a proved felt contact and identification. The method must be to bring to light what the personality is unaware *alienating*, here the interest in the other sex, half the human beings in the world. That is, it is pointless to say, "Why do you act like an 11-year-old?" but it is reasonable to ask, "What is disgusting, immoral, dangerous in acting like a 12-year-old?" Whatever *is* acted has, in so far, been assimilated.[11]

Aside from his therapist's concern for the here and now, Perls himself did not bring much existentialist baggage with him to his new book. If one asks *what* is here and now, how does actuality manifest itself, the answer of Gestalt therapy combines elements from both Gestalt psychology and existentialism. "Awareness" is perhaps the key word in the Goodman and Perls account, and their crucial innovation in psychoanalytic thought was to reformulate the idea of the ego in terms of awareness at the contact boundary between an organism and its environment. Existentialists offered a variety of approaches to the "I" and its awareness, from the Cartesian conception of an isolated and originating consciousness on which the whole burden of existence rests to the more dialectical formula of Buber, the "I" in its dance with the "It" and the "Thou." Buber's dialogue of self and other fit the Gestalt schema of organism and environment neatly. One senses an unspoken assimilation of his views, for instance, in a passage like this from *Gestalt Therapy*: "Finally, spontaneously engaged in a present concern and accepting it as it develops, the self is not aware of itself abstractly, but is aware of itself as contacting something. Its 'I' is polar with a 'You' and an 'It.' The It is the sense of the materials, urges, and background; the You is the directedness of interest; the I is taking the steps and making the progressive identifications and alienations."[12]

Buber's dialogic formula was useful, but it was difficult to avoid reification of the ego in describing awareness; it was built into the pronouns themselves. As Goodman put it in his last book, *Little Prayers and Finite Experience*, "Experience is prior to the 'organism' and the 'environment,' which are abstractions from experience. It is prior to 'I' and 'that there,' which are abstractions. They are plausible, perhaps inevitable abstractions, except for moments of deep absorption. They are said by every natural language, and it is the devil to try to invent a phenomenological language that avoids them."[13] He was thinking, no doubt, of the difficulties he had faced in *Gestalt Therapy* when he was attempting to present the new theory of ego functions in terms that would not do violence to ordinary language.

Perls had already encountered the problem in *Ego, Hunger and Aggression*, where he had attacked Freud's treatment of the ego as "a substance," whereas from his own Gestalt-influenced perspective the ego was "a contact function."[14] Perls thought the focus of Paul Federn on the "ego-boundaries" was useful, but Federn also ended up viewing the ego as "a substance with boundaries, while, in my opinion, only the boundaries, the places of contact, constitute the Ego. Only where and when the Self meets the 'foreign' does the Ego start functioning, come into existence, determine the boundary between the personal and the impersonal 'field.'"[15] One can see Perls struggling here with terminology: he has the distinction between "self" and "ego" under control in much the way that it would serve in *Gestalt Therapy*, but words like "personal" and "impersonal" leap to his tongue to cloud the issue.

Nonetheless, the nature of the new Gestaltized ego—simply a matter of functioning at the contact boundary of organism and environment—is already enunciated here in 1942, though Perls had trouble staying with his insight and did not press it very far. His paragraph wanders off into a discussion of "identification" and "alienation," concomitants of his overriding metaphor, the alimentary canal, though in other sections of his book he returns to the problem since he *is* writing about ego as well as hunger and aggression. There is a chapter on the "First Person Singular" among his concentration exercises in which he urges the reader to say "I thought" rather than "it occurred to me," and another short chapter is devoted to the distinction between self-consciousness and self-awareness.[16] But Perls could not stay with any subject very long—his fertile mind would tempt him to some new idea. In the later chapters he has dropped the concept of contact-boundary and instead applies a figure/ground analysis to the problem of self-consciousness, the self usurping the attention that should be directed to something in the environment, and so forth.

Perls's remarks are offhand, without theoretical push. It is revealing to compare Goodman's treatment of the same issues to see how he keeps the central insight in focus. Here, for example, is a long passage in which he picks his way through the tangle of selves that common speech and psychoanalytic language present to us, in order to explain why the ego has loomed so large and like a substance instead of a function. What appeared here and there as flashes of insight in Perls's book is now pulled together in an accumulating analysis.

> Now all theorizing, and especially introspecting, is delib-
> erate, restrictive, and abstractive; so in theorizing about
> the self, especially from introspections, it is the Ego that
> looms as the central structure of the self. One is aware of
> oneself in a certain isolation, not always in contact with
> something else. The exertion of will and the exercise of
> one's technique impress by their apparent energy.
> Besides there is the following important neurotic factor:
> acts of deliberateness continually recur in quieting
> unfinished situations, so that this habit of the self
> impresses itself on the memory as the pervasive feeling
> of self, whereas spontaneous contacts tend to finish the
> situation and be forgotten.
> . . . Must we not conclude that for the theory of the
> self and its relation to the "I," introspection is a poor *pri-
> mary* method of observation, for it creates a peculiar
> condition? We must begin by exploring a wide range of
> concernful situations and behaviors. Then if we resume
> the introspection, the true situation is apparent: that the
> introspecting ego is a deliberate restrictive attitude of
> the psycho-somatic awareness, temporarily excluding
> the environmental awareness and making the body-
> awareness a passive object.

When this deliberate restricting is *unaware* (when the ego-function of alienation is neurotic), then there is the sense of a fixed boundary of the self, and of an isolated active center. But this existence is created by the attitude. And then, too, we have "mere" thoughts emptied of "reality." But in the context of aware introspection, the thoughts *are* reality: they are the actual situation when excluding the environment; and then the bounded self and its active center are a good gestalt.

But in general, the aware self does not have fixed boundaries; it exists in each case by contacting some actual situation and is limited by the context of concern, by the dominant interest and the consequent identifications and alienations.[17]

As we have seen, in *Ego, Hunger and Aggression* Perls had already formulated this view of the ego as a set of functions—aware experience—at the contact boundary of organism and environment, but this does not mean that Goodman simply took the idea over from him and gave it more elaborate and consistent treatment. Another set of influences must be taken into account, for the fundamental insight that experience takes place prior to either "I" or "that there" had long been a central tenet in Goodman's philosophical psychology. It was so important, indeed, that its history in his thought can be traced with great precision.

In his letter to Köhler Goodman had claimed "affiliation in the way of expressing these ideas" with Husserl and Dewey, but quickly added that ultimately the "most intrinsic—and in many ways still the best—expression of our position is that of Aristotle and Kant." Just as he regarded Husserl and Dewey as mutually translatable in their accounts of experience, so Goodman took Aristotle and Kant as saying the same thing about the psychology of perception and consciousness—"for my purposes it was the same philosophy," he said breezily, knowing how irritating that would be to the professors.[18] The Kantian analysis of "the synthetic unity of apperception" could be considered as restating Aristotle's conception of "the unitary act of mind" in perception.

Starting when he was one of Morris Raphael Cohen's students at City College, Goodman had been reading philosophy since he was eighteen, but his serious devotion to the discipline began after his graduation when he became an unofficial auditor of Richard McKeon's courses at Columbia. He had been studying Aristotle with McKeon for several years at the time of his brief contact with Kurt Goldstein in the fall of 1934, but that was the year McKeon left Manhattan to become dean at the University of Chicago, and Goodman was once again on his own, without formal classes or a mentor. However, after McKeon had invited Goodman to teach at Chicago, he again sat in on McKeon's seminars while working toward his doctorate. In one of his last papers for McKeon, on Aristotle's *De Anima* and the *Posterior Analytics*, Goodman says, in passing (he is discussing Aristotle's conception of the "unitary act of mind" and its relation to the senses), that Section VII of Aristotle's *De Sensu* must be regarded as "the historical beginning of Gestalt psychology."[19] This was a passage in which Aristotle pointed out that the mind does not perceive two things at the same time, but that the "stronger stimulus" displaces the weaker. One sees why Goodman took this as a Gestalt notion, but in fact it was of much less interest to him than another lesson he had learned from Aristotle that was much more central in his psychology of perception.

When Goodman's dissertation was finally published in 1954, it was dedicated to four of his teachers, and in acknowledging his debts to them he said that McKeon had taught him "to notice the actual experience, when he showed that by the object of sight Aristotle means the oval of vision."[20] This lesson was to be found in *De Anima*, where Aristotle's main example happens to be from hearing rather than vision: "when that which can hear is actively hearing and that which can sound is sounding, then the actual hearing and the actual sound are merged in one, . . . the actualities of the sensible object and of the sensitive faculty are *one* actuality in spite of the difference in their modes of being [425b29–426a17]."[21]

It was with this insight, couched in Gestalt terminology, the phenomena lavishly specified, that Goodman began the theoretical section of *Gestalt Therapy*.

We speak of the organism contacting the environment, but it is the contact that is the simplest and first reality. You may feel this at once if, instead of merely looking at the objects before you, you also become aware of the fact that they are objects in your oval field of vision, and if you feel how this oval of vision is, so to speak, close up against your eyes—indeed, it *is* the seeing of your eyes. Notice, then, how in this oval field the objects begin to have esthetic relations, of space and color-value. And so you may experience it with the sounds "out there": their root of reality is at the boundary of contact, and at that boundary they are experienced in unified structures.

And so motorically, if you are aware of throwing a ball, the distance comes close and your motor impulse has, so to speak, rushed to the surface to meet it. Now the purpose of all the practical experiments and theoretical discussions in this book is to analyze the function of contacting and to heighten awareness of reality.[22]

Two pages later, Goodman names Aristotle as the first to have the "saving and accurate insight that 'in act,' in sensing, the object and the organ are identical."[23]

Goodman had only recently learned this lesson about perception when he first met Goldstein in the fall of 1934, and although he was not yet framing it in Gestalt terms, it is at least conceivable that because of that coincidental meeting he began to be interested in the lesson's bearing on Gestalt theory. In any case he immediately understood its relevance for aesthetic theory and twice referred to Aristotle's formulation in articles printed in little magazines of the mid thirties. He first made his point in an essay on music he probably began in the fall of 1934 although it was not published until the spring of 1936, in a magazine his friend Arthur Berger was editing, *Musical Mercury:* "It is clear that there is no difference between an act of hearing and a sound heard, though there is between the ability to hear and the ability to be heard."[24] When Berger's mentor at Harvard, the aesthetician D. W. Prall, published his *Aesthetic Analysis* not long after this, Goodman reviewed it, and citing both Aristotle and Kant he again returned to the point, that "it makes no difference in principle whether we talk of a sensation as an act of experiencing or as a content of experience."[25]

Just how fundamental this insight was in Goodman's thinking can be gathered from these early repetitions and from the dedication to McKeon, as well as from the central place given the idea in *Gestalt Therapy*, where it is fused with Perls's notion of the ego as a function of the contact boundary. Goodman was still relying on the same analysis twenty years later in his last work, *Little Prayers and Finite Experience*, his attempt to sum up the lessons that life had taught him.

> There is no function of an organism that does not essentially involve its environment—we breathe air and walk by gravity and ground. No feeling that does not address the environment—anger that there is an obstacle to reaching, or an insult to organic integrity; grief that there is a hole in the environment, or a loss there that must be mourned through. If emotions did not signal something about the environment, they would not have been inherited and have survived; they tell us the relation of organism and environment, and they spur us to cope.
>
> Conversely, the actual environment, the place, is what is selected, structured, and appropriated by the organism.
>
> Aristotle put it well: When sensory power is actualized, when there *is* experience, the sense organ is the *same* as the sensed object. "The object of sight is the oval of vision."
>
> Experience is neither "subjective" nor "objective." Its proper nouns are Here, Now, Next, Thou, We, rather than I, It, Past, Future. It is impossible to talk such a language, but it is the genius of literature to recapture primary experience by combining narrator and narrative in ongoing plot.[26]

A few pages later he was citing Kurt Goldstein again, to the effect that one does not "see" with the optic nerve, nor with the eye, "but with the whole organism, when there is light, etc."[27] Here was a congeries of ideas and influences that had lasted almost forty years and was as alive for him as ever.

Just as Goodman was eager to assimilate the concepts and terms of the Gestalt psychologists to his Aristotelian (and Kantian) base, so too was he ready to bring the teachings of existentialism to bear and the lessons of the phenomenologists and the murkier wisdom of his Taoist sages. They all helped him understand his own experience and therefore gave him analytic grasp of the theoretical issues he and Perls were rethinking in *Gestalt Therapy*. One must read between the lines to see how very personal the theorizing was in *Gestalt Therapy*, but Goodman's last book reveals the underlying dynamic. Shortly after the passage in *Little Prayers and Finite Experience* on Aristotle's doctrine of perception, Goodman moves to a discussion of what is *beyond* or *outside* awareness, *not* part of the contact boundary, and we see him meditating on his own "finite experience" and the "fertile void" that he posited in order not to feel trapped in awareness or simply at the mercy of who he was and where he was. This too was a sine qua non of psychotherapy in theory and practice.

> "Surrounding" finite experience must be what is not experienced. (This is an article of faith.) What, if anything, can be said about it from what is actual in experience?
> In awareness there is a boundary of which one is still dimly aware, Husserl's "horizon"; and let us consider this

in two different ways. First, if I turn to *it*, then what is beyond the boundary enters awareness. Whichever way I move, comes into being new space. To attend to the boundary is a standard device of psychotherapy: if there is an absence of feeling, trace the boundary of what *is* felt, for example, the air in the nostrils; then how far can you feel beyond the previous boundary, for example, the air in the sinuses. Awareness itself seems to generate energy. They tell me there is a neurophysiological basis for this effect.

But the contrary tack is even more remarkable. If I withdraw further from the boundary by concentrating on the center, then the emptier the background is, the brighter and more structured the figure in the foreground. I take it that this is the idea of Yoga concentration. For my own theoretical purposes, I feign the hypothesis that energy flows from the emptying background and vivifies the figure in the foreground. I rely, by an act of faith, precisely on what I do not experience. Tao says, "Stand out of the Way." The implication is that there is then *new* energy, and theoretically, I like to deny the conservation of energy. But perhaps it is energy that we have dammed up and now set free. . . .

If in either case, attending to the boundary or withdrawing from it, the void is fertile, then it is very well that experience is finite.[28]

We are now in a realm of discourse that has no equivalent in *Ego, Hunger and Aggression* or any other works or reports of Perls's thought. There was little congenial to Perls's character in the injunction to "Stand out of the Way," even though self-regulation was a byword with him. The master of therapeutic technique also found it difficult to trust in the medieval Western saying that Goodman quoted over and over, *Natura sanat non medicus*, "Nature heals, not the physician."

In Goodman's view the goal of therapy ought to be largely "negative," a matter of letting go of tensions and giving up the inhibitions that prevent healthy self-regulation. He had no more taste for trances or transcendences than Perls did, and the idea of escaping either self or world was not part of his Taoism. But he believed that the ability of a patient to stop clinging to his cage of will and habit depended on a kind of faith—call it animal, existential, or religious—faith that he would not dissolve or drown if he relaxed his grip. There would be "new energy" to meet new reality. It did not depend on some esoteric enlightenment sweeping one into bliss. Goodman called his Taoist politics "peasant anarchism," and his Taoist psychology should be similarly construed—the Way was simple and ordinary.

Goodman had been reading Eastern literature—Noh plays and Tu Fu—as long as he had been studying Aristotle, but his interest in Taoism (in Arthur Waley's translations) was an event of the mid forties, occurring about the same time as his discovery of Reich. These were not equal influences on his thought, though it could be said that in the writing of *Gestalt Therapy* he borrowed as much from Lao-tzu as he did from Husserl or Buber. The strands are not easily separated and perhaps one appreciates his eclecticism best by noticing how completely they fuse in passages like the following description of "good contact," where strong echoes of Buber and Aristotle merge with Gestalt, existentialist, and Taoist attitudes in a single synthesis: "The feeling of absorption is 'self-forgetful'; it attends completely to its object, and since this object fills the entire field—anything else is experienced as to the interest of the object—the object becomes a 'Thou,' it is what is addressed. The 'I' lapses altogether into its attentive feeling: we speak of being 'all ears, all eyes.'"[29]

Although certainly not so fashionable as existentialism, especially French existentialism, nonetheless both Waley's version of Taoism and Buber's Hasidism were minor enthusiasms among the intellectuals of 1950. Perls would have had no objection to their inclusion in the recipe for Gestalt therapy, though he himself tended to favor Korzybski's general semantics, the contemporary language-reform craze.

Goodman's absorption of these religious currents into his psychoanalytic thinking was not a matter of fads and fashions. His notion of the psyche had always been a theological one, even before his first efforts to formalize his beliefs in *Kafka's Prayer*, where Lao-tzu, Buber, and Kierkegaard all leave their tracks. Ever since the mid thirties Goodman had been reading the new Protestant theologians with their strong flavor of *Existenz*, especially Karl Barth.[30] And Goodman was a Jew, not a practicing one but aware of that heritage too. However much he was indebted to particular strains of religious thought, by this time in his life he had assimilated them so thoroughly that it is often hard to tell where his faith gets its expression from one, where from another. In any case, Goodman's psychoanalytic faith represented at once a wide claim on the spiritual past and an extremely idiosyncratic and modern theology of the world and the psyche.

One way of understanding Goodman's contribution to *Gestalt Therapy* would be to think of him as an interpreter who was able to seize upon the experience and insights of his collaborator and transform them into doctrine, amalgamating Perls's ideas from psychoanalysis and Gestalt psychology with a range of philosophic traditions into a single new system. Another way of viewing his effort would be to consider it as the Americanization of these strains of thought from Central Europe and the Orient. When he himself looked back on the development of his theories from the perspective of twenty years later, Goodman had a new equation to substitute for the one he had given Ben Nelson in the heat of composition: psychoanalysis plus *Gestalt* plus *Existenz*. In the new equation, the European terms drop out and American ones replace them, as the reader will see.

I have been quoting passages from *Little Prayers and Finite Experience*, written at the end of Goodman's life as a kind of intellectual apologia. This was also a period when the first books were beginning to be written by others about Goodman's contribution to the thought of his times. One such book was Richard King's *The Party of Eros*, a study of the ideas of Reich, Herbert Marcuse, and Goodman.[31] King had been in correspondence with Goodman while preparing a chapter on him, and he sent Goodman a copy of the results once they were in print. Goodman thanked King for the "adequate and fair" discussion of his ideas, but noted that King failed to take account of the religious aspect of his thought, whereas Theodore Roszak in *The Making of a Counter-Culture* had properly emphasized the "Eastern," that is, Taoist strain in him. But Goodman also offered an even more complex genealogy for his psychoanalytic perspective: "*Gestalt Therapy*," he said, "is Freud & Reich & James & Dewey & Laotze."[32]

Leaving to one side Goodman's desire to set the record straight about his religious conception of psychoanalysis and the influence of Lao-tzu, both of which have already been discussed, let us attend to the significance of placing the names of William James and John Dewey next to those of Freud and Reich—and ask what, in this new formula, has become of *Gestalt* and *Existenz*?

The answer is that James and Dewey, in Goodman's backward glance, could stand for their European counterparts, the existentialists, phenomenologists, and Gestalt psychologists. To a large degree their functional psychology already contained the crucial insights that Perls was exposed to in Frankfurt, and although Goodman was content to think through the new theory in the terms that his collaborator was more familiar with— there are no entries for James or Dewey in the index of *Gestalt Therapy* and only a few references to them in the text—the American line of thought would have served equally well, and in the long run Goodman considered himself more solidly in that tradition than in the German one.

Goodman was not the only one to see the congruities between Gestalt psychology and James's *Principles of Psychology*. It was entirely appropriate that so many of the Frankfurt refugees ended up in American universities, and that Köhler and Goldstein had each been invited to give the William James Lectures at Harvard, their respective topics reflecting pragmatist concerns, *The Place of Value in a World of Fact* and *Human Nature in the Light of Psychopathology*. Goldstein was quite explicit about it: James was the first Gestalt psychologist.[33]

Goodman thought Aristotle was the *first*, but he would certainly have agreed that James belonged in the Gestalt and the existentialist camps. Even more to the point, James's habitual philosophic manner, his very tone of voice, can be heard in the pages of *Gestalt Therapy*. It was something Goodman had acquired not merely by study—though he had been reading James and Dewey since his college days—but also by a kind of natural right, as one has one's native tongue and cultural heritage simply by virtue of growing up here rather than there.

Of course there is much in *The Principles of Psychology* outside the range of any theory of psychotherapy, just as there is much in Köhler and Goldstein that never found its way into Goodman and Perls's book. What is remarkable is how much of the basic thought of *Gestalt Therapy* has its parallels in James. To mention a few of the more obvious examples, there is the initial refusal to accept traditional dualisms like mind/body, subject/object, and self/world, and the emphasis instead on organism/environment contact as the locus of experience; the centrality of the here and now; and the reliance on a radical phenomenology as the basis for constructing any theoretical principles. In James's psychology all of these are one thing. Accordingly the self is understood as passing states of awareness organized as succeeding wholes, as *Gestalten,* and this "stream of consciousness" takes place not "inside" some self or ego but at what Goodman and Perls would call the contact-boundary. Like Aristotle, James refuses phenomenologically to distinguish states of mind from their objects when he says "the thoughts themselves are the thinkers."[34]

Perhaps the most important debt *Gestalt Therapy* owed the American tradition was the pragmatic turn James and Dewey had given the phenomenological habit of thought, which took some of the mechanicalness out of the Gestalt theory Perls brought with him and suffused it with human meaning and a powerful impetus toward practical life. The cluster of attitudes we might call the American phenomenology had its own cultural concomitants—for instance, the tradition of progressive education, with its Deweyan emphasis on learning-by-doing, a bias that was especially American in its ideal of the educated citizen who could cope practically with life, who knew his tools and their uses because his training had been *in* the world and not merely *for* it, more like an apprenticeship than schooling. Although Goodman certainly admired much in the work of A. S. Neill, especially the emphasis on self-regulation that Neill shared with Reich, he was more inclined toward this American pedagogy, for which one would have to go back to Montessori or Pestalozzi to find a European source. In practice Gestalt therapy was often conducted on just such a framework of small groups with a mentor, engaged as much as possible in practical life and bringing pressing problems in front of the group for solution, with the ultimate aim being the achievement of master status by every member. At least for Goodman, every group was a training group, somewhat on the model of the Boy Scout patrol.

Also very important, and very American, among the aspects of Jamesian psychology reappearing in Gestalt therapy was its eclecticism, borrowing ideas from many schools and thinkers while refusing to become doctrinaire itself. This last especially was in contrast to European examples. No doubt Köhler was right in supposing that *Gestalt Therapy* was, among other things, a critique of Gestalt psychology, but his desire to protect the integrity of his school and its name from the upstarts Perls and Goodman was far from a spirit of free inquiry and no-property-in-truth. *Gestalt Therapy* does indeed fall into a polemical stance as it takes up the ideas of the various men and movements out of which it is evolving—both Perls and Goodman were fiercely iconoclastic—but the animus of the book is not partisan, and the aim is not to dismiss progenitors so much as it is to make better use of them. "The point of detailing differences among the schools is not to choose among them, nor contrariwise to reject them one and all; nor certainly to discredit psychotherapy as sectarian," wrote Goodman.

> Indeed, by and large the various theories are not logically incompatible and often neatly supplement and indirectly prove one another. . . . But any one who sympathetically surveys the various schools and methods of psychotherapy, as we have been doing, however superficially, also thinks a new thought: the basic human nature is in part given, as they assume, but in part, adjusting to the various therapies, it *creates itself*; and this creative adjustment in favorable circumstances is itself an essential of the basic human nature. . . . The problem of psychotherapy is to enlist the patient's power of creative adjustment without forcing it into the stereotype of the therapist's scientific conception.[35]

When James's *Principles* first appeared it was criticized in some quarters for lacking system. *Gestalt Therapy* is unsystematic in a similar way. That is, the theoretical effort is not put into constructing a rigorous, self-consistent account, for, as just illustrated, the authors do not believe in a human nature amenable to such methods of definition and analysis. As in his other theoretical books, from *Communitas* to *Speaking and Language*, Goodman's aim is to indicate an attitude toward the subject that is suggestive and practical rather than definitive or normative. He has no blueprints to offer, only a humanistic point of view and faith in the methods of natural science. His psychology, like James's, was grounded in experience and experiment. And the goal, as it was for James, was understanding rather than knowledge.

Just as in the case of American pragmatism, catholicity of ideas and eschewing of dogma have also made it easier for elements of the Gestalt point of view to enter into the professional psychoanalytic wisdom and even into the culture at large, often losing their original labels, their attribution, and alas, sometimes their proper sense. In this roundabout way Gestalt therapy has helped infuse something from the Central European tradition— Freud and Reich, *Gestalt* and *Existenz*—into the American line of thought that begins with Emerson, runs through James, Dewey, Thorstein Veblen, and Randolph Bourne, and is our common heritage. Although hardly Fritz Perls's fantasy of his place in intellectual history, it is probably not so far from what Goodman would have welcomed as his own.

One further strand of influence needs to be discussed. Although European rather than American it was not part of Perls's Frankfurt baggage, nor did it grow out of Goodman's own youthful studies. This was the influence of Otto Rank, whose ideas first attracted Goodman as an artist rather than as a philosopher or psychologist. Rank was one of Freud's most promising adherents until their falling out in the mid twenties, when Rank's theories began to diverge too far and too explicitly from psychoanalytic orthodoxy. Like Reich, who was a dozen years his junior and whose break with the master came a decade later, Rank was thought mad by those who remained in the fold, and he pursued his own insights with just as much passionate energy as the discoverer of the orgone.

In their different ways both Rank and Reich had come to doubt the central Freudian project of interpreting repressed childhood contents, the traditional psychoanalytic fixation on the past, and argued for more attention to the current manifestations of repression in the patient and more awareness of how the therapeutic intervention was also part of the patient's plight—in other words, they treated the transference as something more than a pale reflection of buried feelings. As Rank put it, Freud "made the repression historical, that is, misplaced it into the childhood of the individual and then wanted to release it from there, while as a matter of fact the same tendency is working here and now. . . . Some kind of real tying up in addition to the purely psychological relating is naturally necessary for the neurotic, with his hostility to life. In my method this happens not historically, but in the present."[36] It is evident that Gestalt therapy's concern for the here and now did not originate in any single influence—Gestalt, existentialist, or Taoist; Reichian or Jamesian—but Rank's formulation has the therapeutic moment in view more explicitly than any other.

Rank's greatest work, *Art and Artist*, was issued in 1932, just a few years before Reich's *Character Analysis*, but it was the English translation that was published (the original German has yet to be published), whereas Reich's classic had to wait until 1945 before it was translated. Thus Goodman, whose German was never fluent, had read Rank first, though apparently not until 1941 or 1942 when he used some of Rank's material on the Ariadne myth in his novel *Don Juan*. None of Rank's other books had much to say to Goodman, though he seems to have read them, and the intellectual impact Rank's work had on him was slight compared to that of Reich a few years later. Reich's ideas were revolutionary—they undermined and reopened so many old and settled questions—whereas Rank's masterpiece *Art and Artist* was a vast survey and consolidation of knowledge, a final word that could hardly be surpassed and so, in a sense, led nowhere. It too was a critique of Freudian doctrine, but mounted in so stupendous and monumental a treatise that one is simply left with the feeling Goodman expressed about it more than once, "beyond praise."

This partly accounts for the curious way that Rank figures in *Gestalt Therapy*. Other major voices in the psychoanalytic tradition appear in polemical contexts, under headings such as "Gestalt-Therapy and the Trends of Psychoanalysis" or "Critique of Psychoanalytic Theories of the Self," with Freud and Reich always receiving the most attention and the roughest treatment. Mention of Rank is only in passing, often as an aside or in a footnote, though almost invariably with strong approval. Nothing seems to follow from these moments, no contradictions, no insights. Rank is not used to further the argument, and therefore can be neither a hero nor a villain in the story. Yet in those pages where his name appears, the main point usually derives from him: that art (and especially the *play* in art-working) is the key to healthy adjustment, that the neurotic is best regarded "as a failed artist," and that even neurosis is "a creative achievement just as much as any other."[37] These last quotations are from Rank, not Goodman, but *Gestalt Therapy* has its equivalents, in the terminology of the contact-boundary:

All contact is creative adjustment of the organism and environment. . . . [P]sychology is the study of creative adjustments, . . . abnormal psychology is the study of the interruption, inhibition, or other accidents in the course of creative adjustment.[38]

. . . .

We speak of creative adjustment as the essential function of the self (or better the self *is* the system of creative adjustments).[39]

. . . .

[T]he revisionist para-Freudian schools, for instance, the Reichians or the Washington School tend to reduce the self altogether into the system of the organism or the interpersonal society: strictly speaking they are not psychologies at all, but biologies, sociologies, etc. But the self is precisely the integrator; it is the *synthetic* unity, as Kant said. It is the artist of life.[40]

. . . .

[I]n the usual character-analysis, the resistances are "attacked," the "defenses" are dissolved, and so forth. But on the contrary, if the awareness is creative, then these very resistances and defenses—they are really counter-attacks and aggressions against the self—are taken as active expressions of vitality, however neurotic they may be in the total picture.[41]

. . . .

The important part of the psychology of art is not in the dream or in the critical consciousness; it is (where the psychoanalysts do not look for it) in the concentrated sensation and in the playful manipulation of the material medium. With bright sensation and play in the medium as his central acts, the artist then accepts his dream and uses his critical deliberateness: and he spontaneously realizes an objective form. The artist is quite *aware* of what he is doing—after it is done, he can show you the steps in detail; he is not unconscious in his working, but neither is he mainly deliberately calculating. His awareness is in a kind of middle mode, neither active nor passive, but accepting the conditions, attending to the job, and *growing* toward the solution.[42]

One of the chief claims that Goodman and Perls made for their book was that it offered, for the first time, a theory of the self that was not, at best, simply otiose. Gestalt ideas provided them with a locus, the contact-boundary, for the functions of self; Rank's analysis of creativity and the psychology of the artist gave them a way of characterizing the self's activity that fit the contact-boundary model and offered new criteria for the health (and sickness) of the psyche. In this way they were able to bring together much that seemed valuable in life (art, play, the spontaneity of childhood) in a coherent picture of the nature of creative adjustment between organism and environment.

I speak here of Perls and Goodman, but there is no solid evidence that Perls knew Rank's work, whereas Goodman was familiar with the major treatises, and had long experience as an artist, including treatment of his own neurotic behavior in books like *Don Juan* and *Parents' Day,* to confirm Rank's views of art and the self.[43] It is all the more interesting to note how Goodman sets Rank to one side (on a pedestal, to be sure) as a force in psychoanalytic history. Of course it was true. There were no followers to speak of, and Rank's death in 1939, not long before Freud's, put him on the shelf—merely a set of books—in a way that was never to happen to Reich or Perls or

Goodman himself. Even so, the treatment of Rank in *Gestalt Therapy* is puzzling, as if Goodman were reluctant to bring into the analysis any thinkers—not Rank, not James or Dewey either—with whom his collaborator had no genuine affinity or points of contact.

Perhaps it could be said that Goodman's conception of his own contribution to the book was that of an outsider; not a primary thinker or originator but a critic and a synthesizer who could appreciate the value of ideas from many quarters and who, without identifying himself very strongly with any particular position, could be the artist of psychoanalysis, as it were, the theorist without a theory, whose creative act was to bring together and show the compatibility of many lines of thought. Goodman is very comfortable in this book, as he was in *Communitas*, with the "we" of joint authorship, in spite of much rivalry and disagreement with Perls in their encounters outside the collaboration. He has no stance of his own that he wants to insinuate into Perls's Gestaltizing of psychoanalysis; the addition of existentialism to the book was less a matter of inserting new ideas than the use of a phenomenological approach in the exposition. Goodman's importations—his existentialism, his Taoism, his American pragmatism, his Rankian view of art— all of these are worked into the fabric of the book without any sense of their being presented as counterbalances to Perls's insights or authority. Given Goodman's always difficult relations with his peers, this is worth noting. In collaboration he simply assumed he was in charge, and this automatically solved many problems.

The point may be clarified by a glance at the more narrowly *personal* contributions of Perls and Goodman to their book; for in addition to the currents of thought already considered it is possible to identify particular sections that stand out as somewhat isolated from the stream of argument, little islands of special pleading, intellectual fortresses with banners flying above them—to wit, "Verbalizing and Poetry" and "The Anti-Social and Aggression," back-to-back chapters that represent the hobbyhorses of Goodman and Perls respectively.

In the chapter that reflects Goodman's thought, Goodman presents, without saying that he is doing so, the methods he had developed as a teacher of creative writing, for instance, the techniques and rationale of the writing workshop he offered at Black Mountain College during the summer of 1950, immediately after completing the first draft of the book. He begins the chapter by identifying the "verbalizer" as a neurotic type representative of a widespread trend in society which today we would associate with the media: "just as in our culture as a whole there has grown up a symbolic culture devoid of contact or affect, isolated from animal satisfaction and spontaneous social invention, so in each self, when the growth of the original interpersonal relations has been disturbed and the conflicts not fought through but pacified in a premature truce incorporating alien standards, there is formed a 'verbalizing' personality, a speech that is insensitive, prosy, affectless, monotonous, stereotyped in content, inflexible in rhetorical attitude, mechanical in syntax, meaningless."[44] The contrary, healthy use of speech is like poetry, "an organic problem-solving activity." In poetic speech, "the rhythm is given by pulses of breathing (verses), by the gaits of locomotion and dance (meters), by syllogism, antithesis, or other beats of thought (stanzas and paragraphs), and by the orgastic intensification of feeling (climax), then diminishing into silence."[45] All this Goodman contrasted with the rigid speech of the verbalizer.

But poetry is a special case of good, contactful speech in that it occurs in a purely verbal context, whereas ordinary healthy conversation involves a present listener, potential nonverbal behavior, and so forth. The artistic problem solving of the ordinary person leads to acts and alterations in the world of speaker and hearer. The poet, whose situation is entirely verbal, seems therefore to be in much the position of the verbalizer, whose verbalizing "serves as a substitute for life," and "protects one's isolation from both the environment and the organism."[46] Here Goodman leaves the strictly therapeutic issues of his chapter and digresses briefly into his own predicament as an artist—a subject he came back to in several of his articles for *Complex* during this period.

It is often asserted that the art-work does not *solve* any problem or solves it only temporarily, because the artist does not know the latent content of his symbol; and if this were so, poetry would again be an obsessive exhaustion of energy in a repeating situation, like verbalizing. This is both true and false: the problem that the artist does not solve is the one that makes him only an artist, free only in the vital activity of speaking but unable to use the words also instrumentally in further free acts; and many poets feel the obsessiveness of their art in this respect—finishing a work they are exhausted, and still have not regained a lost paradise. (It is not to be seen, by the way, that many other activities—even psychotherapy—win us that lost paradise.) But as for the particular subvocal problems, they *are* really solved, one by one; the proof is that the successive art-works are fundamentally different, there is a deepening of the art-problem; and indeed, this activity sometimes proceeds so far that the poet is finally forced to confront life-problems that he cannot solve by artistic means alone.[47]

These last were prophetic words for Goodman to be uttering in 1950, and perhaps that is part of the reason why, compatible though it is with all the ideas and approaches of the book, the chapter "Verbalizing and Poetry" seems special, a rhetorical island in the midst of the onflowing argument.

Something similar might be said of the next chapter, "The Anti-Social and Aggression," although here Gestalt terminology is brought into play more explicitly, in an attempt to integrate Perls's notion of healthy aggression into the larger conceptual framework without simply reiterating his favorite metabolic metaphors of biting, chewing, digesting, and assimilating. Whatever may be said about Perls's fastidiousness in appropriating ideas from other people's books, or digests of their books, there can be no question that the notion of dental aggression was truly his, an insight that he lived out every day in his own character. Ben Nelson used to tell a story that catches the flavor of it quite well.

One day Perls and Nelson were having dinner together at a restaurant, and Fritz began to harangue Ben about his eating habits, which certainly were greedy and oblivious. "No wonder you have an ulcer!" he exclaimed. "You don't bite. Bite! Use your teeth. Tear into it! Let your aggression out on it! Now chew! Don't swallow it yet, *taste* it! Enjoy it!" By this time Ben had lost his appetite, and he shoved his plate angrily across the table to Fritz. "Here, you eat it." Which Fritz immediately set about doing. "See? Like this." And he gobbled down Ben's dinner with evident satisfaction.[48]

Of course the lesson in these ironies was not the sort of thing that could be captured by a chapter in a book—that was part of the reason Perls turned, late in life, to filmed demonstrations as a way of getting his message across: you had to see him in action, eating his patients alive, to understand what dental aggression was really all about. All the better if his patients bit back.

A certain comprehension of the theory could be gained by diligently working one's way through the awareness exercises in Hefferline's half of *Gestalt Therapy*. Thus, in "Experiment 15: Introjecting and Eating," the self-helping reader is invited to "concentrate" on his eating habits. "Notice your resistances to addressing the food. Do you taste the first few bites and then fall into a trance of 'thinking,' daydreaming, wanting to talk— meantime losing contact with the taste? Do you bite off your food by clean, efficient action of the front teeth? In other words, do you bite through on a meat sandwich held in your hands, or do you close your jaws part way and then tear off a hunk? Do you ever use your molars up to the point of complete destruction of the food, that is, liquefaction?"[49] Further exercises lead the reader from food to thought, the chewing and assimilation (or gulping and indigestion) of mental meals.

All of this is pure Perls. I do not mean that Goodman demurred; on the contrary he regarded the theory of dental aggression as his collaborator's most important contribution to psychoanalytic thought and accepted it fully, down to the last details. However, when it came to writing "The Anti-Social and Aggression," Goodman was obliged, was he not, to do more than regurgitate Fritz's theory? He offered his own assimilated view of the matter, much more politicized than anything that ever came out of Perls. The focus is on the "destroying (destructuring)" which is the natural result of either appetite or the anger arising from the frustration of appetite—that is, less on the negative effects of introjection and more on the liberation of initiative and growth through healthy aggression. The argument broadens out to consideration of antisocial behavior, aggression as a fact of political as well as private life, making a Reichian connection between modern war and the stifling of individual appetite and anger. To all of this Perls would have agreed; he had said something similar, though very briefly, about Hitler and Nazism in *Ego, Hunger and Aggression*.

Whatever overlay of political concern Goodman might bring to it, the chapter was Perls's chapter, just as the preceding one was Goodman's. And although the blood of the general theory of their book circulated through both chapters, they were each animated by a more personal, idiosyncratic spirit. The remarkable thing was that these powerful genies were bottled up in two chapters, while the rest of the book was free of them, and free as well of any sense of underlying antagonism or rivalry in the collaborators.

CHAPTER SIX

The New York Institute and Its Founders

BY THE END of June 1950 the first draft of *Gestalt Therapy* was finished, and both authors left Manhattan, each of them entertaining fantasies of not returning, though neither had solid plans for anything beyond a summer out of the city. I do not mean to imply any violent revulsion from collaborating: their motives seem not to have been linked in any way, though the coincidence makes one look twice. Goodman was off to Black Mountain College to teach in its Summer Arts Program, hoping the school would offer him a permanent job that would solve some of his financial, communal, and domestic problems. Perls was taking a tour of the West Coast, partly prompted by dissatisfaction at home—he and Lore were not happy together—but more basically by his never-ending restlessness.

Goodman returned from North Carolina with his tail between his legs—Black Mountain did not want him—but Perls came back from Los Angeles "top dog," to use one of his favorite expressions. He had found a new group of disciples and a clientele to go with it. He had even been awarded an honorary doctorate—"because of my books"—by a college whose name he could not remember.[1] "Ph.D." would look good on the cover of *Gestalt Therapy*, next to the "M.D." that was not valid in the

U.S. (That made three somewhat dubious sets of initials, for Goodman's Ph.D., earned in 1940, wasn't official until 1954 when his dissertation was published; only Hefferline's degree was beyond question at the time.)

Perls returned to Manhattan long enough to work out final arrangements for the publication of the book and to collect a few followers to take back with him to the West Coast. By this time Isadore From had come far enough in his therapy with Lore to be considered a promising trainee and get an invitation. His twin brother Sam lived in Los Angeles and had served as Fritz's host during the summer, introducing him to a circle of California bohemians that included a number of potential patients and trainees. Jerry Raphel and Richard Kitzler, another of David Sachs's bright young students at Rutgers, went out too, hoping to become part of the second generation of Gestalt therapists. Others joined the ranks in California, for Perls's reputation was growing even though the book would not be in print until the end of 1951. It was just this sort of whirlwind constituency-building that he was to be famous for.[2]

Meanwhile, back in New York, Goodman resumed his therapy with Lore Perls, and its character as training sessions was confirmed when she brought together four more of her professional patients into a group. The nucleus included Goodman, Paul Weisz, and Elliott Shapiro. (Two others were documentary photographers whose names do not figure in the later history of Gestalt therapy.) They met weekly at Lore's apartment on West 95th Street. It was her first group, and she was nervous with her collection of geniuses, as she called them.[3]

Shapiro was a teacher, later to become principal of P.S. 119 in Harlem, a famous community-based school of the sixties. He had spent a dozen years as a reading teacher in the children's wards at Bellevue Hospital, working with Lauretta Bender, and at the time he joined Lore's group he was head of the psychiatric school attached to Kings County Psychiatric Hospital in Brooklyn. Shapiro had been friendly with Bender's husband Paul Schilder, a Gestalt-minded Bellevue psychiatrist with background and interests similar to Kurt Goldstein's. He had also read Jan Christian Smuts and had studied with Max Wertheimer at the New School so that in 1950, when a colleague at Kings County brought to work one day a copy of *Ego, Hunger and Aggression*, Shapiro immediately saw possibilities in Perls's new point of view, especially in the concentration exercises, which he began to use in the night classes on abnormal psychology he was teaching at Brooklyn College. Shapiro looked up Lore Perls (his colleague had been one of her patients) and he began sessions with her in the fall of 1950, shortly before the training group with Goodman and Weisz was formed.[4]

Paul Weisz was a Vienna M.D., trained in neurology and biochemistry as well as internal medicine. His wife Lottie Weisz was a psychiatrist at Bellevue, and it was through her that he met the Perlses and began training therapy with Lore. Of all the Gestalt therapists of the early days, it is said that Weisz was the only one who could hold his own with both Goodman and Perls. He was doing medical research at Montefiore Hospital at this time, and was a cultivated man as well as a serious scientist.[5]

Weisz smoked too much, coughed incessantly, and rasped when he talked. He seemed always to be breaking his legs skiing and having to run his therapy sessions in a cast. His view was somewhat Laingian: if psychosis is the clinging to an old way of dealing with a problem, one solution is to become more

psychotic, to have it out! Perls called him "a killer." Nonetheless, people sent their most difficult cases to him. Once a
patient insisted she couldn't feel anything; he leaned forward
and gave her a crack with his cane: "You feel that, don't you?"[6]
He took patients no one else would see outside an institution,
and his success rate was thought to be better than that of most
Gestalt therapists, though his high-risk cases did not always
respond to the last-ditch techniques he used.

Weisz and Goodman were alike in many ways—somewhat
disoriented in space, compulsive, a bit sloppy, aggressive,
learned. Someone once saw Weisz's passport photo and was
astonished at how "poetic" he had looked as a young man.
There are pictures of Goodman that have the same effect. They
respected one another, and from their very different perspectives tended to agree on things. Weisz was interested in Zen
Buddhism just as Goodman was fascinated by Taoism—but
characteristically Weisz set about mastering his subject, including the languages, whereas Goodman simply assimilated what
he found ready to hand in Arthur Waley's translations. Weisz
knew his Darwin and Whitehead too, and like Goodman, he
relished sharp debate. They were a match for one another.

Elliott Shapiro was the mildest of the three, and he had
been a Golden Gloves boxer in his youth. No wonder Lore
Perls was "scared" when she undertook to train these tigers. But
twenty years of marriage to Fritz gave her plenty of experience
in dealing with unruly genius. And they respected *her* intelligence; they could learn things from her that they could never
learn from Fritz, and she made it possible for them to learn from
one another too. Although only a few years older than her
patients, she had been practicing therapy for almost two

decades. Nor was it irrelevant that she had studied with Gelb and Goldstein, Tillich and Buber.

This practicum group stayed together more than a year. For Goodman it represented an important step. Up to this point he had carried himself as if he were only a kibitzer, a learned kibitzer to be sure, ready to take a turn at theorizing in print, even to give psychoanalytic counseling to his friends, but preferring to keep his amateur status. Now, in a mood of determination, he decided to take himself seriously as a psychotherapist. His career as a writer was at a standstill—he was selling copies of *Kafka's Prayer* and *The Facts of Life* to friends for Christmas presents at a dollar apiece—and after first losing his job in the New York University night school and then being turned down by Black Mountain College, his chances of earning anything as a teacher seemed to be at an end. Editing *Complex* magazine had been worth $50 an issue (for a total of $100) and Perls was going to pay him $500 for his work on the book, so there was a living of sorts on the fringes, but why not move into the center for once? He began to accept patients.

Goodman's first patient was his young friend and disciple George Dennison, then in his mid twenties. In many ways Dennison was the archetype for Goodman's therapeutic career, an ideal figure rarely matched in the actual run of patients but precisely the person for whom Goodman wanted to do something, and could do something.

Dennison was one of three children from a modestly middle-class family living in a small town outside of Pittsburgh. He had a joyous childhood, and his high school days in particular were a series of glories and triumphs—a football hero, a witty

140

writer for the school paper and variety show, a handsome and lucky devil with the girls. After his senior year he had joined the wartime Navy, and he was in a naval engineering program at Columbia when the war ended. By the time he met Goodman a few years later his life was changing fast: he was married now, going to classes at the New School on the GI Bill, passionate about the arts, both literature and painting, and in love with New York City itself. These were his problems as much as they were his delights, for America at midcentury did not smile kindly on such young men. He might have done better to stick with engineering, move to a house in the suburbs, and start raising a family—and his standard of living. Neither his own ideals nor the vision of happiness that society proposed came close to actuality. He already felt trapped in his marriage, cheated in his education, balked as a writer, and apprehensive about earning a living as a housepainter and day laborer once his GI Bill ran out. The world was all before him, in the morning of life, but he was definitely not in paradise.[7]

In the final volume of *The Empire City,* written not long after this, there is a comic scene in which Goodman's hero goes to a psychotherapist. Let me quote a part of their first interview, for parody though it is, it suggests something of Dennison's problem and of Goodman's way of addressing it.

> Horatio did come to Antonicelli's. He came walking up the back street and looking for the house number.
>
> Strangely, on that residential street, a number of pickets with sandwich boards were angrily striding up and down, three men and three women in a close march. At every turning they cried out, "On Strike!"

But their sandwich boards were blank of any information.

"On strike?" said Horatio friendly. "Against whom?"

There was no answer. They came to the turning and they cried out, "On Strike!" They weren't giving out any information. Not for free.

In fact, they didn't know.

Horatio shrugged and went up to the doctor's office. Antonicelli opened the door, ushering him in, motioned him to sit down, sat down himself, and he also said nothing.

Horatio said nothing. There were plenty of matches struck and went out.

"Those pickets downstairs," said Horatio finally, "what's the strike about?"

"Those are Minetta Tyler's people. She's got them out everywhere. Some of them are on strike. Why not here?"

"Minetta Tyler!" cried Horace. "Lord! What is *she* up to? It's been years, hasn't it?"

"*Stop!*" Antonicelli's voice came like the crack of a whip. "Where in hell do you think you are? You can't get away with that stuff with me. You sit there and want to talk about pickets and Minetta Tyler. Those are the things you *want* to talk about. Well, just cut it out."

Horatio swallowed. He looked about him, and said nothing.

Antonicelli said nothing.

The minutes went by.

Horatio said nothing.

142

"This is costing you plenty," said Antonicelli. He had a neat clock that read off the time, $5, $10, $15, $20. . . .

"You've got me," said Horatio. "You won't let me talk about what I want to talk about, and I'm damned if I can think of what I don't want to talk about. I'm at a loss."

"*Now*, we're getting somewhere!" said the physician, cracking his knuckles like thunder. "You're at a loss! Hop! Hop! Stay there, stay with it. That's the place to be—at a loss. It's the fertile void from which come all beautiful things."[8]

Actually it was Dennison himself and not Goodman who thought up this emblem of the postwar generation, blank sandwich boards. No doubt it would be better to know exactly what one was demanding or refusing, but if not, it was perhaps a way of finding out, to yell, "On Strike!" and see what happened next, a peculiar mixture of stirring up trouble and standing out of the way.

What *did* Dennison want? And what did Goodman advise? *The Empire City* will not tell us much more, for the hero there is really a surrogate for Goodman himself and no one else. However, the point is not to recover the case history but to get a sense of how Goodman worked with his patients. For that, the following fragmentary sketch about Dennison, found among Goodman's papers, may help. I quote it in full.

Having separated from his wife, by whom he was frustrated and felt caged, George was in a state of precarious freedom. For alas! our freedom to create a better life for ourselves, that should be a solid oak to bring forth new leaves in the spring, is, as we are, a hot-house plant, easily discouraged. He wanted room, room for himself to walk about in his home, and he had the adventurous thought to look in Hoboken across the river from the tired city. Sure enough, he found a vast loft, the top of a nearly empty building, with a grand view of the Hudson. He paid the rent and moved in his cot and boxes. Carillo, the owner, was willing to give him a good price in hopes that he would lead other cultivated New Yorkers—artists, journalists, college-graduates—across the river, and revive blighted Hoboken.

The loft was in good shape, warm & dry; yet it required a lot of work to make it livable. The walls were 60 feet long to scrape and paint, and the ceiling was 15 feet high. The big window needed nearly 100 yards of curtain. It was the kind of job that a man could easily do in two weeks, provided that every stroke of effort were fired by the prospect of moving in with his new wife and hearing her surprised exclamation. George felt lost, and a little afraid, in the big dirty space. He chose not to sweep the floor, because he was going to start scraping the walls. He put up his cot in the middle of the room.

I visited & admired the premises and gave my opinion on the colors-to-be. But I could see that his heart was sinking. As he looked at the ceiling, that for technical reasons he had to paint first, he began to feel the old intolerable pressure that he knew so well how to resist. Urgently I advised him to make the place as livable as possible at once. To fix up one corner, real neat—with a lamp & table—and get a hot-plate to make coffee—and make up the bed, as if he were indeed awake for the day.

Then little by little he could decorate the rest. As for the ceiling, it was not bad as it was, rusty iron, provided one chose to consider that that was its color.

My advice was good, to get the indispensable & grow from there. That is, it was good for me if I were in his place. Buoyed up by the security of my years (mine was no solid oak, but it was a good tough bush with lots of roots), I did not have to confront myself with a great task in order to mobilize myself at all. But George felt that he was resourceless; and therefore unless he embarked on a project that was in itself worth doing, he could not embark at all. He rejected my advice with passionate scorn; and indeed this passion seemed to hearten him anew for his enterprise, to create all at once a better life, if only to spite me.

So I drove him about town to buy lumber for the closet & partition. The April sun was lively. It was a prettier town in its dilapidation than our city where the sun was not lively. With anticipation George looked at the comely girls and called out to them. He decided that he was not going to suffer from loneliness; he was going to make use of solitude. I envied him that he was living in Hoboken with everything that that meant. We went into an old restaurant and had steamed clams & their broth, which was for him a new taste.[9]

Of course these are not notes of treatment, nor do they quite fall into any category, scientific or literary, and I cannot say for what purpose Goodman wrote them. Nonetheless they show him and his patient in characteristic relations at the early

145

stage of treatment. Obviously there were sessions in which their roles were much more easily identifiable in the usual way, but Gestalt therapy, especially in Goodman's practice, cultivated the collaborative possibilities of life, not the boundary between the professional and his client.

In the private journal he kept for a while during his Gestalt therapy years, Goodman asked of himself, "[S]hall he be 'therapist' in ordinary company? shall he marry? and so forth thru the list of questions that would apply to the cloth. But this is presumptuous in the way the problem is first set: the distinction is as if there were a prophetic vocation; there is none. A man should be as compassionate & wise as he can in society, & not otherwise with his patients. If others expect him to be other than his ordinary self, that is their lookout."[10]

Goodman took on his young friends as patients, he used to say, because he was already counseling them informally, and it seemed reasonable to regularize the treatment. Making appointments ahead of time gave a different weight to conversations about their troubles. Sometimes they paid him, sometimes not. What are you going to charge? people asked. "What does a good electrician get?" he wondered. Indeed, once a friend of his rewired his loft as recompense for treatment, but there was no formal arrangement between them, no balancing of services rendered. You could call it urban barter, but being a friend in need was probably closer to the truth. In discussing fees with trainees later in his career, Goodman used to say, "What does a philosopher get?" A special service gets a professional emolument.[11] At the outset no one paid him more than a couple of bucks, and his fees were always at the bottom of the scale. By the end of the fifties he was charging $5, $10, or $25 depending on his patient's means. Friends without money, like George Dennison, were treated free—just as Goodman's sessions with Lore Perls were free.

In Dennison's case the formal structure soon fell away, and they were on the same old footing, as the story of his Hoboken loft dramatizes, except that now it was taken for granted that Dennison was Goodman's trainee, preparing himself for a possible career as a therapist, like their friends in training with Fritz on the West Coast. After a year or so Dennison would sometimes take over group sessions while Goodman went on vacation. Of course their therapist's absence always made a tremendous difference, both symbolically and practically, but everyone was used to Dennison's style of running the group, for he often took a strong hand when Goodman was present, as did many of the patients—that was part of what it meant to be in a Gestalt therapy group. And for some of them, Goodman's vacation was an occasion for breakthroughs.[12]

Dennison did not go on to set up a practice of his own, though he later worked with severely disturbed children in a semi-institutional setting for a few years, background for the period in the sixties when he was teacher/therapist at the First Street School, the subject of his famous book *The Lives of Children*. What he wanted was to be a writer, and not long after his move to Hoboken he took his meager savings and went off to Mexico where he could live cheaply and practice his art.

Dennison's relations with Goodman continued to be important for him wherever he was, and for a long time his career was very much on the model of his mentor's—writer, therapist, educator, living a bohemian life on practically no income. He also became very much one of Goodman's family, so that on his

147

travels he wrote "letters home" and received Christmas packages from Paul and Sally. Goodman's letters to him included
gossip about the therapy group and gloomy reports on the
progress of his own case. Here again we can observe the recip-
rocal nature of the therapeutic apprenticeship. "You're right,"
Goodman wrote in reply to a letter of self-analysis from Dennison,"your problem is to find out where your honor is, since
you have such a quick sense of it (it's one of the things I love in
you); you understand, I am sure, that it's all a lot of nonsense,
but that's something to feel afterwards. My problem, I'm afraid,
is to find where *I* am. For years and years now I seem to operate
at all well only paying attention to the other—either writing
something I haven't chosen, or some other fellow, and so forth.
With regard to things *I* want and have an eros for, I'm quite
childish, as you know. . . ."[13] Such a passage is especially touching for its moments of affection and acceptance. "It's one of the
things I love in you" gives Dennison his problem back as a
potential strength rather than a weakness; and the comment,
"I'm quite childish, as you know," perhaps made possible by the
first remark, short-circuits the self-pity that usually afflicted
Goodman when he looked inward, but that could evaporate,
and more and more *did* evaporate, when he paid attention to
something or someone else. The great recompense of his new
career was just this, that through his efforts to rescue others he
finally, painfully, wrenched himself free of the self-analysis and
self-pity that was souring his own life. He mulled it over in his
notebooks again and again.

> I have to do 2 things apparently incompatible. (1)
> Simply disregard evil, folly, prejudice, lethargy, provok-
> ing timidity; cheerfully assume that you aim at the sensi-

ble & pleasant—rousing, of course, first your disbelief
(& disregard), then your irritation, but finally without a
frontal fight—you're laughing at yourself. This is right
behavior—I always have done it when at my best. (2)
But it is too thin in content. I must learn to take seriously your world as it is for you—& richly for me;—*not*
glibly bypass it, and yet use it without acquiescence or
frontal assault. God is in the world, not in my soundest
intuitions. . . . Perhaps my difficulty is that I do not
understand the conventional motivations (my "psycho-
pathic personality"). I haunt the bars, the fringes, and so
forth, because I understand the simple passional motives
there; but of course I am very thinly engaged there. The
psychotherapeutic situation seems to be the only one
where I am animatedly engaged.[14]

Lore's training group adjourned for the summer of 1951, and she
went out to California to taste for herself the charms that Fritz
had been reporting. She stayed two months, didn't like it, and
returned to her own friends and practice. Something in her
reaction seems to have made Fritz reconsider his own choice
and before long he too returned to New York, leaving Isadore
From behind to finish off those California clients who were not
allowed or able to follow him. There were colleagues who
thought this was not quite ethical, but Perls had never encouraged strong attachments or promised his clients they could rely
on him. That was not what he had to offer. Jerry Raphel chauf-
feured him back, his analyst's armchair part of the baggage.
Driving through Texas, Perls would call ahead for reservations
to spend the night, describing himself as South African to see
what response he could provoke. *That* was his style.[15]

149

Gestalt therapy was beginning to have a reputation within the profession. The William Alanson White Institute remained friendly and was sending trainees. Word spread among the like-minded at Bellevue, at Kings County, at the VA hospital in New Jersey. When *Gestalt Therapy* came out in December 1951, new converts were made. Allison Montague, another psychiatrist at Bellevue, read it and immediately called Perls and asked to be taken on as a patient. There were others. The time was ripe, and Perls decided to start his own institute.[16]

Several different constituencies intermingled in the Gestalt Therapy Institute. The inner core developed out of Lore's training group, enlarged and no longer working with her as guide. This was now the professional group, meeting weekly at the Perls's apartment to learn from one another. Besides Goodman, Weisz, and Shapiro there were Allison Montague, Sylvester ("Buck") Eastman, Leo Chalfin, Jim Simkin, Paul Oliver, sometimes Lottie Weisz, or Ralph Hefferline (who sat rather silently), and then a bit later, Isadore From, Richard Kitzler, and others of the second generation of therapists. Usually there were ten or twelve at a meeting. At first Fritz and Lore acted as leaders, but that changed as the dynamics of the group emerged. To some extent it was still a training group, to which individuals would bring their cases for discussion and where the expertise might be shared among colleagues. It was also an exploratory seminar, an ongoing brainstorming session where the theory and practice of Gestalt therapy was being invented—for Perls and Goodman's book was only a beginning that set forth the terms of discourse, and the movement was still in its formative stages. Sometimes arguments would arise that had to do with just this, Gestalt therapy as a movement or school. How formal should it be? Someone would say, we ought to have a secretary, or, I resign as secretary. It was impossible to make this group toe any line. Perls complained, "I'm trying to build a house and they're fighting over the nails!"[17]

Finally and perhaps most fundamentally, it was a group therapy session where everyone's character was fair game and the goal was increased awareness and self-discovery. "We hammered at each other," said Elliott Shapiro,

> and hammered, and hammered—every week. And it was the most vigorous hammering you can imagine. . . . If you could live through these groups and take the corrections, the insults, the remarks. . . . All these remarks were offered in some kind of professional way, in a professional sense, but with great emotion. And often, even though they were offered in a professional sense they were picked up by the recipient as being unprofessional; that this doesn't come from your professional self, this comes from you. And then that person gets hammered after having hammered somebody else, and then the next person immediately gets hammered, and so on. . . . The interesting thing was that no matter how they hammered at each other at these meetings, after they were over many of us would go out and have coffee together. We'd all be in good spirits and forget that we'd been almost murdering each other.[18]

No one was immune from the hammering, but some took it harder than others. Jim Simkin later wrote that he finally left New York because Paul Goodman and Elliott Shapiro were "loading elephant shit on him."[19] Others, like Hefferline, sat mum in the corner, or attended only a few sessions. But most of the regulars were thick-skinned veterans who could take it as well as dish it out. Perhaps Perls himself was the most interesting case. As the expert on dental aggression, always ready with an unsettling insight into his victim's character, it was no wonder if he was often the object of similar assaults from others. He would return from one of his more and more frequent campaign trips—Los Angeles, Cleveland, Miami—full of excitement and basking in prestige. Whereupon his colleagues would take him to task for descending to showmanship, and shoot holes in the innovations that had been so warmly received elsewhere. "Instant cure? Hah! Hyperventilation!"

Goodman was particularly hard on Perls's theoretical pretensions. Face it, Fritz, he would say, you're not an intellectual. Lore's an intellectual. You're not an intellectual. Indeed, Perls sometimes boasted that he no longer read books. But he had his retorts for intellectuals like Goodman and Weisz: The problem with you, he said to Weisz one night, is that you're so clear inside your head it comes out confused. And you!—turning to Goodman—you're so confused inside it always comes out crystal clear. According to Kitzler, who tells the story, this was Perls in a charitable if somewhat paradoxical mood. Yet at other times he was heard to say that Goodman was the only person he had learned anything from in twenty years.[20]

In fact Perls did not like criticism, and there were those who thought his eagerness to set up institutes everywhere had as one of its motives the desire to live continually in the glow of an intellectual honeymoon—off to Los Angeles, Cleveland, Miami, where he would be the center of adulation. Yet he never altered his style to protect his ego. On the contrary. One day, when the institute and its courses were well established, he walked into the middle of one of Goodman's classes. Goodman continued expatiating for a few minutes, made his point, and offered his colleague a bone, asking, "Would you agree, Fritz?"

"No."

"That's the trouble with you, Fritz; you come in late, haven't heard what's going on, and immediately begin throwing monkey-wrenches."

"*Ja*, because I am not afraid!"[21]

Meetings of the professional group continued weekly for a number of years, and they remained the nucleus of Gestalt ideas and practice. But almost from the start Perls was agitating for more structure and enterprise. Elliott Shapiro recalled the uneasiness this aroused in group members: "We were clear that if anything was going to be developed in regard to this Institute, it must not be a bureaucratic Institute—one that gives degrees or gives certificates. . . . Yes we ought to develop this as an institute but we have to be careful that nobody's in charge, nobody's authoritative, that we were all equals, one way or another, that we were all equals."[22]

It was in 1952 they decided to offer a few courses, although there was uncertainty whether even this might not be self-aggrandizing. At first Lore Perls refused to be involved. She was already overcommitted, she said, spending one day a week in Philadelphia, working the other five or six days in New York, plus running a household with two children still at home. "It's your baby," she told Fritz, "I won't have anything to do with it." But when forty people showed up for the first seminar, she gave in and took half of them.[23]

Others of the inner circle also offered classes. Goodman sent round to his colleagues the following announcement:

I shall lead a course of 8 discussions during April and May (April 8 to May 24) on the relations of

PSYCHOTHERAPY, RELIGION, AND ETHICS
including in Ethics fundamental Politics.

Readings will be assigned from the Bible, Lao-tzu, Shakespere, Spinoza, Nietzsche, Freud, Reich, Rank, Schweitzer, Buber.

At each session I shall speak for half an hour and lead a discussion for about an hour and a half. The group will be restricted to not more than 12.

The fee for the course is $20. Register by April 1.

Tuesdays from 8:45 to 10:45 P.M., at Dr. Lore Perls', 311 W. 95 St.[24]

In the fall the institute published a brochure, complete with five courses, a list of the fellows and their credentials, and announced a monthly "open house" at new offices of "The New York Institute for Gestalt Therapy." Fritz offered a ten-week series on "Principles" and "Techniques," while Lore was accepting new participants in her "Practicum for Group Therapy" (beginning and advanced groups, both "in progress"). Shapiro's workshop was "The Classroom as a Laboratory for Psychotherapy," Weisz's "The Problem of Psycho/Somatic Medicine," and Goodman's "The Pathology of Speech and Writing, and Speech-analysis as a Tool of Therapy." The Perlses had moved to larger quarters on Central Park West, where the institute could meet, courses could be conducted, and where several of the fellows could have space for private consultations. It was about this time, too, that Lore decided, at least for professional occasions, that she was "Laura," and so her name appeared in the brochures, and so her friends, including Goodman, now wrote it. (Here too, from now on, she will be Laura Perls.)

There was a certain amount of ritual display in all of this, no doubt, but even Fritz, who was the most fanatical about the trappings of power, enjoyed them only for the glory and had no desire to follow through with bureaucratic zeal, tightening every nut. The institute was a model of anarchist self-regulation. A dozen years later, at the height of alternative education experiments in the colleges of the country, Goodman liked to hold the institute up as an example of how such things ought to be done:

> We didn't want to go through the business of getting accredited so we couldn't give units of credit or degrees. Nevertheless we sent out a little brochure saying that I would give a course in religion and psychopathology of speech, that Paul Weisz would give a course in the philosophy of medicine, Elliott a course in educational psychology, and Laura Perls a course called "Contact and Support"—it was a course in physiotherapy and its relations to the emotions. Now these were simply crackerjack. I used to sit in on the other courses. Lots of people came. Twenty, thirty, you know, they were far too big for what we wanted. We kept it up for two years and then, because we had too many other things to do, we let it go to pot. . . . The Institute wasn't a college because there wasn't enough of a community. People weren't together enough to talk and share what they got in the courses. That would have taken more arranging than any of us was willing to do.

The lapse after two years did not make it a failure in Goodman's eyes. He thought such institutions "should be evanescent. Yes, that's right. And I don't think that's so bad. . . . Yet there's no reason why it can't be continually self-renewing. You have connections and you inveigle people in for a couple of years. By the time they want to go you've lined up enough people so that not everyone's leaving at once. And you go yourself and come back yourself."[25]

Goodman's memory of actual courses and their titles was a little hazy. In fact, he offered "Psychotherapy, Religion, and Ethics" in the spring, "Psychopathology of Speech and Writing" in the fall, and in following sessions, "Psychology of Sex" and "Theory of Reaction Formation." The numbers also varied. Fritz and Laura may have had twenty or thirty in their classes, but "Theory of Reaction Formation," scheduled for four sessions in January and February of 1954, drew but three auditors, as did a final (unadvertised) seminar Goodman gave in the fall of the same year, "What is Man?"[26]

At the first meeting of "Psychotherapy, Religion, and Ethics," Goodman sketched out his intention to present the "quintessence of what is problematical for me—not what is obviously sacred. For example, not the impassive Laotze but the dark, unsettled idiotic. Not the Sh[akespeare] who lives *thru* a love dream, but the poet who is in deep-conflict about his art." These would not be lectures, and even the half hour announced as preliminary to discussion would be Goodman "thinking aloud with your help." Nor did he suppose that what was problematical for him would be so for others: "we are not likely to meet on what troubles us. My attitude," he further admitted, "is either caviling or impatient."[27]

156

He did not spend equal amounts of time with all the authors on his list. At the outset he gave some attention to Nietzsche and Rank, using their ideas on art and religion, along with familiar Freudian notions, to provide a framework for discussion. He devoted much more of the course to Shakespeare, sometimes going through the sonnets one by one, and looking very closely at *Othello*. The themes of homosexual love and of heterosexual jealousy were perhaps part of what he meant when he said that "we are not likely to meet on what troubles us"; these certainly were problematical for him.

When he came back to religious problems in more traditional terms, it was Buber and Lao-tzu that he ended with, both much Goodmanized, even more than Gestaltized. Buber was presented through a reading of the Gospel of Mark, a story of miracles that fascinated Goodman so much he later wrote a short story and a play based on it ("The Young Disciple"). In these seminars, as in *Gestalt Therapy*, the placing of emphasis on the miracle of existence made an important counterweight against Goodman's Taoist impulse, which however much he might deny it tended toward nonattachment as well as awareness of the here and now. Goodman tempered his Taoism with Buber, and vice versa.

His view of psychotherapy as a kind of religion was explicit and insisted upon. It was the working premise for everything else. Here is the brief formulation he left in his notes:

Superego: introjections: "reality"; this is the system of resignations. Religion is the tension of life—these factual resignations. Ordinarily it is the attempt to domesticate the mystery; for example, the Catholic mysteries, they are irreducible but they are "only that," in their place. Psychotherapy is a religion to liberate the mystery, and dissolve the resignation. It is a ritual, a compulsion, a faith, attested by miracles.

My faith is that this obsession cures itself.

And then, finally,

the person is the art-work demanded by the muse (the immortal thing worth doing). The structured self.[28]

This opening seminar in the spring of 1952 was Goodman's most ambitious contribution to the institute series, both in its scope and in the hopes he had for learning something from it himself. Later seminars were not so saturated with high seriousness, though he always went into them seeking new ideas rather than rehearsing what he already knew. In all of his offerings, he gave fair warning that not only he but also the members of the class would be at risk, as in the usual group therapy situation. Thus in his second seminar, "The Psychopathology of Speech and Writing," he announced at the beginning that "the speech of individuals in the group will be subjected to analysis by the group."[29]

He stuck to topics that felt problematic for him personally. In the fall of 1953 he wrote George Dennison, "I began my course at the I.G.T.—'Psychology of Sex'—heh! heh! 'what you can't do, teach.' First session not bad, it raised (in me) a certain interest. I kind of generated the question how it is in our generation we (all) have as a great goal to achieve 'a mature sexual relation'—and why? A Renaissance or ancient would never even have thought of such a thing."[30] And the following February he reported: "My course 'Theory of Reaction-Formation—4 sessions' has 3 members: Monty (that's Allison Montague, a psychiatrist who, I think, has the hots for me), Humphrey, and Bob A. I'm trying to show that the creative process, as opposed to ordinary growth and activity, always contains a 'normal' reaction-formation: namely, a denial and a systematic effort to prove the denial (including sublimation and overcompensation). I'm using 3 examples: compassion, art, and ego-ideal love. I announced the course on a hunch, and now I know I have a thought."[31]

This was Goodman's chief motive in offering these seminars, to "have a thought." Auditors were a necessary ingredient, at once admiring and demanding. Allison Montague was a traditionally trained psychiatrist with much experience at Bellevue. Humphrey Noyes (a descendant of the famed patriarch of the Oneida Community) was a children's therapist who had been one of Reich's patients. Bob A. was one of Goodman's young friends considering a career as a therapist. Although at any moment they could become a therapy group, most of the time they functioned as a study group, with Goodman as leader but with steady contributions from all the participants.

This format appealed to Goodman so much that he organized still another version of it in the fall of 1954, even though the institute had stopped offering its full array of seminars. "I'm giving a little class," he wrote Dennison. "I'm learning something from it." His students this time were two young friends from one of his therapy groups, and Isadore From. "We do a kind of directed free-speculation in the manner of Husserl," he explained to Dennison. "I have been noting down the proceedings after every meeting, and they make interesting reading."[32]

Although explicitly a collaborative enterprise, Goodman led the discussions in directions that were becoming more and more central for him as the decade progressed—raising questions that seem not to grow out of psychotherapy as such, except as they concern the overarching problem of defining human nature. "What Is Man?" was the title he gave the seminar.[33] It is worth taking a close look at this last seminar he gave at the institute, simply to notice the difference that four years of practical experience had made in the attitudes he held as the theorist of *Gestalt Therapy*. Here too, perhaps, we can once again see Goodman without Perls hovering in the background.

"What Is Man?" tells us something about Goodman's future as well as his past. Shortly after the seminar ended he began to keep a notebook or journal in which he often returned to these same questions about human nature—entries of a page or two at a time, intermingled with all sorts of other thoughts, but separated out under the heading "Method" (rather than "Psychology") in the published version of his journals, *Five Years*.[34] Such questions fascinated him for the rest of his life, and one reason that his later friendship with the cultural theorist Gregory Bateson meant so much to him was that they shared a passion for philosophical anthropology. In a way this represents Goodman's gradual withdrawal from his love affair with psychology and a return to the larger concerns aroused when he was a young man studying Aristotle and Kant. I have only one subject, he was wont to say: "the human beings I know in their man-made scene."[35]

The little seminar met for eight weeks, and Goodman's brief reports on the members' discussions, a few typed pages each time, reveal them coming back again and again to two or three touchstones for what it is to be human. At the start there was some attention paid to their own methodology as "naturalists" attending to wholes of experience or observation, and attempting to explore these through phenomenological description and analysis, not unlike the method of *Gestalt Therapy*. But there was little terminology taken over from Gestalt theory, little talk of figure and ground or organism and environment. Some familiar issues emerge. For instance, there is much discussion of sensation and perception, whether or not they are the "same thing," and if not, whether the ability to distinguish them might be an essential human trait. ("Does perception entail responsibility—for example, to look and listen, to answer in the dialogue? Is this the human factor?")[36] But the treatment of such matters is not schematic in the way it tends to be in *Gestalt Therapy*, and there is no attempt to organize a conceptual framework.

Among the criteria offered for what it is to be human, the most insisted-on seems to be the capability of communication, dialogue, response. The human being is "reachable," and "must answer *back* and not merely reflect like a mirror."[37] A focus on human initiative and response seemed inescapable during the first month of their discussions, whether they talked about perception or curiosity or the conflict between will and desire. Several times the seminar came round to Buber's conception of I-Thou relationships as a paradigm of human engagement in the world. (Buber himself was the author of lectures on philosophical anthropology, published as *Was Ist der Mensch?* and translated in 1947.) Kurt Lewin and Paul Schilder were the only psychologists mentioned at all in Goodman's résumés of their conversations—not Freud or Reich or Rank or Perls. In addition to Buber, there were frequent references to Aristotle and Kant, Plato and Kierkegaard, as well as to Wordsworth, Rilke, and Kafka. As the second month began, the group moved to topics that suggest why their authorities tended to be philosophers and poets. Sleep and dreaming, confusion and bafflement, aging and death, grief and mourning—these were rather different from the phenomena they had addressed at the outset: perception, curiosity, problem solving and play, and the bodily imperatives with their satisfactions and inhibitions.

About the time their focus shifted, Goodman interrupted himself as he summarized a discussion of curiosity to note, in a parenthesis, "Our activity here, on the question 'What is the case?' is not, on the part of PG [Paul Goodman], bona fide curiosity, to find out the answer, but rather to allay superstition and prejudice, to increase non-verbal and non-intellectual freedom."[38] This parenthetical aside is a bit obscure, but seems to signal Goodman's personal interest in the themes that were emerging in their discussions, a particular range of conflicts and dilemmas that might be regarded as the most disturbing characteristics of being human. For example, "In general we will find this conflict of 'urge to' and 'ought to.' It is certainly human to be prone to this conflict; also tolerant of this conflict."

Or again, "We are confused: by the excessive subtlety or by the great variety of differences. These parts do not 'add up.' Confusion as a feeling that it 'ought to make sense'—betrayal by the body.

"(Too much absence of confusion or dark area is likely highly neurotic.)"

Or yet again, "If we say that 'over-control' is neurotic and not human, we must say that it is human to be prone to this neurosis, equivalent to a constitutional original sin."[39]

What Goodman was saying about himself at this time, for example in letters to George Dennison, was, "My whole life is a kind of clutching to presence" and "I lead very little inner life in the form of interior dialogues, and so forth."[40] Perhaps this self-description clarifies what Goodman meant when he said that for him the seminar served "to allay superstition and prejudice." They were discussing those areas of life that were for him the most fearful and risky—the problem of distinguishing appetite from duty, the animal anxiety about his own body, and the deep need he felt to solve problems and make sense in every situation.

One other significant topic the seminar raised probably tells us something more about Goodman's "superstition and prejudice." The final two meetings were devoted to the fact of mortality and whether "knowing" we must die is not an essential human trait. Goodman pointed out that "things pertaining to death like funerals, are 'different,' awesome, magical."[41] There is little about death or dying in *Gestalt Therapy*. It was a subject he seemed to steer clear of. "We never talk about death," George Dennison said to him one day after a group session. Goodman merely nodded.[42]

But in this seminar death was discussed, primarily in terms of loss or emptiness. We fear death, Goodman suggested, because we have not yet achieved our hopes of life, we long for our paradise on earth. And the deaths of others leave us alone, abandoned. The idea of immortality is a "reaction formation" to make good these losses. Only the barest mention is given to the fear of dying itself, which Goodman conjectures must be "a panic of choking." Given his own proneness to panic reactions in hospital environments, one wonders how much feeling is being kept down here by talking about death as "unfulfilled possibility." One feels him avoiding the murky or confused, and preferring to "make sense."[43] Not so different, perhaps, from the rest of us at age forty-three.

CHAPTER SEVEN

Goodman the Therapist

THERE WAS USUALLY some overlap in the membership of the Gestalt Institute seminars and Goodman's therapy groups. Those who came to both were getting two rather different sides of Goodman, in spite of his principle that the therapist should simply be himself in all situations. Although he might very well speculate theoretically in a therapy session and it was not unknown for someone to shout or weep in his seminars, the underlying mood was obviously not the same.

The very idea of group therapy was relatively new at mid-century, and there was no strong tradition of successful practice; in particular, there was no weighty European legacy from the generation of Freud. Several of the earliest experimenters were Europeans like Jacob Moreno or Paul Schilder, but they did their group work in very American contexts. Although the model of the classroom as an instrument of social progress may have been an important influence, the conceptual starting place was simply the idea of certain preselected communities in need of therapy—hospitals, prisons, the army, and other institutional settings. These settings helped shape the group therapy dynamic in its formative decades, the thirties and forties. One might also point to older phenomena like the "mutual criticism" sessions that kept the Oneida Community going for a whole generation in the nineteenth century, or the Quaker meetings, which, as Goodman once remarked, were similar to group sessions in their exclusion of both objective structuring and small talk.[1]

Among the Gestalt therapists several different group styles can be identified, and it is their blend that is most interesting. From an early age Laura Perls had studied in various schools of movement and modern dance, and their techniques informed her work, both its emphasis on body-awareness exercises and the concentration on group dynamics. Her chief role in the institute was as the leader of its practicum for prospective therapists, and of course it was her first group, Goodman, Weisz, Shapiro, and others, that gave Gestalt therapy its founding congregation.

In *his* early years Fritz Perls had been fascinated by the theater, and Laura thought he would have been happiest as a director.[2] It is not surprising then that his own work with groups extended the line Moreno had pioneered, psychodrama and other sorts of role-playing, with Perls more and more a kind of impresario, with a growing separation between his "cast" and the "audience" of disciples, until finally his demonstration films were being shown to an anonymous public that was simply curious.

Another sort of group was that developed by Elliott Shapiro, whose institute seminars were primarily for teachers and whose own experience was so centrally in the classroom. This group was a workshop model, developed over his years spent with children in Bellevue Hospital, Kings County Psychiatric Hospital, and at P.S. 119 in Harlem.

Goodman's expertise combined elements from all of these traditions. He too had worked with children and adolescents, in isolated communal settings where, among other things, he had directed plays as therapeutic vehicles for both cast and audience. He had also run writing workshops and had taken part in anarchist editorial collectives. Although nothing in his experience matched Laura Perls's background in physiotherapy, he had some practical knowledge of Reich's vegetotherapy from his six months with Alexander Lowen, not to mention his year of technical training with Laura herself. To all of this experience must be added the circumstance that Goodman said led him into practice in the first place—that so many of his young friends were already his informal patients, coming to him with their problems. His inveterate haranguing, mentoring, and pestering of the young had entered into a new phase by the time *Gestalt Therapy* was published. A little band of disciples had grown up around him, drawn from the circles of anarchists and artists and theater people that he frequented. In addition to the *Why?* circle and the Living Theatre circle there was now a Goodman circle. Not only did this little community provide many of the recruits for his therapy groups, but it also set the tone for them, established their ambience.

Although his was certainly the dominant voice, Goodman did not lord it over his disciples, who were also his friends, who ate at his table, slept on his couch, borrowed money from him, played handball and poker with him, came to him for advice, and sometimes made love to him. These were hardly the admiring throngs that were to sit at Perls's feet in Big Sur, but they were not just patients off the street either. In *Gestalt Therapy* Goodman made much of the fact that the particular "run of patients" had largely determined the major varieties of psychoanalytic theory, "for they are both the observed material and the confirmatory evidence of response to the method."[3] In his own case it made a crucial difference that so many of his patients were his friends and disciples and that they already knew each other.

They met at his apartment, on a regular night of the week—Mondays or Fridays—beginning about 7:30 or 8:00 and running for several hours. There would be six or eight of them, though attendance was irregular, less predictable than a poker game, more so than a party. At least two-thirds of the company would be acquainted outside of the group and saw one another frequently, if nowhere else, at least at the San Remo bar. They sat around the fireplace at one end of Goodman's loft on 23rd Street, with the dining table and the kitchen sink at their backs. There were chairs for everyone though the bookcases were homemade and several of the canvases on the wall were without frames. Goodman's children, Susan and Mathew, would wander through on the way to the bathroom. Sometimes Sally Goodman joined the group, though everyone agreed that was not such a good idea because Paul was too hard on her, and she usually stayed out of sight until it was time for the session to end, when she would emerge to serve coffee and cake. There followed a social hour which confirmed the underlying community and during which one might recover one's balance or relax one's grip, depending on how the session had gone.[4]

Goodman was a full participant, taking his turn at various exercises, with much weeping. It was not a bad way to know him, as George Dennison once said, for the group session fostered give-and-take, and on other kinds of occasions Paul was likely to do too much of the talking.[5] It was part of his task here to coax people forth and to encourage them in helping one another. Although his groups formed and grew somewhat haphazardly, he had a principle of composition in the back of his mind that they should consist of a variety of types selected for "interest and/or antagonism."[6] If possible he wanted all his private patients in groups as well, and he sometimes invited people to join. On at least one occasion he asked someone to stop coming because he was not really participating.[7] A good group would provide opportunities to "make connections with something else," to "integrate" in a situation full of potential anxiety. Serious group work meant "moving on the edge, one of the critical moments of living," and a condition for this was "secure fellowship."[8]

I am quoting here from advice he gave to Gestalt trainees in the workshops he later led in Cleveland. It was earnest advice, grounded in more than his recent clinical experience. All his life Goodman had been a passionate devotee of small, close-knit communities, beginning with his childhood on 151st Street when he was first accepted as a member of the gang of neighborhood kids. Indeed, one night he asked members of his therapy group to "walk" for one another, commenting on the various gaits and stances, and when it was his turn one of the group told him he reminded her of a little boy, no older than eight, the age he had reached living on 151st Street. This brought tears to his eyes, but when she tried to comfort him, he did not want her to touch him—no mothering![9] However one interprets this particular occasion, there is no doubt that Goodman was often deeply moved by things that happened in his group sessions. Individual therapy with patients, even with those who mattered most to him as friends, held no such charms.

Was he good at it? Did his patients get well? And what did it do for him to turn to the plight of others as his means of livelihood and way of life?

Though aware of failings and blind spots, his patients—at least the ones I've talked to—all praise him now. At the time, of course, they often complained and sometimes grew furious with him, as he with them. "Paul spends entire sessions insulting me. Why does he do this?" wrote one patient in her diary.[10] That same month Goodman mentioned her in a letter to George Dennison: "Judith has been terribly pissed off at me and comes around faithfully to tell me how she hates me and to inform everybody else how I am a son of a bitch."[11] But feelings like these were part of the therapy itself, something to be worked with. More disturbing criticisms came chiefly from others, some from his intimates—family, friends, and colleagues at the institute—and some from outsiders who heard rumors or caught glimpses of his practice and raised their eyebrows in disapproval.

Goodman was clear about his competence and its limits. He did not treat borderline psychotics, as Perls or Paul Weisz did, and none of *his* patients ever committed suicide. His colleagues were comfortable referring people to him, but they did not send risky cases.[12] He was said to specialize in "career block," a rubric that suggests his therapeutic orientation more than it does any particular set of presenting symptoms among his patients. If their subsequent careers are any measure, it would have to be said that the majority of patients found their way, though there are some gloomy histories among them.

But judgments of competence in therapeutic or pedagogic pursuits are almost never based on outcomes but on training, experience, and credentials. Gestalt therapy being a tiny unorthodox sprout in a corner of the psychotherapeutic garden, it is not surprising to find it frowned on by the straitlaced establishment. The chief form such criticism took was a blank look and a cold shoulder. Goodman was used to this. When had he been treated in any other way by the powers that be? And so he was not downcast when his new book with Perls and Hefferline got exactly one review, a mild, patronizing notice in the *American Journal of Psychology*.[13] That was better than the few sentences of passing mention bestowed by magazines on his last two novels.

It was one thing to be dismissed by distant experts who controlled the institutions and channels, another to be sneered at by his enemies or brushed aside by old friends. The arbiters of culture at the *Partisan Review* took no public notice of Goodman's new career, but word got back to him of their contempt. It was fashionable then to make psychoanalytic pronouncements about literary texts, and some of the *Partisan* clique were regarded as authorities on such matters. Lionel Trilling's *Liberal Imagination*, for instance, handled Freudian topics with such confidence and urbanity that it had been favorably reviewed in Goodman's own magazine *Complex*. When Goodman heard that Trilling was saying Goodman had no business practicing therapy, he was furious.[14] Had Trilling any real experience of psychoanalysis? Had he been in treatment or training or practice? He was just a self-important literary critic—and not a very good one, whatever Laura Perls might have said in *Complex*. Trilling was perhaps especially invested in systems of credentialing and licensing, but none of the *Partisan Review* circle had any patience with intellectual upstarts and ideological adventurers like Goodman. This was the period when the magazine harnessed itself to the American bandwagon, publishing symposia with titles like "Our Country and Our Culture" and defending its readers against every sort of insurgency.

The centenary of Freud's birth in 1956 provided an occasion for the New York intellectuals to show off their psychoanalytic sophistication. Everyone had a speech or an article ready for May 6th. Trilling made a book out of his centenary lecture, *Freud and the Crisis of Our Culture*; Alfred Kazin wrote the showpiece for *The New York Times*; Stanley Edgar Hyman celebrated in the *Partisan Review*. No one thought of inviting Goodman to speak or write—with one peculiarly aggravating exception, his old friend Benjamin Nelson.

Nelson was back in New York City after a couple of dead-end teaching jobs in Chicago and Minneapolis. He had been through a lot during the last ten years: unable to secure an appointment in a history department, he had refurbished himself as a sociologist, only to have difficulty establishing himself in that field too; then his wife ran off with a graduate student, and he had a nervous breakdown. But recovering from all of this, he turned adversity to advantage; he had made himself a lay expert on the modern cure of psyches (psychoanalysis) as well as the medieval cure of souls. And not only did he find a job teaching social science, at Hofstra College, but he was becoming an important force in American intellectual life by virtue of connections he had made with the newly invented world of quality paperback publishing, as a consulting editor first for Meridian Books and then for Harper & Row.

The Freud centenary was one of Nelson's early opportunities to bring his new interests and influences together. A year in advance he began to plan a symposium of "outstanding contemporary thinkers" that might suitably mark the occasion. There was to be a formal presentation of papers on the eve of Freud's birthday, sponsored by Meridian, which would then print the best of these along with others gathered from similar celebrations elsewhere. Ben Nelson loved such events. He was in his element that night at the 92nd Street Y, introducing famous speakers and sounding the trumpet for Freud as the genius of the century. Of course he knew that his old friend should be one of the speakers, but Goodman was not invited to the birthday party, and he was bitterly angry with Ben for leaving him out.

Nelson claimed that he had *meant* to invite Paul to speak. As he put it, years later, "I was absolutely insistent that Paul be invited to be on that program."[15] But the person at Meridian who was arranging the funds for the symposium, and would publish the proceedings, said, "NO PAUL GOODMAN! NO PAUL GOODMAN! NO PAUL GOODMAN!"

Ben wailed, "We have to have Paul Goodman! He really is the person who will be able to do this better than anyone else."

The reply was, "Well, if you think so, hire a hall."

But the worst was yet to come. According to Ben, "The result was that I was obliged—we were already in the works, there was a book being made, I had gotten a lot of essays, I knew I wanted to get Paul in to talk about it, but I had not given Paul a formal invitation, I didn't until I definitely knew I could—I was forced to ask Philip Rahv."

Insult upon injury! Philip Rahv was the man who had blacklisted Goodman at *Partisan Review*. It was he who had sneered at *Kafka's Prayer* in the *Saturday Review of Literature*, characterizing Goodman's "purely speculative application of Freudian concepts to literature" as "so far fetched as to provoke immediate dissent."[16]

Nelson blamed it all on the publisher: "To me, you don't know what that meant. I just never would have asked him. I asked Rahv, and he gave a talk which was the most pretentious thing I've ever heard, in a manner that he absolutely ought never to have affected on a subject that he shouldn't have touched. It was so awful in my view that I wouldn't dream of having it in the book. You won't find it there, there's no reference to it even."[17] At the same time Nelson tried to make amends by putting *Gestalt Therapy* in the bibliography, along with the following cryptic apology in his preface: "Even the omissions which seem flagrant are likely to have accident rather than design for their explanation. Wherever possible, an effort has been made to amend this lack by appropriate matter in the footnotes and in the Selected References."[18]

Thinking about it later, Nelson felt that Goodman's reaction to his exclusion was extravagant, somehow in excess of what was called for, and charged it to his friend's desperate hunger for recognition. There had been a time when Goodman could do no wrong in Nelson's eyes, but as his own career finally began to take shape, Nelson seemed to regard himself as an elder statesman who, having paid a great price for his own place in the world, felt constrained to admonish the prodigal who had never given up anything out of prudence or propriety. They weathered the storm of the Freud centenary and remained friends, but very much at arm's length.

Several of Goodman's old friends were disturbed by his new career, though each one put a different face on it. Only Ben Nelson was in a position to assess the theoretical achievement of *Gestalt Therapy,* but after twenty years of intimacy they all knew Goodman's character inside and out. It was not so much that he was too playful, too driven, too irresponsible, too indiscreet, though all of these traits might be held against him as a psychotherapist. The real problem was that he was too Paul! They simply *knew* him too well, and one was not supposed to know a psychotherapist: he was supposed to know *you*. It was a measure of the radicalism of Gestalt therapy that people found it so hard to accept the therapist as just a person, not a priest or sage.

Consider the prediction Ben Nelson made (in his preface to yet another symposium for the Freud centenary—to which Goodman was also not invited).

> In the years ahead, if this observer is not deceived, vast pressures will be placed on psychoanalysis to present itself as a gospel of glad tidings and to evolve a *mystique* and a hierocratic structure like that of a church. Forces working at cross-purposes will drive many analysts to affect the role of wonder-working healers and seers. . . . Men today are in desperate need of mediators through whose good offices and ministrations they may have themselves declared healed, justified, and solvent. In this crisis, we shall yet witness a veritable War of the Titans—the battle of the mediators. Already, indeed, an excessively large part of our cultural life takes its coloration from this unseemly wrangle among the rival ideologies and claims of the myriad sorts of mediators— commissars, yogis, corporation executives, labor leaders, artist-heroes, ministers, priests and the endless varieties of psychologists and therapists.[19]

For all its oracular pomposity this was not a foolish assessment. Hindsight makes it ring a bit hollow as a prophecy for the sixties, yet Nelson was surely right in predicting a period of religious crisis, cultural confusion, and bluster. It was what Goodman was to call the New Reformation, though unlike

Nelson and other old friends, he welcomed it, and perhaps aspired to be a Hus or Wycliffe. But the sixties had not yet arrived; this was the decade of McCarthyism. Ben and the other clever young comrades of Goodman's college days were now in their forties. They were no longer the brash know-it-alls they once were. Still, having chattered their youth away on the intellectual sidelines, connoisseurs of folly, they were permanently inoculated against enthusiasm of whatever stripe. What then were they to make of their friend Paul when he set up shop as a "wonder-working healer and seer"? There was much shaking of heads in private, and biting of tongues when they chanced to meet.

Stories that came back to them about Goodman's disciples sitting at his feet in therapy sessions would have been particularly distressing since they themselves had swarmed about him in their youth—though never at the price of personal dignity, which friends surely gave up when they became patients. Such feelings were somewhat allayed by closer experience. Ben Nelson and Meyer Liben still saw enough of Goodman to meet his young friends and judge the therapeutic relationship for themselves. Another member of the old crowd, the youngest of the Wadsworth Terrace Social and Literary Society, had still more immediate evidence of Goodman's probity in his new calling. In the mid fifties, at the height of the anticommunist witch hunts, this old friend suddenly found himself in serious trouble. He was fired from his job, one he had held for ten years, because of his undergraduate history as a Red (actually a Social Democrat, anathema to the Communists), a history that had come to light at the same time it became known that he was homosexual. To top it all, he and his lover had just parted. Although he had not been seeing much of Goodman, he knew Goodman was in lay practice, and so he called for help. As he later put it, "I asked him to say I was in therapy, as part of the defense of my job, and Paul said, 'I think you could use a little.'"[20] They arranged that Goodman's fee would consist of a visit to the cottage his friend rented on Fire Island that summer, where Goodman would have been welcome in any case. The therapy lasted only a few sessions—to no great result, since the job proved irrecoverable—but one night the friend attended a group session at the Goodman apartment and was surprised by how earnest and professional it all was. At the end of the evening, when the newcomer was told that he must now say something critical and something positive about everyone, he chose this for his remark on Paul: "I don't know if it's positive or negative," he said, "but I'm impressed by your conscientiousness."

A similar anecdote of therapy bestowed on old friends showed a different outcome. Goodman's brother Percy had not always approved of everything his little brother did, yet he was very proud of him and ready to give him the benefit of the doubt, and if necessary a helping hand. Percy was a modern man. He did not hold back from the movements of his time but joined them early and stayed with them loyally. He was among the earliest American disciples of Le Corbusier. Until the Moscow trials and the Spanish Civil War, he had been a Communist too. His friends were the cultural avant-garde. He knew Alexander Calder and Jacques Lipchitz, and among his dinner guests were various psychoanalysts, including Reich's translator Theodore Wolfe. Though never again the enthusiast he had been for the Paris International Style, his brother Paul's respect for Reichian ideas encouraged Percy to explore a bit further on his own. Characteristically, it was the "architectural" side of Reichianism that intrigued him, and he was one of the first to rent an orgone box.

About the time that Percy's son Joel was born, Paul decided that his brother could use a little therapy. The birth of his own son not long before had brought disturbing childhood memories to the surface, but he and Percy had never talked about these, and especially not about their reactions to abandonment by their father. Perhaps now was the time. Furthermore, there was a physical complaint to serve as the occasion for Gestalt exercises, bursitis in Percy's arm.[21] So Paul began showing up once or twice a week for dinner, after which he and Percy would closet themselves for a few hours while Naomi Goodman tidied up and tended the children. She resented this encroachment on her already rather brief hours with her husband, whose booming practice designing modernist synagogues kept him away from home much of the time. But Percy did not seem to relish these sessions with his therapist brother any more than Naomi did. Awareness exercises were one thing; probing the painful past was another. Percy had dealt with his own unhappy childhood by willful amnesia, and his brother's eagerness and obvious personal investment in laying it bare proved more than he could tolerate, even from Paul. As they neared these explosive subjects, Percy became more and more convinced that Paul was unqualified and ought not to be practicing therapy, with him or anyone else. The sessions were finally broken off one night when he lost his temper and took a swing at Paul. For a while after that they did not speak to one another, and there was a hint of reserve between them through the rest of the fifties, as long as Goodman continued to take patients. However, that swing at

Paul seemed to have cured Percy's bursitis. It could be called successful termination, on the Rankian model—Enough![22]

In any case, Goodman was satisfied if the reactions of his intimates to his new calling were responses to the way he actually conducted himself. One of his cardinal tenets was that the therapist was only a person, not a shaman or healer, and especially not a strategic "person," that is, standing in for a person for purposes of the transference a patient might make. No special treatment or regard for the therapist then, except that he ought to be the first to shoulder the burden of change: "What world can *I* live in? How to cope with the fact that *he* exists? I can live here if I bring about such & such changes, in him & me."[23] If his old friends could understand that, they would have less difficulty accepting his new temerity.

The other side of this coin had to do with the sort of person Goodman had always been and declared he would remain. It was *this* Goodman to whose inclusion in their programs the impresarios of the world shouted No! No! No! and to whose public behavior Ben Nelson's word "unseemly" applied. The problem was not his competence. "I'm not exactly the village idiot," he would say, "I've written a book on the subject."[24] But he could not be trusted to keep to the decorums. Were he allowed to speak at the Freud centenary, there was no telling what he might say.

It was not only publishers and funders who worried about such things; so too did the leader of his own faction, his collaborator Fritz Perls. In 1953 the New York Institute for Gestalt Therapy had offered special seminars designed for out-of-town therapists who wanted a practical introduction to the new methods. A product of Perls's drumming through the provinces, this experiment soon resulted in the establishment of a Gestalt Therapy Institute in Cleveland, to which Fritz and Laura, and Paul Weisz, would travel periodically to hold seminars and run training sessions.[25] After a year or so Isadore From was asked to take responsibility for training the Cleveland group, and it was proposed that Goodman also fly to Ohio once every two months to give a set of workshops. Goodman did this for a number of years, traveling not only to Cleveland but also Columbus and to Grand Rapids, Michigan. But at the outset there was opposition to his going, primarily from Perls, who complained that all his labors building up the movement would be jeopardized by Goodman's notorious lack of discretion. With all due respect for Goodman's genius, he said, could Paul behave himself properly among the new converts, most of whom were M.D.'s working in the hospitals or at the university, and who were, after all, Midwesterners?

Coming from Fritz Perls, these compunctions struck his friends as absurd. He himself was much more likely to get into nasty scrapes with patients and his growing cult of acolytes. If Paul could not be trusted in the same room with a pretty boy neither could Fritz with a young woman. At a party on Central Park West, for example, Perls singled out one of Goodman's patients and, she reports, "corners me upstairs in the bedroom. He does not for a moment drop his role nor I mine. This is singularly European. Our culture requires that at the first love-pass, one drops one's role, or at the least, takes on a different role, that of simulated sincerity. Though this is customary, it does seem more honest not to attempt it. He catches hold of me and murmurs, 'Tell me, Judith, do you have orgasms?'"[26] This sort of indiscretion bothered Perls precisely because it was his own failing too. In this regard neither he nor Goodman really had a role to drop—these were their habitual selves—but Fritz was courtly where Paul was gauche.

The more orthodox professionals among Goodman's colleagues, and also some of his patients, were troubled by another form of indiscretion. He was known to blab. His failing was not exactly gossip, more a kind of shop talk among members of his group, but however one named it, he certainly did reveal the intimate details of his patients' lives—that A has been fucking B's wife, who in turn seems to have designs on C; that X sleeps in a fetal position and still wets her bed; that Y made love to his mother on Mother's Day. (When Y told him that, Goodman's reaction was as uncanny as the incestuous fact itself: he reported feeling suddenly disembodied, his consciousness strangely rising in the room until he seemed to be listening to his patient from somewhere near the corner of the ceiling.)[27]

Should we condemn these revelations as breaches of professional ethics, violations of the therapist's rule of confidentiality? Goodman had no rule of confidentiality. When he offered Judith Malina private therapy sessions without charge, she was "surprised and pleased," but told him she was worried that he would not be discreet. "Why are you afraid to be discussed?" he asked. She had no reply.[28] Another new patient was warned, "I'm a sociopath."[29] Once in treatment, people soon learned what to expect, since he was constantly violating the taboos and pushing others to do the same. He took his chances along with everyone else: "In the group . . . Paul, lying on the floor, central and vulnerable, doesn't play the antagonist that he has been of late. He accepts everyone's remarks."[30]

As it turned out, most of the Cleveland therapists were charmed by the very qualities that gave some people the willies.

No one could ever measure up to Fritz Perls, whom Erving Polster called "a magician." But Goodman too was "exciting" and
held in "awe," "a combination of the beatific and the outra-
geous." Insofar as his workshop style was concerned, although
"occasionally provocative," Goodman's sessions were much less
aggressive than those his colleagues ran. "He was not a man to
create a tension system," as Perls and Paul Weisz typically did;
"in a workshop with him, the personal threat was not continu-
ingly as high as it was in workshops with Fritz." Polster was surprised to find Goodman "more curious about the person he was
working with than interested in whether there would be a
cure." That was what made him different from other Gestalt
therapists: "What Paul did was bring through his own personal
function, he brought in humanity."[31]

It was just this attitude that Goodman made the essence of
Gestalt training and practice. His Cleveland seminars were centered on the distinction between therapy as a "special discipline" and as "a way of life." A whole set of oppositions
followed from this basic dichotomy:

Specialty	Way of Life
Profession	Differential Friends
"Person"	Vulnerable Person
Fee	Support (Community)
Hour	Visit
Professional & Private Life	Single Life
Plan	Projection & Need

Goodman explained, for example, that in the classic psychoanalytic relationship there was always an "attempt to avoid
projection" on the part of the analyst, to "efface self," whereas

181

in his own practice, "I immediately project: attend to what my interest is: empathize."[32]

Attitudes like these may have been implicit in *Gestalt Therapy*, but as a theoretical tract it was more focused on what the therapist needs to know than on how he should behave. During the twenty years Isadore From ran his training groups in Cleveland, the book was always in front of them, the starting point for working through Gestalt principles and practice. When Fritz Perls came, his approach was the opposite. He acted as though the book didn't exist and Gestalt therapy was being invented under their very eyes, at a wave of his wand. The Cleveland disciples were expecting one or another version of these styles when Goodman began to visit them too and were surprised to find that he did not present himself either as the author of their sacred text or as the intellectual fountainhead of the movement. As Polster put it, "He was more like a street philosopher than a Gestalt theoretician."[33]

In discussing therapy as a way of life rather than a special discipline, Goodman raised the question of professional ethics. When his critics complained that he was not professional, they usually had in mind something under this heading. Often the question boiled down to, did he exploit his patients? His Cleveland seminars shed light on such issues and help us understand his practice and the accusations it occasioned.

To begin with a simple case, consider the opposition between "Fee" and "Support (Community)." As we have already seen, Goodman's was a sliding scale, with many special arrangements. In some respects his attitude was that of the old-fashioned professional, who offered treatment as needed and accepted payment according to ability. But Goodman's version of this was more communitarian, and had a different rationale behind it. Among his friends there were some he treated for nothing, though friendship and community are surely not nothing, as he would have been quick to point out. "Nothing" might also translate as "I like you" or "I think we can get somewhere."[34] Or his recompense might be a potential "something," a disposition to return gifts and favors. When Goodman offered to take on Judith Malina as a patient, he was not just a friend in need but also a playwright whose work was going to be directed by her for the Living Theatre, if the Living Theatre could ever struggle itself into existence. This he saw not so much as casting bread upon the waters as a form of anarchist mutual aid.

Even his fee-in-kind was on a sliding scale. As we saw, when an old friend needed help Goodman proposed a visit to Fire Island as his payment, a favor he could have asked and received in any case. At the other end of the scale, a few years later Goodman accepted the invitation of a wealthy patient to accompany him, all expenses paid, on a trip to Europe. Was this ethical? In fact, each of these cases was too complicated to be judged in any simple way. That was what happened when therapy was regarded as part of life rather than a commodity in sixty-minute packages. When he went to Fire Island, Goodman was in his element, the same bohemian gay community that he consorted with most summers, where he always had a place to stay with his family—Percy and Naomi and their children; his sister, Alice; his wife, Sally, and his own children. When he went to Europe with his wealthy patient, there were old friends to stay with there too, like Edouard Roditi, but Goodman also felt an obligation to keep company with his benefactor, whose middle-class tastes in hotels and social life put a certain strain on Goodman. He liked him well enough, but it was a relief when the agreed-upon period of companionship, and free room and board, came to an end and Goodman could wander off on his own to the cheaper, riskier, dirtier world of back streets and quais along the Seine that made him happy.[35]

Another example shows how such mutual aid worked not only on vacations but also at home. In 1953 when Goodman's family moved from their apartment on Ninth Avenue to a loft on West 23rd Street, a number of their friends helped fix the place up, not just carting books and furniture but making substantial repairs, painting, putting in new wiring. Among the helpers were several patients, former patients, and even wives and husbands of patients. One did the electrical work, George Dennison wielded a brush—he was painting apartments for a living at the time—and there was a swarm of Gestalt elves making the place livable. In the midst of this it happened that Paul Mattick, a "Council Communist," who frequented the anarchist hall on lower Broadway to argue his brand of syndicalism, came by to see Goodman's new apartment—perhaps after a meeting, but more likely because he and his wife Ilse were bringing six-year-old Mathew Goodman home from the Hudson Guild day-care center where Ilse worked.

Mattick had no use for the psychoanalytic invasion of politics that had been going on for several years at the anarchist hall, nor did he find much of anything to admire in Goodman's work or character. (Once Goodman announced that he had just been sitting in an orgone box. "What did you get out of it?" asked Mattick. "Nothing," said Goodman, "nothing. But that's it, that's *what* you get out of it." This sort of talk baffled Mattick when it did not simply disgust him.) When Mattick saw all the Goodman patients and disciples busily making the loft habitable for their sage, he thought to himself how shrewd Paul was in making a living. True, he charged very little for therapy, but there were these other benefits. Mattick did not think it exploitative or mean so much as it was comic. But the joke was on him, for he did not understand what was going on. Mattick's misconception perfectly illustrates the difference between his notions of community and those of the anarchists he debated with on Saturday afternoons. He could not see Goodman's circle as a community, only as a set of economic relations and roles.[36]

What would Mattick have thought had he observed this same group at work on another refurbishing of new quarters a year later? On that occasion Goodman wrote to George Dennison, now in Mexico: "Biggest organized incident is the Andersons moving into a house where they're to be caretakers & fix it up. Perry, Bill, Dave Andree, Dave Riff, Isad, Hans, Sally, Bruce De John, Glenn have been working on the job (+ MR [seven-year-old Mathew Ready Goodman] & Bruce's cocker spaniel). Various truncated triangles involved, but much less velvet-bordered neurosis than in working on 142 W. 23. The reason is, I think, the absence of 1. B.B. and (poor 2nd) you. I haven't been there yet—Sally says that, with all the effort, it really isn't superior to what they are leaving."[37] All this, including the fact that Goodman had not been one of the work crew "yet," gives his community of patients, disciples, and friends a comic coloring, to be sure, but without the acid that Paul Mattick's account injected. Was this exploitation? Or was it an example of how psychotherapy could be "a way of life," as he put it in his Cleveland workshops?

But of course it was sexual exploitation that Goodman was most often accused of. Since he was already notorious for his shameless importunity of every young man who struck his fancy, his detractors were quick to suspect him of seducing his patients. Even his friends made jokes about his preference for the young and beautiful in making up his groups. But this too was a more complicated story than first meets the eye. Goodman had been obsessed with his sexual delinquency so long and so publicly, and this had already cost him so much, that it hardly makes sense to take his case as another example of the hanky-panky that has always pervaded the medical and therapeutic professions. Nor did he hide his history from his patients. On the contrary, he was likely to boast of having been thrown out of three different schools for seducing his students—or more accurately, for not keeping quiet about it, for refusing to be discreet.

Yes, Goodman sometimes made love to his patients, though I know of no one who had not been to bed with him first, before entering therapy. Perhaps there were such cases too; it would have been unlike Goodman to make a distinction. Did the Freudian dictum hold here: no important life-changes during the analysis? Goodman would have been amused at the question. In fact his own attitude toward sexuality and therapy was Reichian: often what was being dealt with was not *psycho-*neurosis but *actual*-neurosis, a physical deprivation that could be treated, at least in part, by more sexual pleasure. The goal of therapy was precisely to change such life circumstances, the sooner the better.

He discussed these problems with his Cleveland trainees. Given the Gestalt therapist's commitment to being a person, not just a strategic "person," in his relations with patients, what could he do to promote their actual well-being, their sexual, vocational, or domestic health? His question was framed in the context of group therapy, so that it was not the therapist's amorous behavior that counted—which would fall out as it might—but the possibility of mutual aid within the entire group. A group would be put together in the first place for "variety," that is, "interest and/or antagonism."[38] This would include sexual attractions, and as we have just seen, Goodman was alive to the "truncated triangles" among them, well illustrated in another letter to Dennison, which I quote with the names changed:

> There's the usual almanac of sexual news, gripes,
> attempted suicides. Joe Doe (!) has, it turns out, for
> months been fucking Tom Jones's lethargic wife; Tom
> doesn't know how to take this, but has been ever so
> slowly working himself up into the beginnings of a pon-
> derous anger; otherwise he's much more merry and alive,
> and seems to have designs on (!) Jill Jackson. John
> Smith, you know, is living with Chuck and Jim. I have a
> kind of semi-official room there—to where Max and I
> repair to get away from our respective households. I don't
> see anything of John. He avoids me since he got a job
> and blew on liquor thirty bucks that I lent him to pay a
> month's rent. Frank has become a patient of mine, I
> think I can do him some good. Laura and I have a weekly
> session with Jane and Ed Brown, and afterwards, over
> supper, we marvel at the way some people can carry on.[39]

Obviously Goodman saw no difficulty in violating the Freudian taboo on important life changes during therapy. He was less sure of himself when it came to upsetting his own prin-ciple that there should be no pretense in the therapeutic relation, no merely strategic "person" with whom the patient practiced being a person himself. Wasn't this inconsistent with his view that the therapist, and others in the group, were there to provide a "safe emergency situation" for the patient, including even sexual exploration?

He argued the issue out in front of his Cleveland audience, as his seminar notes make clear: "Sexual 'person' as strategy: sexual or employment auxiliary: but the fact that just to find his own is his problem, and so forth; but in education, the apt object is thrown in the way in a good form." Although the debate swings back and forth, he ends with the formula that he never seriously doubted: a Gestalt therapy group might occasionally have among its proper functions those of "Bawdy-House & Employment-Agency."[40] And so his own groups sometimes served. There were evenings, for example, when someone complained of a lack of sexual companionship, and Goodman would set about finding a solution in the room, if not one of the group then a date with some outside acquaintance. He turned to one person after another and asked each, What are you doing on Monday, on Tuesday, and so forth, and set up appointments for a whole week. There! See, that's not so hard, is it? he said.[41]

Was this an example of a safe emergency situation or was it a case of "strategizing" the sexual relations of his patients? And regardless of principles and rules of thumb, was it likely to be of therapeutic value? I do not pretend to know the answers to such questions. Goodman certainly took the issues of transference and countertransference more lightly, even humorously, than therapists do today, or did then, including those in Gestalt circles. I do not mean that he took his relations with his patients lightly, but that he treated those relations as immediate and practical, not cases for the application of abstract principles.

Another sort of story has circulated about Goodman's exploiting his patients sexually. He is supposed to have required several of them, often at the first private session, to produce their penises. When one tracks these stories down, they sometimes turn out to be true but not as examples of seduction or exploitation. Typically these cases involve patients with some sexual complaint—impotence, for instance, with feelings of inferiority and self-consciousness about having a small penis. "Well," Goodman would say, "let's have a look."

In two other cases that I know of—one of a man a good deal older than Goodman, and definitely *not* his type (no one older was), the other of a man much younger and therefore a possibility—Goodman suspected that repressed homosexual impulses were part of the problem. To aid his diagnosis he unbuttoned his own fly, took out his cock, and asked his patient to touch it. These patients were old friends, he had known one of them twenty years, and if he had ever had any sexual interest in them they would have known about it long before. However unorthodox, the action was perhaps a useful maneuver, for it tended to reduce anxiety about Goodman's own sexual threat at the same time that it raised the issue of homosexuality in the most demystifying way.[42]

Even if Goodman had never opened his fly in the line of duty, so to speak, his reputation was already such as to guarantee that there would be rumors about his using the therapeutic situation as a staging-area for his own amours. Neither friends nor enemies could resist repeating and embellishing the gossip. They all knew, for instance, that he and a (female) lover had once joked about setting up a "College of Sex" in which they would put their vast experience to work pedagogically. Now Goodman was literally offering Gestalt seminars on "The

Psychology of Sex." It was hilarious. Although Goodman was not running a sex clinic, other Gestalt therapists did sometimes think of him when they encountered patients with specific sexual disorders, as if he were their specialist. Once, for example, a female colleague referred a man who had just had prostate surgery and was worried about the quality of his orgasms. The consultation, as reported back to her, was sensitive and reassuring.[43]

In assessing Goodman's contributions to psychotherapeutic practice, we should remember the squeamish, guilty, punishing attitude toward sexuality common not only in polite society, the conventional middle class, or the blue-collar masses, but almost as widespread among doctors, clinical psychologists, and psychoanalysts of just a generation ago. This attitude was all the more rigid and unyielding in the fifties simply because the repression was breaking down at last, and we were on the verge of the sexual revolution of the sixties, whose reverberations are still echoing today. Goodman's championing of sexual freedom, especially for the young, was as much a part of his politics as it was of his psychology, and in fact it predated his discovery of Reich's *The Function of the Orgasm* and *The Sexual Revolution*. Speaking out on this issue was one of the chief reasons for the difficulties he faced in earning a living before he turned to psychotherapy. A teacher could get in trouble very fast by advocating the rights of students to sexual experience (no matter what their ages), and if you made it known that you believed in such rights, you would probably never be hired at all. And although many editors and publishers were happy enough to promote works sprinkled with whatever measure of sexual explicitness would titillate readers without offending them (something Goodman *never* did), nonetheless to speak frankly and earnestly about the sexual mores, arguing for more honesty and permissiveness, was enough to keep you out of the respectable journals or bookstores. Straightforward sexual libertarianism was also frowned on by most schools of psychotherapy. Yes, sex certainly had to be dealt with in the treatment of neurosis—after all, the sexuality of infants and small children had been one of Freud's great discoveries—but direct confrontation of the patient's actual sexual plight was taboo. Aside from a few practitioners who followed their own lights, the only therapists of the postwar boom in psychotherapy who took actual sexual misery and its treatment seriously were the Reichians and the Gestalt therapists. They were the pioneers, in league (whether they chose to be or not) with the libertarian anarchists, the bohemian artists, and in the later fifties with the beatniks of North Beach and Greenwich Village—not to mention the native impulse of human beings, the practice of very many adolescents, and the changing mores.

But even the Reichians were notoriously homophobic. A friend of Goodman's who practiced as a children's therapist—not Gestalt-trained though he came to some of the seminars—went through a complete therapy with Reich himself without ever daring to reveal that he was homosexual! In contrast, a number of Gestalt therapists were either bisexual, like Goodman, or homosexual, but whether they were or not, patients in Gestalt treatment never had to be in the closet. The Gestalt view of homosexuality was laid down by Goodman more or less along these lines: there were a number of different etiologies, just as at different stages of life there were different proclivities, but the problem was never what gave pleasure or satisfaction, only what prevented it. It was not the love of either one's own or the opposite sex that needed explaining and treatment (except insofar as society made one suffer for it) but rather the disgust or hatred for men or for women as erotic objects. A similar argument would be made regarding sensuality and its gratifications in more general terms—as against, for example, the Reichian dogma that genital potency was the sine qua non of health and the final benchmark of cure. Finally, it should be added that Goodman did not consider sexuality a gloomy or solemn topic, however serious and important. He often spoke of sexual "fun and games," and found plenty to laugh about, even in his own bad luck. Sex was something to enjoy, with the emphasis on joy.

To illustrate the dynamic involved in all this, let me offer a few anecdotes that suggest the prevailing attitudes of the time and some typical reactions to Goodman's sexual libertarianism. The first has to do with a story he wrote in the late thirties, "The Continuum of the Libido." This story covers a good deal of erotic ground, including both the polymorphously perverse sexuality of infants (and of the infant-in-the-adult) and also the homosexual love of adolescents (and their resistance to any awareness of it). One comic episode concerns the hero when he finds that he is "in love with his mother-in-law's collie-dog Tippy, and indeed with all of a class of large woolly female beasts, such as sheep and the she-bears in the zoo."[44] Because the character in the story in fact made love to his dog, Philip Rahv, who rejected the story at *Partisan Review* in the early forties, had spread the rumor that Goodman himself practiced bestiality. "Goodman? he fucks dogs!" This calumny and its source got around, and became a joke among Goodman's friends, who would call him up to report, "Paul, they've got a new bear at the zoo; interested?"[45] It is also true that Goodman once told one of his patients that, in "the human struggle with passion," he aspired to direct animal lust: "He says that he wishes to be a dog, an animal"—which had been the point of his story so many years earlier.[46]

My second, somewhat related anecdote is also slightly off target as regards Goodman's sexual behavior as a therapist, but it took place in the Gestalt community, among colleagues, patients, and friends, and displays his provoking behavior and some typical reactions to it with extraordinary vividness. It happened at a party given by one of the more orthodoxly credentialed Gestalt therapists, Allison Montague. George Dennison was present, and it is in his words that the event comes to life, in the memoir Dennison wrote for Goodman's *Collected Poems*:

I remember Paul at a party during his forty-sixth year. It was a stressful period. He had written twenty books, among them his best, and had seen no reward. He had much need, certainly, of love and pleasure. The party was lively. There were a great many young women, and they were conventional, were scrubbed and scented and prettily dressed. There were no intellectuals. The young actor he had been waiting for arrived with a woman. And it seemed that all the young men had come with women. He talked with this one and talked with that one. Soon he was looking into the distance, his jaw clenched and his eyes vacant in exasperation. But a handsome mongrel dog, part shepherd, was ambling about pausing at this one and at that one. Paul by now was sitting on the floor, leaning against the wall, dismayed and contemptuous. The dog went to him and wagged its tail. Paul took its head caressingly in both hands and spoke to it. There was self-pity in his voice, but also admiration and outright gratitude. "Yes, my darling," he said, "you're the prettiest one here." The dog licked him, and Paul licked him back, and for a full twenty minutes they exchanged kisses. The voices in the room fell silent, started up, fell silent. The two red tongues touched again and again, and Paul opened his mouth to the dog's tongue.

He meant to offend the human company. It was an effective display of contempt. But much more than this could be seen. The longing expressed by his open mouth was real, and was disquieting, as of something beyond placation. His affection for the dog was real, too; his fingers liked its fur, and he welcomed the closeness. Yet in the entire event there was a quality of will. I don't mean that he willed to kiss the dog in order to express his contempt, but that he willed—now, and had in the past—to overcome the squeamishness, that is, the way of life, and the entire tradition of that way, that appeared in those other faces. For in fact their fascination—persistently staring eyes, and nauseated mouths—was neurotic disgust: unlived life.

Dennison went on to discuss this rich event as an example of Goodman's attitude toward issues much larger than sexual appetite or neurotic squeamishness:

During his years as a therapist he devoted a great deal of time to the Gestalt exercises, and more time still to an investigation of breathing (about which he had considered writing). Certainly in all this he was concerned with his competence as a therapist; but more deeply it was simply another aspect of the examined life, and, as such, was nothing new, was all of a piece with the task he had long made his own.

The didactic burden of his display with the dog was obvious: if you would affirm and not suppress your animal nature, and so forth, if you would be as direct as this dog instead of wasting life in idiotic avoidances, the world would be more practicable, and I not so alone. The message, in the event, was both true and false. To some extent his dismay was a private matter. Generalized, the message is true and familiar; it comes from many quarters, not least from Paul.[47]

It is not difficult to see in this story what it was that his detractors found infuriating about Goodman. He insisted on bringing his animal nature, the continuum of the libido, into every human encounter. He did not leave his sexuality behind when he practiced therapy, or taught school, or gave speeches and workshops. On the contrary, he was likely to rub your nose in it. There was something of the kid on 151st Street in this behavior, ribald and smirking and determined to resist the adult world of inhibition and taboo, whatever the cost. Dennison draws attention to this side of Goodman's character too, with an example from his own family life:

When my younger brother was three or four, he and the family bulldog were much enamored of each other. One night my father could bear it no longer, and said, "Stop kissing the dog on the mouth." But the kissing went on.

195

My father grew angry and sent my brother up to bed. Ten minutes went by. They heard his footsteps coming down the stairs, and then he stalked into the room, both fists clenched, and made for the dog shouting, "I don't care! I love Skippy and I'm gonna kiss 'im on the mouth!"

There really was a child like that alive in Paul, both problematically and as a reservoir of power.[48]

Dennison's story brings Goodman to life in all his childishness and charisma, but let us turn the perspective around for a final look at how this and other incidents must have been regarded by his community, whether among his friends in Gestalt circles or out in the wider habitat of the New York intellectuals. Not everyone would have seen the event at the party as Dennison did, a parable of the Garden.

Allison Montague, a Bellevue psychiatrist who went on to become head of psychiatry for students at Columbia University, was part of the original Gestalt Institute and, it will be recalled, was a member of Goodman's seminar on "Reaction-Formation"—the one Goodman thought had "the hots" for him. The incident took place in Montague's apartment, with Montague's dog. In trying to imagine the effect of Goodman's behavior we should keep in mind that among the staring eyes and gaping mouths were many of Goodman's professional connections, well practiced in Gestalt exercises designed to combat squeamishness and enhance awareness of bodily functions. Goodman knew how to get under their skins too—"The voices in the room fell silent, started up, fell silent."

Finally Montague collared his dog and dragged him to a bedroom, shut the door, and locked it.

"But Monty, . . ." Goodman protested.

His host replied, "It's *my* dog, Paul."[49]

It is not hard to imagine what people were saying to one another when the party started up again, its crisis having been acted out so satisfyingly in front of their very eyes. Those who had always pursed their lips at Goodman's impudence did so with all the more distaste. Those who wished he would stop offending people who might otherwise be his friends and supporters, or at least not his enemies, frowned and clucked. A few, like George Dennison, laughed.

One final accusation of unprofessional behavior was leveled against him, not by his enemies among the intellectuals nor by his friends in the institute but by his patients themselves, who on most other counts judged him innocent, or at least not guilty. Almost everyone who saw him in the group setting seems to have felt that when, as sometimes happened, Sally was tempted or persuaded to join a session, he was much too hard on her.[50]

Although Goodman's groups rarely indulged in the hammering at one another that went on among colleagues at meetings of the institute, there was plenty of brutal frankness to keep the safe emergency from becoming too safe. An early participant likened it to "hazing," and remembered that it was not just a matter of taking it; she for one had been good at giving it out and recalled being praised one night for going after another member of the group in a "challenging" spirit.[51] Although he himself tended to be gentle in these sessions, Goodman relished a bit of nastiness in others and appreciated a wicked turn of phrase. All the better if it brought his patients into stronger contact. But sometimes people couldn't take it. One woman ran out screaming, "You're just doing this to drive me crazy!"[52] Another wrote in her diary:

"I cannot withstand attack.

"I left quickly at the end of last night's group and didn't even stop to taste the cake Sally had baked for us during the session.

"Then, after crying it out in the doorway, I trudged back upstairs, apologized cheerfully, and had my coffee and cake."[53]

This little sequence—from agitation and flight, through weeping and licking one's wounds, and finally back to the gathering of friends for comfort and support—may be taken as a typical arc of feeling, though not often acted out so dramatically. One function of the social hour at the end, when Sally joined them for coffee and cake, was simply to cordon off behavior that was "group sesh" and preserve its pitch of intensity—things would relax later, and there would be a chance to recover one's spirits.[54] Usually Sally stayed on the comfort-and-support side of this divide, but sometimes, especially during the first years of Paul's groups, that is, before she learned to keep away, she would take a chair in the circle and see what happened. There was much weeping during sessions, and Paul himself probably shed more tears than anyone else—it counted as a virtue—but when Sally cried, as she did under the onslaught of candor her presence called forth from him, she cried bitter tears that were not so easily wiped away when it was time for the coffee and cake.

Goodman also addressed this problem in his Cleveland workshops. If the Gestalt therapist had a duty to be a person rather than a "person," that meant entering into groups without inhibition, not bracketing off the professional from the personal. Some would say that this was just an elaborate excuse to do as one pleased. Goodman was not blind to the risk, but after all, being "objective" and not allowing one's own feelings into the session could hardly be called a neutral stance. It immediately set up authority dynamics and rules of the game that were just as susceptible of professional abuse, whatever the pretense. Rather, Goodman told his trainees in Cleveland, the goal was "to be 'subjective' without using the patient for *other* unfinished situations."[55]

All well and good, but just where Goodman was most vulnerable, that is, in his domestic life, he was at the mercy of his unfinished situations and quite merciless in his use of Sally to repeat them over and over. No doubt she made her own contribution to their impasse, and of course he suffered too. However the blame was placed, everyone agreed that it was better for her not to join the group until it was time for coffee and cake.

There was never any illusion that Paul could serve as Sally's therapist in one-to-one sessions, except in the sense that, merely by virtue of living with a man who made no distinction between being a therapist and being a person, she risked finding herself under therapeutic scrutiny at any moment. She partially protected herself against this by having her own therapist, someone she could count on to be on her side and whose unfinished situations were not automatically locked in a neurotic dance with hers. Sometimes her sessions were arranged to coincide with Paul's groups, so that she would get home just in time to join in the general posttherapeutic social hour. She had consulted Wilhelm Reich himself briefly in 1946 and then Alexander Lowen for a while, just before Paul's sessions with him. She moved on to Gestalt therapists in the fifties, seeing both Isadore From and Paul Weisz at different periods and even Perls himself, though his methods were clearly not for her. She lay down on the couch in Fritz's office, and said nothing. He waited. She waited. Nothing. Their thoughts would surely have been interesting to each other, but there were too many reasons for withholding them, not the least of which was that she did not like Fritz personally. She did like From and Weisz.[56]

Others noted that Goodman's relations with his colleagues at the institute, especially with Weisz, who was his rival in a number of ways, became seriously strained while Sally was their patient.[57] Goodman's own confusions and anxieties were so thoroughly bound up in his marriage that he could not let go of the reins. Indeed, it was precisely the problems of his marriage—jealousy and blocked feeling—that also baffled him as a therapist, with all his patients. He wrote about it in his journal.

There are two states that balk me as a therapist: (1) Jealousy. I empathize completely. I can predict the next sentence and the course of resentment, anger, fear, and grief. I even know how to alleviate suffering by holding oneself more erect and lessening depression (the mind goes blank). But I have no perspective. I do not know how to drain energy from the insanity. It is with the patient as with myself, we are forced to rely on time and chance and flattering rationalizations and resolutions. (2) Blocked blank inability to speak or have a next thought or feeling. Here my bother is just the contrary. I often have to deal with this state and recognize it, but I have no empathy with it, I do not believe it. It leaves me out, and I don't know how to woo him forth. I myself can always think of something—except just when I am balked. I can write something even when I am balked.[58]

Goodman claims here to know how to lessen jealous suffering by techniques that cause the mind to "go blank"—but then, he says, the "blank" mind is just what he doesn't know how to deal with. Furthermore, he speaks of patients "blocked" in thought and feeling, and of himself as "balked" and "without empathy" when faced with their "blankness." Who is he really talking about? One way of understanding what Goodman says here would be to take jealousy as his problem, blocked feeling and thought (which might be interpreted as passive resistance) as Sally's problem. From his perspective that was how it looked sometimes, whether or not he meant to be speaking of his own domestic situation in this journal entry. But there is another way of reading his account. If one focuses on what he says about himself, it is possible to see him circling round a peculiar concomitant of his own jealousy—not wordlessness, which was so alien to him, but its opposite, intellectualism or "verbalizing," which was his closer enemy. This too might produce a kind of blankness and failure of empathy—in Gestalt terms lack of contact. The journal entry could then be understood as about two related topics, jealousy and the panic states it occasions. It is not too much to say that Goodman had spent most of his self-analysis, and much of his soul-work in stories and poems, trying to solve the riddle of just how these disturbances went together, how his fear of betrayal and abandonment and his ready tongue and wit were part of a single dynamic.

There was still another side to it. The anxiety about betrayal and abandonment could also manifest itself as a deep-seated sense of some ultimate loss already suffered, an archaic expulsion from the Garden which gave rise to his lifelong identification with the outcasts, the Ishmaels of the world, and which also lay behind all his talk about having been "cut out for an archangel" and "searching for Paradise," metaphors for the two sides of his continually thwarted but also continually renewed ambitions in life, to be acclaimed as an artist and to be blissfully in love. So every morning he wrote stories and poems, in touch with the Creator Spirit, and many an afternoon he cruised the streets looking for his erotic Adam.

Other fears and desires were also twisted into Goodman's psychic knot, but during this period, the decade of his practice as a therapist, these were the cords that chafed him most. Self-analysis had tugged at the tangle, but its loosening would only come as a result of shifts of tension that were less willfully achieved, that in fact were felt, one by one, as defeats and catastrophes rather than triumphs. In important ways Gestalt therapy was the means by which he coped with these blows of fate and turned them to a kind of advantage, yet at the same time the working through of his problems led him ultimately to give up his therapeutic career and answer the call of the sixties as a social critic and philosopher of the New Left. Let us now consider this process and try to assess the part that Gestalt therapy played in freeing Goodman for his next vocation.

CHAPTER EIGHT

"Can Anything Be Salvaged from All That Effort?"

GOODMAN'S MARITAL PROBLEMS went back a long way. Being bisexual complicated matters, though perhaps not in the way one might think. He himself regarded his dual sex life as a kind of solution or at least a neat compartmentalizing of two basic impulses in him, domestic and promiscuous. He was constantly cruising for sex, but almost all of his pick-ups and affairs were homosexual; home life was strictly heterosexual and monogamous—he was a one-woman man. Sally did not find this an impossible situation, though she was jealous of any woman who might appear to interest Paul, as for instance his first wife. The problems in their marriage had more to do with love than lust. Each felt the other did not really care, and they staged secret little tests of affection that were impossible to pass and so created just the estrangement they feared: "If only he . . ."; "If only she . . ."

There was also a peculiar double standard operating in their relationship. They agreed, on principle, that each of them had the right to take lovers outside their marriage, and especially that if one of them had this right the other did too. But Paul's stream of young men did not make Sally jealous, whereas her occasional lovers sent him into fits. He did not suffer silently, though he understood that his own promiscuity, not to mention his general advocacy of sexual freedom, left him no grounds to complain of her infidelity.

The inconsistencies and ironies here were worthy of Molière. At one point Paul's jealousy raised things to such a pitch that he decided he had actually fallen in love with Sally, something he had never been able to feel during their first years together. One can imagine her reaction to this announcement. Of course this phase did not last very long, but all through the fifties Goodman's unhappiness and self-pity were kept at the boil by his obsession with the classic torments of romantic novels—love and its absence, desire and its rejection, jealousy and the threat of abandonment. In his self-analysis he tended to locate the origin of such conflicts in his childhood relations with his mother, who had suitors and who went off to work every day of his infancy, leaving him with his aunts. Perhaps he was right, but of course it was the unfinished situation in the present that he had to deal with.

Goodman's homosexual life was no less difficult. Here jealousy played no part, but there were other sources of anxiety and dismay. Let me emphasize here what I have already said, that Goodman did not regard homosexuality, his or anyone else's, as abnormal or neurotic in itself. How one felt about it, acted on it, and the satisfactions that did or did not meet one's expectations—those were issues that might be judged against some notion of health. But the love of young men struck him as a perfectly ordinary passion. What was neurotic or unhealthy was whatever behavior cut off feeling and denied pleasure or love. In his own case Goodman realized that there were aspects of the way he pursued his desire that were unrealistic, self-thwarting, and caused him great unhappiness. To be sure, many a lover has suffered from similar follies, whether the beloved objects were heterosexual or homosexual, though of course our society has made the latter pursuit more of a gauntlet to be run. But Goodman's path was a particularly thorny one, and he felt its windings more and more as a tortuous maze he was lost in.

He complained, for instance, of sheer lack of success—his cruising the parks and waterfront was often fruitless—or he would spend hours in a bar waiting for a partner who failed to keep the appointment. Obviously his sense of deprivation was an artifact of the fanatical quest itself. In fact he had many lovers, both strangers and friends, and his laments over being stood up were so numerous because that was what he did while waiting, write lonely and self-pitying poems.

Another element of anxiety in his relentless sexual "hunt" (as he often called it) was the likelihood that success would bring dangers and humiliation rather than pleasure. He knew through painful experience that he might be beaten or robbed if not arrested and disgraced. This was part of the excitement, though he would have gladly settled for safer thrills.

When he wrote, near the end of his life, an essay on his homosexual experience, Goodman spoke first of the price that a "sexual nigger" paid for his behavior, the ostracism and contempt, and the defensive reactions to these attitudes that might be equally damaging to character; but he also dwelt on the positive side, including the advantages of promiscuous cruising: "It can be profoundly democratizing, throwing together every class and group."[1] The accusation that such contacts were appallingly superficial, "a kind of archetype of the inanity of mass urban life," he answered by saying that in his case, at least, "I have always followed up in exactly the opposite way and many of my lifelong personal loyalties had sexual beginnings. . . . Given the usual coldness and fragmentation of community life at present, my hunch is that homosexual promiscuity enriches more lives than it desensitizes."[2] Goodman discussed the problems and possibilities in greater detail, but he ended with this sobering summation, especially applicable to his own case: "Yet it is true that an evil of the hardship and danger of queer life in our society, as with any situation of scarcity and starvation, is that we become obsessional and one-track-minded about it. I have certainly spent far too many anxious hours of my life fruitlessly cruising, which I might have spent sauntering for other purposes or for nothing at all, pasturing my soul. . . . On balance, I don't know whether my choice, or compulsion, of a bisexual life has made me especially unhappy or only averagely unhappy."[3]

The neurotic character of Goodman's promiscuity can be glimpsed in its obsessional pattern, a kind of addiction, and the very compulsion to go out again into the streets day after day suggests the hollow satisfaction he often found there. He knew that his desire was a sickness of some kind and tried to track its origins down in his past too. His earliest homosexual experiences, at age eight to ten, had taken place in the context of boyhood gangs, street life among the tough young Jews and Irish boys who lived on his block and whose comradeship he envied and yearned for. He was clear about the sequence of his obsession: first he took the risk, made the pass, had the sex, and then, sometimes, felt the lust. If he was lucky he might also make a friend, the final motive. He certainly did make some lifelong friends this way. But rarely if ever did the series reverse itself: friendliness, lust, satisfaction.

Goodman's love life, domestic and promiscuous, had its symbolic as well as its practical significance. Most of his relations with the world were figured here. He made demands on the loyalty of others, especially his hoped-for readers, that were like those he made on Sally. And he wanted editors and publishers to "come across" with the same largesse that he courted, with equal bad luck, in the San Remo bar. The audience for his writing was tested for its affection before it was wooed. Were his readers willing to love him no matter what? He could be a jolly companion, but first one must accept his crochets of style, insulting tone, shocking opinions, and above all his importunity. He was not interested in making himself lovable; he just wanted to be loved. As a frank friend put it, he offered himself and his wares as if he were selling dirty postcards.[4]

One pattern that was apparent in most of his behavior was the refusal of responsibility. It shone through even when he was working hard to come to terms with his neurotic habits. In the early fifties, almost immediately after writing *Gestalt Therapy*, he produced a series of essays on his career as a writer that attempted to explain why he had failed to win an audience. The most personal and self-questioning of these was "On Being a Writer: An Essay for My Fortieth Birthday," which he never published, perhaps because it had not been framed as an objective study, as other pieces in the same effort were, like the psychoanalytic "On a Writer's Block" or the literary-historical "Advance-Guard Writing, 1900–1950."[5] His chief theme in this study of his own case was that he never really *chose* to be a writer but just drifted into it and that few of his works were things he *wanted* to write, at least so far as he was aware of it. This sounds very much like a denial of responsibility, especially when he goes on to say that "rather than tending toward a goal,

207

my work has rather contradicted, or at best wandered from, my better judgment of what I wanted. I have done work that made me be taken as I did not want to be taken, that could not be rewarded, that did not enlist my sharpest abilities, that was indifferent to the present state of the art or my felt concerns."[6] The exceptions, and he thought they were few, were chiefly works called forth by particular occasions—love poems, commissions, answering an opponent. Goodman was fond of quoting Goethe's opinion that "occasional poetry" was the highest kind—one suspects because this view took the burden of wanting anything himself off his shoulders. Obviously this was a convoluted neurotic strategy, full of truth and falsity, but one motive that seems powerful in it is the avoidance of rejection. It was never *his* wish that produced the work, and so if his audience did not like it—if in fact it was written so that his reader *could not* like it—his *real* abilities and performance were not being judged, and some day, when he was called to his true occasion, all these minor failures would be swept away in his triumph. Meanwhile he hunted his occasion as relentlessly as he hunted sex, with similar results.

The foregoing hardly does justice to the complexities of Goodman's engagement with life, but let it serve as a starting place for an examination of how, during the decade that he practiced psychotherapy, he came to grips with his neurosis and managed to find more practical ways of discovering what it was he really wanted, of identifying with his desire, and of acting on it so that he might sometimes actually get some satisfaction.

The self-examining essays Paul Goodman wrote at the beginning of this period came from a kind of desperation and despair.

At just the point when much else in his life—his marriage, his obsessive cruising for sex—was also under great strain, he had come to the conclusion that he was a failure as an artist and that he had best give up writing and seek a new career. Psychotherapy offered itself, and one of his first uses of its insights was to turn them on his failed art, at once taking stock and mourning his loss. Again and again he went over the same ground, steeling himself for the blow of separation: Should he leave his wife? Would she perhaps leave him? Should he give up writing? Had he already lost his chance for an audience? If only he could fall in love, and all else be swept away by irresistible passion!

"If only I knew the truth," he told himself in poems and in his journal, "I should act on it." But he was "sick with fear and ignorance," and did not know "whether or not my 'deep impulse' to aim at the best was really my deep impulse, or just another illusion."[7] As he wrote his friend George Dennison in a passage already quoted, his problem was one of wishes and desires—of clinging to the unobtainable, of no longer knowing what he wanted. "For years & years now I seem to operate at all well only paying attention to the other—either writing something I haven't chosen, or some other fellow, etc. With regard to things I want and have an eros for, I'm quite childish, as you know."[8]

Like a good Taoist he tried to live with this confusion rather than banish it. He may have given up on his career, but he did not stop writing. He tried to confront his problems in his stories, sometimes writing explicitly about his marriage ("Our Visit to Niagara," "Bathers at Westover Pond"), sometimes about his inveterate cruising of bars and bus stations ("Chester's Birthday"), sometimes about his griping and self-thwarting

("The Complaint of Richard Savage") or his resolutions to do better ("Dogwood"), or about practicing psychotherapy on others while he himself was miserable and at a loss ("An Asclepiad," "The Death of Aesculapius," "A Rescue").[9] In these stories he did his best to let his imagination play in the medium or, speaking in Gestalt terms, to find and finish the unfinished situation, relying on art as a safe emergency and the creative powers as a means of discovery. If he hoped for solutions or greater clarity, he was disappointed, but more likely he sought only to stir the depths and let the surface be murky. There is much talk during this period of patience and fortitude, the "theological virtues" necessary to faith. In his way of thinking about it, writing could be a form of prayer, simply defined as "saying how it is with me." If he could tell that honestly, perhaps something would come of it.

Of course this was not writing what he *wanted* to write either. It would take most of the decade to get to that point. *Growing Up Absurd* was still a long way in the future. Meanwhile the world kept turning. Goodman gave a good deal of his time to psychotherapy, but there were other activities to engage him as well. His friends Judith Malina and Julian Beck had finally gotten The Living Theatre established, and they performed one of Goodman's plays every couple of years throughout the fifties. He was in love with the theater then, and told himself that *that* was the art he could be successful at. Every afternoon he would show up for rehearsals, and soon he would be in love with the young man playing the lead—much to the disruption of production. The bringing together of his sexual yearning and his fantasies of artistic success made those afternoons in the darkened orchestra as exciting as anything in life.

Even so he had time on his hands. He decided to improve his piano technique enough to be able to compose little melodies for some of his poems, and with the help of one of his friends and patients, he taught himself to sight-read the simpler classics. He filled a few copybooks with songs.

In 1954 the University of Chicago Press was convinced by the combined arguments of Benjamin Nelson, who had the ear of an editor there, and Goodman's one-time mentor Richard McKeon that Goodman's dissertation, completed in 1940, was worth publishing. Goodman revised it, adding a chapter on Kafka and an elaborate glossary, and began to hope for academic recognition. But like *Gestalt Therapy*, this extraordinary book of theory was treated by the orthodox professionals as wrongheaded and perverse. Nonetheless his doctorate was at last confirmed and bestowed, the ritual being complete when the university library accepted a copy of *The Structure of Literature* in lieu of the required typescript of "The Formal Analysis of Poems" for its archives.[10] Goodman went to Chicago for the ceremony. It was a little like having one of his plays produced—including the letdown afterwards. He tried somewhat half-heartedly to find an academic job—in the Midwest, in England—but even if he had been in earnest it was unlikely that negotiations would have gotten very far beyond the usual tests he put to those who might possibly do him some good.

Aside from psychotherapy, the only area where his carping style and uncompromising intelligence were welcome was politics. This was the first decade of the Cold War, the years of McCarthyism, air-raid drills, and the great buildup of what General Eisenhower first presided over and then named the "military-industrial complex." Beginning in the mid fifties several new magazines with political aims were founded, and soon Goodman was appearing in their pages, especially in *Dissent* and *Liberation*. The audience was small but it did not have its fingers in its ears. Goodman could write for it with as much anger as he liked, for it was angry too; the official world of state power and corporate greed drew all his fire, and there was no temptation to complain about his readers as well. Moreover this audience was gradually increasing, particularly among the young. The beatnik movement of "disaffiliation" from the affluent society and its commodities, the civil rights movement with its call for social justice, the pacifists and their protests against bomb tests and shelter drills—all of these were gathering numbers and visibility.

Goodman's experience as a Gestalt therapist saw him through the career crisis that he faced at the beginning of the fifties. It was not really an alternative path for him, but it allowed him to cope with his disappointment and move on to work that would use his powers and reward him as nothing else ever had. His practice was never large, and he kept trimming it down "to my size—and income needs," which were modest indeed. By 1954 he was writing George Dennison that "it's not for me as a vocation," even though he considered himself good at it: "the sessions I do have are excellent with surprising frequency."[11] Part of the problem was that to do it right required more commitment to individuals than he wanted to make, as he explained some years later when asked why he had given up his practice. He often scheduled appointments "with an hour before and an hour after free—so the patient couldn't pull the racket of producing interesting material two minutes before the hour and then run out."[12] It was not just the time, however, but the drain on the spirit: "you are continually giving out and giving out and paying attention and concentrating. And I just was not happy enough to have the energy. At the same time," he added, "there is enormous satisfaction in the sense of overcoming one's solitude, in knowing you are in contact with real people." He meant it in both ways, overcoming his own solitude as well as that of his patients. "It's beautiful, like taking care of a child. You give yourself and you expect nothing in return."[13]

There are many passages in Goodman's letters, poems, and journal entries that attest to the fact that he understood that his work as a therapist was curative for himself as well as his patients. Simply to be attending responsibly to other people, without feeling that they ought to be attending to *him*, was perhaps the essence of it. Gestalt therapy, at least in his version of it, did not even demand that the patient be cured, only that enough contact be established to allow for creative adjustment and growth. Patients were not problems to be solved but people to be cared for and cared about. For someone with Goodman's neurotic need to test his welcome and put his worst foot forward, this was very important practice in the safe emergency situation.

However, Goodman also got bored with his patients and complained sometimes that they did not do enough for him.

> I break off sessions with Dick—who has been treating
> the sessions with the sullen dutifulness he otherwise
> reserves for his wife; but *this* duty, I tell him, he does not
> have to fulfill, & and it costs him money too!—he says,
> "I do not want to lose your friendship (but you will
> come to the poker games)." What friendship? in which

he neither gives or gets anything; but it is important to him that I be there somewhere in the background. Oh, it's a great role for me! Which I do *not* invite, but effectuate (1) by coming across in their need, and (2) by muffling my own need.[14]

Usually he could remember that this role was why *he* was the therapist and *they* were the patients. And if he resented the role and finally abandoned his practice because it was too often like this, giving and never getting, he also knew that it was good for him to be needed and to hush his own wailing for attention.

Goodman's novel *The Holy Terror*—the final volume of *The Empire City*—which he wrote in 1952 and 1953, expresses some early ambivalence about the new relations with people that being a therapist entailed. All of his chief characters make some effort in this section of *The Empire City* to get into better contact with the society that surrounds them. The preceding volume, *The Dead of Spring,* had presented the hero with the great dilemma of Goodman's own existence: "If we conformed to the mad society, we became mad; but if we did not conform to the only society that there is, we became mad."[15] In *The Holy Terror* Goodman played out some of the further comic possibilities of this grim formulation. I will describe only the case of his hero Horatio, who in all the earlier volumes had stood apart from the mad society. Now he chooses to be part of it, to accept "the World of the *Herald Tribune*" and all that it represents. His friends are in dismay: their champion has clearly gone nuts, the primary symptom being that he supports "the General for president"—that is, he is an Eisenhower man. Horatio is urged to seek help, and goes to a therapist. The treatment is simple: he is advised to join the local PTA. Since he is in all respects but one the same person he has always been, his comic adventures among the parents and teachers quickly convince him that it is better to be insane the *other* way.

"Well," said his therapist, "at least you see that it's not worthwhile to be demented just to have *their* president." But Horatio had wanted to have *his* president, to identify with *his* country, and have *his* share of the social goods.[16]

The story was not merely to show that society was sick, the country "betrayed" and its citizens "mesmerized." Nor was it a lesson in self-protection, advice to dissenters. At the end of the book we find the hero "spoiling for a fight," ready to do battle, though he is not certain who his enemy is. Surely not the PTA, and not even the General with his smile of "arrested adolescence" and his absurd habits of speech.[17] In his journal Goodman pondered the problem: "For what fight? I do not definitely envisage the fight. This is because I am myself a coward; if I were not a coward, I would recognize *my* fight, and then I could invent a great fight."[18]

A few years later he would write in the same journal that he had found "the fight I wanted for Horatio." It was Goodman's own "war against the Organized System," the first volley of which was *Growing Up Absurd,* followed by many others throughout the sixties.[19] And how had he come to this realization? Horatio arrives at his stance only by working through his alienation from the society that surrounds him. He is not *against* the PTA or its members, and without his experience there he would not have felt so robbed of his birthright, angry enough to fight. The attempt to join in the only society that there is—instead of pushing it away and griping about its absurdities—turned out to be the necessary condition for Horatio's anger to be aroused and find its proper target, though not in fiction. It was not irrelevant that the group Horatio joined *was* the PTA, that is, a body whose responsibility was the welfare of the young.

We can find two important meanings in the story of Horatio's madness and cure that shed light on Goodman's own experience with Gestalt therapy. He too had long felt the pinch of the dilemma that in defying the insane society he was himself somewhat demented. The cure was to try to join the society, to take it and its citizens more seriously. He worked at this in a number of ways, but chiefly by taking patients and helping them cope with their lives in this world. Like Horatio, and like himself, they were variously demented—because they accepted the roles society offered them or because they did not, it made little difference. The chief need for Goodman was to feel concern for others, that they were his friends, his audience, his allies, and not just the mesmerized victims of a vicious social order. That was one meaning. The other had to do with what sort of a fight could be fought against the enemy Horatio intuited. In a novel of the sort Goodman was writing, this opponent had to have some symbolic form or other. There had to be some way of personifying the evil. But even if that had been possible, what would be the point, for Goodman, of fighting out an imaginary battle with a symbolic antagonist in a work of art? The struggle had to take place in the real world. That was the meaning of Horatio's baffled defiance of his unknown enemy.

Goodman put it this way in his journal: "Obviously art does not do the right thing for me: in principle the work should help solve my inner conflict; rather, when my conflict is solved, then I find I have a work. What the work does is to affirm & define for me whither I have arrived."[20] Yes, but as he was soon to see, the work that affirmed and defined his new cause was not to be a work of fiction at all, but an actual attack on his enemy, now identified as the organized system—which, to be sure, was a kind of personification but no fantasy. *Growing Up Absurd* was not just one more search for an answer to his dilemma but an angry blow aimed at his true enemy.

When he finished *The Holy Terror* in 1953, Goodman not only had no place to send his hero to do battle, but also had no place to send his manuscript. The preceding volume, *The Dead of Spring,* had finally been published by subscription. But now he wanted to collect all four volumes in a single book. It would run close to 600 pages, and deserved a wider audience than his little community of the like-minded. He had no hope whatsoever, and for a while he did not even bother to send it out to editors.

Goodman had ended *The Holy Terror* with a scene in which the characters come together to discuss how to persist in their struggle with the larger society. Three answers were proposed, mottoes for survival: "Have another ounce of strength." "Go about your business." "Get a handyman." These might be translated from Goodman's *Empire City* Taoism to something like fortitude, patience, and pragmatism. It was advice meant for himself. One must not give up, but neither must one stay in the clench of the dilemma, insisting on one's integrity. Attend instead to practical matters. Perhaps a therapist would be helpful, though one could be one's own handyman by simply paying heed to some actual detail. "Consider it this way," explained his hero, "it's always some particular problem for you or me . . . it's some detail that can be remedied."[21]

As he sometimes did in his fictions, Goodman made himself one of the speakers in this discussion at the end of *The Holy Terror*. It was he who proposed the formula Have another ounce of strength. And now, astoundingly, he saw that people were listening to him—alas, only in the book, not in life! There was a round of applause. How could that be?

"I understood what it was that had occurred and wherein lay the difference in my relation to my audience. Despite their reasonable disbelief, they had come to realize that I did have still another ounce of strength, and so they unanimously rallied to me, for people care for that.

"And *therefore*, I saw, my cursed victory (of integrity) that nobody wants to win by such strenuous means and die, was now proving unnecessary. It was not such a hard matter after all to be accepted for oneself. The clench of twenty, thirty years was loosing in my breast."[22]

Probably this self-assessment ought to be turned upside down. It was not by having another ounce of strength that Goodman found his audience, but by realizing that he need not hold himself so self-righteously apart, insisting always on *his* correct analysis, *his* integrity, *his* insanity. It had done him good to send his hero to the PTA for a while.

In any case it was true that he was making progress in the treatment of his own case. He was trading his fantasy of paradise for a simply tolerable real world that had a place for him. Gestalt therapy was not only giving him principles for this exchange but also offering support for his efforts. In this sense he was right to say that people rallied to him because of his extra ounce of strength. Patients and colleagues alike respected him and maintained him in a position of dignity—something that had never happened to him before, not even in his days at the University of Chicago, where he was just a lowly teaching assistant and never part of the club. Now he was one of the founding fathers, a theorist and a practitioner whose wisdom was sought in other cities, whose group sessions went "surprisingly" well, and whose patients actually got better.

Here were three kinds of audience for him to practice on, so to speak—patients, trainees, and peers. He was invited even farther than Cleveland to run his workshops; there were people in Los Angeles who wanted training sessions with him too, and he spent a month there early in 1955. This was new to him, being in demand and getting well paid for it. (He made $120 a week in Los Angeles, a little fortune for him.)[23] But most important was his association with genuine peers in New York. He had been surrounded by young disciples for a number of years now, and his groups of patients were not so very different, but he had never been able to find a body of age-mates, fellow artists or teachers or simply intellectuals who would welcome him into their midst and let him be part of their give-and-take. Partly this was merely the way of the world. Bohemian life in Manhattan in the middle of the twentieth century was not very communal, and though there were cliques and circles, there were not many settings of the sort that the Gestalt Institute provided where peers met regularly to share their expertise to hammer in a friendly way on one another's steel. Goodman needed this more than the admiration of the young; he needed both the respect and the resistance of equals who paid close attention and were not overawed by his genius, and whom he therefore had to take seriously when they disagreed with him or gave him advice.

The institute did not function this way for Goodman very long. By the middle fifties the weekly groups had become monthly, or even less frequent, and there were no seminars offered. People had too much else to do. Perls was in Los Angeles or Miami or Columbus, setting up new institutes and gathering new followers, while Laura Perls and Isadore From had their hands full with trainees in New York and Cleveland. Shapiro was the principal of P.S. 119 in Harlem. Weisz was busy with his patients and his research. Goodman himself had his other interests, though of the original Gestalt therapists he was the only one who had not yet found his task.

His experience with peers in the institute had a lasting effect however. A few years later he was invited to join the Columbia University Seminar in Hermeneutics, another group of true professionals—primarily historians and theologians, including several like Goodman without regular academic appointments. Habits formed at the Gestalt Institute helped him get something out of this association too. Still later when he became a member of the editorial board of *Liberation*, and later yet as a fellow at the Institute for Policy Studies in Washington and a participant in innumerable conferences and public forums, Goodman could play a major role and be more than just a gadfly because he had learned something about high seriousness, mutual respect, and the spirit of inquiry from his colleagues at the institute.

The training workshops Goodman ran in Cleveland and other cities were a kind of middle ground between this experience with his colleagues and his therapy sessions with patients. Here too he discovered much of importance to him in his later career. He wrote in his journal a description of one of his trips to the Midwest that is worth quoting at length because it sums up much of this history and gives us a sense of how hard the lessons were to learn. He is speaking of a visit to Cleveland in the spring of 1956:

> Then again, a day later, I am presented with a third, resounding experience: teaching, leading a company of my peers, who seem to accord me boundless attention & love—including interesting sex. I work well, with almost complete absorption and plenty of spontaneity—a good deal pans out—I down my misgivings, ask for what I want, and somewhat get it. The activity seems worthwhile, humanly valuable, and I am rewarded with good pay. Indeed, I am in love with this situation. But the uneasiness comes afterwards: I was not clinging to myself or an idea of myself, but was indeed in the situation & borne along; now afterwards—for alas! it was ephemeral (that was no doubt a condition of it, for myself and was it not also for them?—I am back to the railroad train) *where* was I? what kind of a figure did I look? what is their reaction now that I am gone?
>
> I wrote this feeling at a pause: after the situation in which I was more completely absorbed, sexually & with my academic learning, and where I did not cling to myself—again I am faced with the empty day, what to

do, but I have less impulse to throw myself back into the wild world & its fearful desire.[24]

Here we see not only the growth of Goodman's power to engage others with mutual respect and profit, but also the way in which such experiences were precisely what he needed to wean himself from his neurotic pacing of the city streets, hunting Sex and Desire rather than any actual partner, to force some capital-letter meaning out of life.

But there was no single experience or lesson that would unknot the snarl. Patience! Another ounce of strength! Pay attention to details! Such was the counsel of *The Empire City*.

I have been quoting more and more frequently from the journal Goodman kept during the last half of the decade and later edited and published as *Five Years*. He bought himself the first little notebook in May 1955, and thereafter he always had one in his pocket, filling it with what he called his "hermit" thoughts. At first he gloomily considered this as a kind of penitential activity, marking time while he waited for life to offer some larger commission. "Thoughts During a Useless Time" was the subtitle he gave *Five Years*. But if his journal thoughts failed to bring him into contact with the world ("These thoughts do not develop beyond themselves, do not set going or set me going") they were nonetheless valuable, for "they state me where I am and allay that much tension to sue the world for a clue or remedy." That was what he said after about a year of keeping these notes, and a few weeks later he added that perhaps they were "closer to the social world" than he had supposed.[25] He used them in something like the way he used the short poems he called "little prayers"—"saying at certain moments just how it was, however it was"—but the prose record shows him reaching out as well as looking inward.[26] One might say that journal keeping was one of the ways he exercised patience and paid attention to details. At times he forgot himself entirely, thinking only about something or someone he had noticed in the world. And even if he often lied to himself or indulged in self-pity, there was also much occasion for honest self-criticism. With no one to answer back, some of his defensiveness could be relaxed. He would read his entries over and comment on them, and a hollow bluff might ultimately lead to a new insight. They were like the awareness exercises of therapy, practice at the here and now.

The crisis in his neurotic history—his nadir, that led to his breakthrough—came in the summer and fall of 1956, the second year of his journal keeping. A series of major disasters occurred that shook him out of his routines, made him frantic and desperate.

First there was some good old-fashioned dashing of hopes. He had forestalled disappointment by not sending *The Empire City* to publishers who had already told him they were not interested when he finished volume three. Who would want volume four? But a few literary figures of importance had taken notice of him. W. H. Auden had written him a letter of praise for *The Dead of Spring* and had even nominated him for an award. And Norman Mailer, who was throwing his weight around in a number of quarters—*Dissent, The Village Voice*, Madison Avenue—decided that *his* publishers, Putnam's, should print *The Empire City*. Goodman was cautiously delighted: "I have been subjected," he wrote in his journal, "to a real stroke of luck, with all the earmarks of surprise, extreme unlikelihood, & great utility for my further activity . . . and not undeserved either."[27]

Soon he was thinking hopefully about the changes he would make in his life:

> I am beginning to sense that there must be some other value, some quite different kind of experience; for consider: I fret about my wife or agitate myself about some young fellow on 38th St., and, I see quite clearly that this is mere folly, "unworthy of a man," etc.; the human enterprise is much bigger. Yet it is just such as I who carry on that enterprise at its best—the music of Beethoven, policy of Jefferson or [illegible]—I am quite adequate to that, I could play in the same game tho not so well; I *do* play in the game from time to time. If I could be all there for a spell, I'd make a mark, of that kind.[28]

But then word came that Putnam's would not publish his book—"as I had expected," he quickly added. "I am not crushed nor terribly cast down," he lied, "only saddened & empty."[29] He got the news while vacationing on Cape Cod, where he was frequently in company with the successful writers and editors who summered there, and he took it out on them: "my tone has been so harsh & savage as to be ludicrous . . . a dry growl, sweeping negations, pointed personal accusations, a stubborn will to be displeased, and nothing concrete in my head to provide any interest to what I'm saying." Now he was being honest.[30]

In the background of this bitter recapitulation of what had been over and over again his fate, another rejection was looming threateningly. In April the New York State Legislature had passed a law requiring the licensing of psychologists and psychotherapists. Requirements included advanced degrees in psychological disciplines, which of course Goodman did not have, even though his Ph.D. in aesthetics was at last official. There was a grandfather clause in the new law, allowing persons to be certified who had one of several combinations of psychological training and practice. Goodman had until July 1957 to make his case. After that he would be subject to prosecution.

Most of his colleagues at the institute had no trouble fitting into the grandfather categories, though their careers were as mixed and unorthodox as Goodman's. But few were so skittish of institutions as he. It was humiliating to be in the position of a supplicant to the bureaucrats in Albany, and although there was certainly talk of the new regulations among his Gestalt friends Goodman did not discuss his own case with any of them. He asked several of the people at the Cleveland Gestalt Institute to serve as referees for him, testifying to his expertise, but his peers in New York knew nothing about it.[31] He who was so brazen and proud was now shamed. He did not even mention the matter in his journal.

He chose to apply under one of the grandfather categories and produced a résumé of his education and experience fudged just enough to meet the requirements—his time with Lowen expanded six months, the date of his first patients pushed back a year or so—except that he miscalculated the requirements themselves.[32] He was not eligible in the category he chose because he lacked the basic thirty hours of credit in academic psychology—an orthodox master's degree. As a result the nine years of therapeutic practice which he offered (beginning in

1948, as far as he could stretch his conscience) were insufficient. Without the master's degree he needed twelve years' experience.

Negotiations over his credentialing went on for a long time. Although at first he thought he could squeak by, it was soon evident that he would not. But then the case was reopened in 1960 when Albany sent a form letter announcing that he could appeal the decision. He decided it was worth trying and put together a remarkable dossier of his accomplishments, including a day-by-day account of his current activities on the campus lecture circuit, but even his growing reputation as an expert on the young did not help him at the state capital.

In 1956 he was calling himself a "psychological consultant" for official purposes like tax returns. He was making over $2,000 a year from his patients, another $600 from the workshops in Cleveland.[33] For the first time in his life he was bringing in as much money as his wife did as a secretary or office manager, a true breadwinner. In 1957 he called himself a "career consultant," to avoid prosecution, but he was still practicing therapy. He told his daughter one day that he thought he would give his practice up—not, however, because he could not be credentialed (he never mentioned that problem to her) but because he wanted more time to write. He did not want to devote his life to his patients, as he felt he must to be as good a therapist as he could be.[34] No doubt it was *all* true. But he kept on seeing his patients anyway.

Neither the disappointment of his hopes for *The Empire City* nor the possible loss of his career as a therapist hit him so hard as the next catastrophe he had to face. His daughter, Susan, now seventeen years old and about to begin her sophomore year at Bard College, had gone out to Fire Island with Percy and

Naomi's family for a week at the seashore before returning to school in September. Paul and Sally got a phone call saying she was dreadfully ill and had been taken to a hospital. She could not walk—it was polio.

Goodman panicked. He was more or less prepared for the other blows of this season, ready with his anger and resentment at the injustice of his lot. But his little daughter! It could not be.

She was his first child, and soon after her birth he had written of her as his hostage to fate. Her name was Susan Elizabeth Goodman, but her father invented the sobriquet "Likely" for her when she was born—she was his "likely" child. After his first marriage broke up, when Susie was three, it was he who had mostly raised her, though she spent brief periods with her mother and one whole year with her maternal grandmother in Chicago. For a while Goodman had been a single parent, and since his marriage to Sally, Susie had lived with Paul and Sally. Because Sally was the chief breadwinner during much of Susie's childhood, and continued to work even after therapy money began to come in, this meant that a good deal of the parenting in the family devolved on Goodman, who had a strong nurturant streak in him. Indeed, there was a Jewish mother side to him, fussing over the children when they were sick with ear complaints and such, worrying over the color of their cheeks, and making sure they got out of the city during the summer for health and happiness—just as he bragged his own mother had done for him, poor as she was. Goodman was also one to examine report cards from school and bestow praise. In short he was an unusually involved father, especially for those times— bestowing love and affection, concern and anxieties, directions, opinions, morals, values, duties, the works. He was there every night for dinner, yapping away and insisting that Susie yap back. They talked to each other steadily from the time he took full charge of her at age three until his death. Obviously such relations had to be problematic at times, but there can be no doubt that Goodman and his daughter were close.

Susie had a bright happy face and was gay and mercurial like her mother. Goodman thought of her as a wildflower, and all his poems about her use that image.

> How like a wildflower untended
> among garden flowers no fairer
> is Susan and these kempt
> children, beauties all.
> . . . . . .
>
> In our unhappy home
> still sometimes the sun
> and wind and fresh rain blow
> and these nourish our darling.[35]

Goodman had written those lines when Susie was nine or ten. A few years before that, when she was ill, he had written:

> . . . beautiful as a fieldflower to me
> is Susan as she goes and shines and dances
> in all the freeborn motions of mankind.
> I cannot hide how heavy my head hangs
> to see hers drooping low—in this mad spring
> when the late frost has killed the apple-blossoms
> and now the unlucky heat
> seeks out and parches the brave violet.[36]

Now he wrote:

> . . . I cannot sleep, obsessed by Susie's colorless
>   cheerless face
> and bony body in my arms too light,
>   she who was bright
> comparable to the meadowflowers
>   alas! that the mowers
> passed and did not spare, their petals droop
>   my shoulders stoop
> for fear and neither can I breathe for fear.
>
>   No, hear my prayer,
> Nature! who alone healest and not wishes
>   nor art nor pity,
> and do thou Creator Spirit visit her
>   with the quick future
> that alone stirs to courage and to walk
>   and to work.[37]

Ten years later, when his son Mathew was killed in a fall on a mountainside, Goodman also wrote poems. They were his prayers and mourning labor. At that time some ungenerous person accused him of making literature out of his child's death, and perhaps it would also be possible to say that his response to Susie's illness was too literary. But that was how he got in touch with suffering and loss.

His first impulse was to deny the truth. Susie was very ill, to be sure, but soon the crisis would pass and she would get out of the hospital bed and stand and walk. His panic was of that order, full flight from reality. As a psychotherapist he had a somewhat shamanistic attitude toward health and sickness in any case. He spoke of it in many places—for instance, in "An Asclepiad," where he said, "Our [physicianly] compassion is our refusal to accept our disaster. We *will* not accept it. . . . When you are here, we turn this stubbornness of ours to your advantage; we will not accept for you to be hurt, to have been hurt . . . we will to undo it."[38] This was no literary fancy on Goodman's part but a real belief not in miracles but in nature and spirit. And of course as a therapist he had plenty of evidence for it. But it did not apply to *this* disease. He could not *will* Susie to walk. There was something quite crazy in his insistence as he dutifully recorded it in his notebooks:

"My daughter is stricken with polio and her legs are seriously involved, but I want her to get out of bed and walking in a few days. I am set on this one thought and nothing else will allay my hope and fear.

"At the hospital, however, the doctor speaks of transfer, after the acute stage, to another hospital for rehabilitation. He mentions months of time and wearing braces, or even sitting in a wheelchair. I reject these ideas violently and hate the man who utters them."[39]

Finally, after much frantic activity—consulting with other doctors, asking advice from medical friends, all undertaken in a spirit that flip-flopped from perfect sense to utter irrationality—he began to get his bearings again. As his own panic subsided he at last glimpsed that Susie too was "in a panic of fear, and this I can alleviate": "I give myself to all-day visits, I somewhat calm her fears and lighten the long hours. And since action leads to feeling and feeling to understanding, I now have her as a real object of affection, and I see the whole matter in perspective and more practically."[40]

Once past his own shock, Goodman acted with remarkably good judgment as well as compassion. He dealt with the doctors and made sure Susie had the right care, protecting her from operations that were then in fashion and being recommended for her, such as "switching" muscles and nerves, or fusing the ankle in her weak leg to prevent its "drop," procedures that in other cases were to prove counterproductive. After she passed the acute stage he arranged for her transfer to a hospital in Manhattan where he could visit her daily—as he did for the next six months, arranging for substitutes whenever he could not come himself. And all of this close attention and support did make a difference, steadying Susie in the midst of her turmoil, helping her face away from despair. Patience and fortitude were relevant virtues here, for father and daughter both.

When Goodman revised his journals for publication some years later, he gave these entries on his reactions to Susie's polio their own space and title, unlike anything else in his diary. He titled the entries "Growing Up," with obvious reference to himself, and he was intent on looking hard at his panic reaction, which was almost as disturbing to him as his daughter's illness. Were his own resources so thin? Was he that close to the brink? For there was no doubt that he had lost his hold on reality. Sitting in the hospital lobby waiting for the doctor, for example, he observes his own condition.

> The door of the elevator opens, but it is a Negress in a green dress. The outer door opens and a red-haired mother comes in with her little boy. Suddenly the inner door opens, a Puerto Rican orderly limps by. One would think that it is just this arbitrary factuality that would convince us that the world is material, is not our idea.

231

But indeed, it is just in these cases of anxiety that the world seems most like paranoia, rife with "reference." Certainly the world is not our idea; but the contrary *proposition*, that "there is an objective world," feels very much like either obsessional disowning or paranoia.[41]

Fifteen years later he still remembered this moment, and retold it in *Little Prayers and Finite Experience* as an example of how "I dare not let the new be new." The sudden appearance of any element not already part of his structured awareness loomed, at this crisis, with such portentousness he could not integrate it into his experience—a classic "delusion of reference."[42]

Goodman was very near to hitting bottom. Life was battering him. If he seemed at times to be out of control, surely there was good reason for it. His daughter was stricken down. The book to which he had devoted a dozen years of his life would never be published. The one talent that brought him recognition and livelihood was to be taken from him. But he was too shrewd a therapist to suppose that his own character was not playing its part in bringing on disaster. There was surely some better way to face the world than the defiance he had always thrown back at it. During the next few months his journal was full of signs that the ice floes were breaking up, with what result he could not foresee.

I am sick. I am a sick man being in the world as I am.[43]

. . . .

I am left out . . . isolated . . . I alone am close to the nature of the situation, yet I am powerless to change it because I don't live in the same world as the powers-

232

that-be. Now this looks suspiciously like a psychotic response on my part. What is the more likely case, at a quick frank glance? That I am a seedy unsuccessful writer who has some talent but doesn't make the effort to communicate. I blow a good deal and impress a few unimportant persons whose ego I support, as they support mine. I am a sexual failure and a medical quack with a flair. And all this I hedge around with reservations and interpretations to make it colorable and painless. I'll be more and more isolated. We'll see.[44]

. . . .

And here are some further reflections about myself that occur to me soberly but with little affect. (1) Either I was crazy then, or I am now. Then when I felt I was excellent and was angry and bitter that others did not accept the love and art that I was eager to give them; or now when I suspect my abilities are mediocre, and also that the others are what they are, not interested and not interesting, and I am not excluded but isolated in the know. (2) I, like everybody else, am in physical jeopardy in the city, from a crushing blow with the butt end of a revolver, the tortures of the cops, the gang of queer-killers, etc.; but I do not accept the Social Compact that Hobbes thought up for this; it is not my Way. (3) When occasion arises—but it arises rarely—I can become alert, friendly, self-reliant, scarred by healed suffering. Certainly I have done some good things to be proud of and have little to be remorseful for. I can hold my head up and I do hold it up. What does it mean that I think of these 3 things? That I am freeing myself from clinging.

Good! But "just now I do not love anybody" and it seems that without the illusion that I am right, great, misunderstood, etc. I do not know how to take the world at all; I have never learned how. Oh God! *can anything be salvaged from all that effort?*[45]

At this point, in the very depths of his despair, it counted very much to have another ounce of strength, for he was close to the truth about himself, and to know the truth would give him the footing and leverage for change. He was ready to change, for he was thoroughly sick of himself as he was. And he did have another ounce of strength, for he was not a mediocre writer, a medical quack, or a psychotic; he was Paul Goodman. Soon, like his hero Horatio, he would be spoiling for a fight.

Susie's crisis passed, and she entered the early stages of rehabilitation. Her own will to walk was as strong as her father's frantic wish, and she would ultimately succeed, though the struggle was long and hard. There was no chapter on "Convalescence" in *Gestalt Therapy*. What was required was physical and spiritual effort that analysis could not ease nor poetry comfort. In any case, his daughter's crisis was not Goodman's crisis, however much he might behave as if it were. He had his own soul-work to do. His practice as a therapist had helped him shift his gaze from his own complaints to the plight of his patients. Susie was too close to him, too essential a part of his self-image, for him to maintain the compassionate distance that served with others. As his panic subsided, Goodman found himself more or less at the same impasse in life that he had faced before the polio struck, and yet there was a deep shift in perspective beginning to appear in his journals. When he asked himself, for instance, whether anything could be "salvaged" from all his efforts and ambitions, it was not unrelated to the trials and recuperation of his daughter.

Then came a bit of luck. It was at this time that a patient wanted Goodman's company on a trip to Europe. He offered to pay Goodman's fares, they would travel together for a week or two, and then Goodman would be on his own. It was now the summer of 1957 and the nick of time. Nothing could have been better for Goodman at this moment than to leave home and family, patients and colleagues, friends and enemies, and go where he would be surrounded by a new and interesting culture, where he did not know the rules or speak the language, had no routines or duties, no hopes or commitments.

He did not approach his journey as therapy, though it certainly promised to be a respite. He simply hoped to have a good time. One way to think of it would be as a long, leisurely cruising of the European young while also enjoying their culture and tradition. As a tourist he might find his sexual adventures to have a more serendipitous cast. To some extent this was the way it worked out, but there were a number of surprises that made the trip a real turning point. Perhaps that term gives a false impression of breakthrough, since Goodman's conversion was full of backsliding, yet there is no doubt that this was a season of great spiritual upheaval in him. The most immediate and momentous discovery was that he regretted the life he had been in such a hurry to escape. He missed his family, especially Sally, to whom he wrote long letters twice a week, full of detailed reports of his travels, sharing his thoughts and frankly avowing his affection. He missed his city too, and his countrymen "the Americans," as he had always called them as if to distinguish himself from them. Now he felt *he* was an American, and although there were things about America to be ashamed of, all in all he was proud of it.

As soon as he was on the boat he began to think about the differences between his sojourn and his usual world. Should he make a pass at one of the sailors? It wasn't worth it, he decided; his stay on shipboard would be too brief for him to "brusque the situation," as he oddly put it, imposing himself where he was "not wanted," in hopes that he might be wanted after all. This was his usual pattern, to brusque the situation out of daring and desperation, rather than letting it "calmly become as it will." But, he went on, "I am dark as to any other way of living than the way I live." To say this was already to be thinking about another way. Suppose he were to stay on this boat "forever"? he asked.[46]

After a few weeks on his own during which he "brusqued" many situations, he could not complain about his luck—the young would still make themselves available oftener than not. Indeed, his lust was either sated or beginning to fade, for he found himself regarding the young simply as another category of wonderful artworks to be admired. "I cannot even weep for it, but throw wide my hands in despair. This beautiful adolescent, Renato, hard on with desire and determined to be satisfied—why should he favor me, except that I look at him with admiration and make his advances for him? But *I* am without lust and such satisfaction as I get is in his pleasure. Such an animal! a few short years ago I would have burned for him and trembled for joy. What has become of me? and what is to become of me?"[47]

There were other things on his mind. Like any tourist spending so much time in front of great works of art, he felt

himself somewhat healed by their beauty and grandeur, and especially by the admiration which welled up in him and crowded out meaner emotions. His own ambition was touched and purified. "Praise, and in it nothing grudging," he wrote in his journal; "As I see this, and hear the silent praise resound, I think, 'I too!' Instead of feeling as usual that my time is slipped away, I feel I have plenty of time to carry out something worthy of praise, as indeed I have the soul & knowledge. It is simply necessary to put away my yearning that betrays me, to be supported, loved, and happy. Isn't it what I always urge on my young, to do something great to make me proud?"[48]
Such hopeful feelings grew in him with every day he spent there, but he knew his weakness as well as his strength:

> If only—as indeed we ought—I could take this world as my home, for it is my home; but I guess I do so regard it. Yes, this explains why in these little trips to old museums, or sometimes sitting in concert-halls or reading, or sometimes with a patient, or sometimes in a bar making a page of verse, I am both content & happy, for I am at home: they speak directly to me or I do as I please (it comes to the same thing). But unless I look for sexual pleasure or human understanding, I am in pain & miserable, for they do not directly speak to me and I cannot do as I please, I am a stranger.[49]

The irony was not lost on him: here where he was a stranger he could feel at home in the company of great artists of the past; at home he often behaved as a stranger.

More and more during his travels he thought of home, family, and country. He was homesick. It helped to set the date for his return and get the tickets.[50] He realized how relieved he was, and immediately began to enjoy himself more. He took one last trip, to Amsterdam to see the Vermeers, and while he was there wandered down to the docks and happened on the spot from which Henry Hudson had set sail in the early 1600s. One of Goodman's best poems was written then, on the back of a cafe menu, celebrating his beloved Hudson River and the New World he was longing for. "I see I've come a pilgrimage," he wrote. And soon he was saying:

> What do you want, my Captain? what you want
> is impossible, therefore you must want nothing.
> "I am looking for the Northwest Passage to
> India; if I had made the world
> that would exist."

The Northwest Passage did not exist, but the Hudson and all the other "lovely Northern rivers" did:

the Housatonic and Connecticut
and Charles and James and Thames and Roanoke
and the St. Lawrence and the Kennebec
and the Potomac and the sweet Delaware.[51]

It was true that they all flowed into the sea, none opened the passage to India, but he found himself weeping as he wrote down the names of his native waters. They were enough.[52]

As the day of embarkation approached, he felt a wave of anxiety. Sally and Susie had written to him regularly, as he to them, but what had really been happening while he was gone?

"I have these dreams of the events most painful to me, yet supportable—most often Susie's leg crippled or Sally openly & regularly cuckolding me; as if the wish were finally to resign myself & live on & stop investing so much energy in fearful denial. For my entire existence at present is like a Bourbon insistence that nothing has changed, nothing has been settled, no real defeat has been suffered, even of things not only irremediable but now fairly uninteresting: I cling to their denial to save face." He saw these dreams as a sort of "practice in reality-acceptance," as an infant plays "the blanket game" to get used to mama's leaving. "The dream says: set free some of that energy invested in narcissism."[53]

When he returned at the end of the summer, he was able to make some use of the lessons of his long retreat. The passage from fearful denial to resignation could not be quick or easy, but it was gradually happening. His dreams proved prophetic in both senses: Sally had indeed had an affair while he was gone, Susie's legs were crippled; but Sally was glad to have him back, not at all tempted to abandon the marriage, and Susie was gallantly at work to rehabilitate herself, growing stronger and coping with braces and canes.

In spite of everything, Goodman soon took up his old life, but his journal reveals that it was not quite the same round of "looking for love where it can't be found," one of his favorite self-characterizations. He complained less about his fate, and noted more moments of satisfaction. Both in his marriage and in his cruising the streets, more reasonable expectations took the pressure off. His advice to patients with marital problems reflected his own accommodation: the criterion should be whether "there is ever in any respect *any* satisfaction that they get from one another: is there occasionally a pleasant shared meal, a moment of teasing, a moment of feeling protected, a good fuck once a month?" If there were three such good hours a week, his principle was to encourage couples to stay together. He began to think of his own case as a "normal neurosis"—that is, a marriage not ideally healthy, but providing the "secondary gain of illness," advantages of comfort and security that made sense in a society "where nearly everybody is pretty impractical." In addition, "it is good if marriages are given a more rational meaning by being forced with real necessities—primarily the children—that must be coped with unquestionably; for this limits the working of the essential underlying fantasies that wreak havoc with the happiness of the partners. . . . In the course of time, too, these shared necessities become a fund of remembered experience, unsoured by hurt feelings, and with demonstrable products, that is a more rational bond of union, a kind of friendship."[54]

At the same time that such realizations were calming his domestic torments, other important lessons were beginning to affect his obsessive hunting for sex outside the home. Several journal pages of complaints about his frustrations and "lousy luck" are followed by a passage of acute insight into his condition: "My sexual behavior—devoid of desire and satisfaction—may now be fairly equated to a false cultus-religion (an obsession). My seeking and waiting are its pieties and austerities; and the sexual act itself has just about the meaning of a ritual communion sacrifice. It is a false religion, an idolatry, unlike the psychoanalysis that I believe in as a true religion. . . . It all has a promise in it of Paradise (for me the apparently sensible & available aim of finding someone to love), but that promise

is an abstraction & a fraud that I dare not, however, expose."[55]
Of course he *was* exposing it, in this very entry in his journal,
and in fact the compulsion itself was changing and abating. His
yearning for an impossible paradise was diminished, though not
yet his ritual worship. He did not stop cruising, but he was less
blinkered and enthralled. At the same time other interests were
growing stronger.

Although Goodman does not go so far as to say that psychotherapy, his "true religion," has begun to undermine the
"false cultus-religion" of his sexual cruising, surely it is significant that he juxtaposes the two in this passage. Gestalt therapy
did not promise to install him in paradise, but it was a practical
means of staying in touch with the here and now of experience,
including the actual possibilities of love and lust. Let us pursue
this question of therapeutic efficacy further.

The idea of a "normal neurosis" of married life, a creative
adjustment to the realities of sexual partnership and familial
bonds, was a kind of footnote to the chapter of *Gestalt Therapy*
where he had explained the anthropology of neurosis. "There
is an important difference between the normal and neurotic,
but it is not such that when a neurotic comes as a patient and
poses an earnest *practical* problem for the doctor, the doctor can
set as his goal a normal adjustment, any more than he could
give an arrested tuberculosis a clean bill of health, though he
might have to discharge the patient. Rather he must hope that,
as the patient begins to reintegrate himself, he will turn out to
be more 'human' than is expected, or than the doctor is."[56]

For Goodman, who was both doctor and patient, reintegra-
tion depended in part on taking his case as more or less representative, not so different from the rest of his patients, and

doing something about it not only as therapist/patient, but also
as anthropologist or sociologist.

> And so again, if we speak, as we must, of a social or epi-
> demic neurosis, it is not the symptomatic social eccen-
> tricities (dictators, wars, incomprehensible art, and the
> like) that are pathologically important, but the normal
> knowledge and technique, the average way of life.
>
> The problem of abnormal anthropology is to show
> how the average way of a culture, or even of the human
> state, is neurotic and has become so. It is to show what
> of human nature has been "lost" and, practically, to
> devise experiments for its recovery. (The therapeutic
> part of anthropology and sociology is politics; but we see
> that politics—perhaps fortunately—does not devote
> itself to this at all.)[57]

At the end of the same chapter in *Gestalt Therapy*, Goodman said something that was also relevant to his obsession with
sexual "hunting" and its goal, the entry into "Paradise." The
conditions of civilization—civil security and technical plenty,
for instance—"seem to make important powers of human
nature not only neurotically unused but rationally unusable. . . .
It is not surprising if such an animal should often complicate
quite irrelevant needs—for example, sexuality—with danger
and hunting, in order to rouse excitement."[58] Furthermore, he
pointed out that "repressed or unused natures then tend to
return as Images of the Golden Age, or Paradise."

When Goodman wrote these words in 1950, he was inclined
to view the conflict as irreconcilable. The opposed claims of the

social order and the individual organism were "the human condition." It might be that in "a transitional stage toward a tighter sociality" there were necessarily some like himself who seemed full of neurotic yearnings for the virtues and excitements of a previous era. Or, equally the case, these conflicts have always been the human condition, and "the attendant suffering and motion toward an unknown solution are the grounds of human excitement."[59] But only half a dozen years later Goodman was not so sure, at least about his own suffering or excitement. Even if it were true that his neurotic longing was "originally" for some lost power of the species, the problem of a "repressed or unused nature" was more likely to be solved in the present moment by creative interaction in the community of family, friends, and fellow citizens than by defiance and risk taking in the alienated Society, with a capital S. Psychotherapy might be described as the "re-education of the emotions"—and Goodman bowed to the classic formulation[60]—but this could not occur in a vacuum, not even the safe emergency situation of Gestalt therapy. "Above all we must remember that where the contestants are natural drives—aggressions, special gifts, sexual practices that in fact give pleasure, and so forth—they cannot be reduced, but their manifestations only deliberately suppressed, bullied or shamed out. When all the contestants are in awareness and in contact, a man may make his own hard decisions; he is not a patient. The hope is that in such a case a difficult drive will spontaneously find its measure in a new configuration, by creative adjustment and convalescent organismic self-regulation."[61] For Goodman, the "new configuration" was to be a political one, and instead of paradise his search would be for utopia— that is, for a more practical and communitarian polity.

Goodman's summer in Europe had awakened new patriotism in him, and he was alive to political issues as he had never been before: "In dismay, I see my country going to its doom." He reminded himself that all along he and his friends had seen it coming and cried out, Woe! Woe! But what had he actually done? "I was not in a fight—for at no moment, no not for one moment, did I put myself . . . to helping the commonwealth."[62] Now he felt guilty and that he ought to do something. Anarchist though he was, he even considered *voting*!— for Adlai Stevenson, the darling of the liberals. Like Horatio, he yearned to have *his* president.

All of this thought surprised him into the realization that his "feeling of alienation seems to have immensely diminished." He immediately saw a connection with other parts of his life: "it is the lapse in my erotic desire that makes the whole structure that was inspired by desire now seem empty. Furthermore, this loss of outgoing desire lays me open to the sense of doom (by some projection). I do not get a hard on—i.e. I am in dismay."[63] Soon he would be hunting ways of improving his country as obsessively as he had always hunted sex.

If it were true that the neglect and lack of reward for his writing—much of his misfortune in life—were due to his own bristling hostility to publishers and readers, then it ought to have happened that now, as his alienation and spite lessened, his work might find its audience. During the winter of 1957–1958 the first sign of such a possibility appeared when a young friend, Leo Raditsa, managed to arrange the publication of *The Empire City*. Raditsa had just graduated from Harvard, where he had founded a literary magazine that published a lot of Goodman's writing, and now he had a job as secretary of the

Readers' Subscription book club, and had talked the editorial board into naming Goodman's opus as one of its selections. With the club's minimum of guaranteed sales, Raditsa was then able to convince Farrar Straus's Roger Straus to undertake the actual publication.[64]

Goodman could not quite believe it, but he was energized enough to start working on a fifth volume of his chronicle, and to make plans for a visit to Ireland in the spring of 1958, where he would revise the whole manuscript. This was to be a different sort of vacation: Sally would join him for part of it, and although he never admitted the obvious fact to himself, it was a kind of middle-age honeymoon—bound to have its disappointments.

Indeed, the disappointments began before he had even sailed. Negotiations with Farrar Straus fell through when they asked him to cut his manuscript to 500 pages and Goodman lost his temper.[65] That same month he got the news that the State of New York had turned down his application for licensing as a psychologist. But Goodman was no longer at the mercy of outward circumstances. His inner man was growing and changing, and the lessons were irreversible. He got on the boat anyway, and Raditsa promised to find another publisher while Goodman revised the manuscript.

It was not so important to be certified as a psychologist either. He was satisfied as a "career consultant," and anyway, perhaps his book would sell and he could be a writer again. The pattern of his earnings over the next few years confirmed these hopes. In 1956 he had made $2,850 from his psychological work and only $300 from his writings. By 1958 his writing income had more than doubled while that from his career consulting remained about the same. In 1959 the ratio reversed itself: $575 for consulting, $300 for Cleveland workshops, and $1,880 for writing and lecturing. By 1960 he was taking in nothing for psychotherapy and $3,613 for literary activities.[66]

The Irish trip was pleasant, and when Goodman came back Raditsa had arranged for Bobbs-Merrill to publish his book. That summer he began what he hoped would be a new novel, though it never got beyond the stage of a short story—"Jeremy Owen." The fifth volume of *The Empire City* had not panned out, and the new fiction was quite explicitly another attempt to find the "fight" he had wanted for Horatio—but this fight was not to be found in the imagination, only in reality. He had actually thrown a few tentative punches in the pages of the new political and cultural magazines—*Liberation, Dissent, Cambridge Review, Midstream*—and as a result he was also being courted by some mainstream editors looking for a bit of saucy social criticism, and he found himself being offered speaking engagements as well. *Esquire* commissioned the article "The Mass Leisure Class" and various university groups invited him to take part in panel discussions, where he met peers and felt surprisingly at home. Nor did he give up his patients immediately. In his journal he patted himself on the back as a therapist: "I am a 'good technician,' I can get on confident paths and bring something about." It was in fact what he had achieved in his own hard case. He was proud of his "pastoral letter" in *Esquire* too, and pleased when Sally read the typescript and was "unusually enthusiastic. In her eyes I have avoided both the Scylla of bending to please them and the Charybdis of purposely offending them."[67]

The winter of 1958–1959 he began reading patriotic literature—Washington and Jefferson, Emerson and Thoreau—obviously moving toward some intervention of his own in the fate of his country.[68] There was less and less griping in his letters and journals about his wife or his sexual *malchances*. For the first time in many years he had more inviting possibilities to fantasize about. The Living Theatre proposed to stage his *Abraham* play cycle in early June, just after his novel was to appear. There was wind in his sails at last.

Of course it was too good to be true. The play was a terrible flop, and *The Empire City*, though it got many splendid reviews and even a story with a photo in *Time* magazine, never caught on with the public.[69] Book stores sent their copies back, and Goodman was quite cast down. Perhaps he should have known better than to count on favorable response to works which, after all, he had written in his days of alienation and intransigence. No one wanted to hear his caviling and cawing. He might be a different person now, but these works were not by that person.

Yet he had another ounce of strength. His gloom actually dissipated very quickly for he *was* a different person and had reserves of energy for new work. A publisher commissioned a study of juvenile delinquency, and he sat down to it as to a table spread before him "in the presence of mine enemies." He wrote the first draft of *Growing Up Absurd* in a few weeks of the fall of 1959, quickly seeing that *this* was the fight he had been looking for.[70] It did not even matter when once again his publishers reneged—it was not the work on juvenile delinquency *they* had in mind! He found another publisher immediately, for this time he had written a book that did have an audience. His time had come.

CHAPTER NINE

Gestalt and Politics in the Sixties

THE SIXTIES BROUGHT their own problems, but they were not the sort that one dealt with in a lonely diary. Soon Goodman had given up carrying his little pocket notebooks; instead he had desk calendars filled with speaking engagements. He stopped seeing patients too. There was no time for it even if he had wanted to keep running his groups. He could see most of those friends in Hoboken on poker nights, if he wasn't in some other city.

Growing Up Absurd set the mold for his work in the new decade. In it there came together many of the impulses that had been crowding one another if not actually warring in previous years. For once he felt completely comfortable with the project in hand, whether in its initial guise as a study of juvenile delinquency—these toughs were just his type—or in its ultimate dress as an attack on the organized system and its failure to provide the young with an adequate world to grow up in. With this meeting of what he wanted and what he needed, Goodman could focus all his powers, and he wrote the book in what was for him a new and powerful style, not antagonistic and spiteful and yet not withholding or circumspect. He could afford to be patient and earnest with his audience because he was confident that he would be understood and that many of his readers would even agree with him.

His political stance in the past—the time of "The May Pamphlet" for instance, which he wrote at the end of World War II to defend his anarcho-pacifism—had been apocalyptic, rather in the manner of his approach to sexual partners, full of bold insistence and a certain recklessness. In those days he had argued that "free action" for the anarchist was "to live in present society as though it were a natural society," and furthermore that the touchstone for a libertarian was "to advocate a large number of precisely those acts and words for which persons are in fact thrown into jail."[1] He drew out the implications a bit when he wrote *The Dead of Spring* a few years later: if one lived the way his hero did in that novel society would certainly regard one as mad or criminal, and therefore when advocating punishable acts it would be wise to avoid being caught and prosecuted. Goodman was not recruiting for the prisons.[2]

Generously interpreted, there was much to be said for these principles, but the way he put them betrayed an anxiety to have it out with the reader immediately, either to win you over at once or to be rejected and have it done with. *Growing Up Absurd* had much the same politics behind it, but its strategy was not to make demands of immediate acceptance. Goodman argued his case with more patience, treating his reader not exactly with kid gloves but frankly and concernfully, as he had learned to treat his therapy groups.

His new book was the first long work of nonfiction he had written since *Gestalt Therapy*, and in important ways it was a sequel to it. He spoke later of how, just as there was abnormal

psychology, "the therapy of disturbances of creative adjustment," so too there was an abnormal sociology: "it is politics,
to remedy institutions that hinder experience from occurring,
for example, roles rather than vocations, individuals or collectives rather than people in community, whatever prevents citizens from initiating and deciding, or makes it complicated for
craftsmen and professionals to practice."[3] *Growing Up Absurd*
was his first large work in abnormal sociology.

He was not just carping. Goodman had a program, a set of
therapies if you will. In his journal, which he continued to keep
while writing the book, he congratulated himself on the strategy he used to make his proposals.

In the chapter on the Missing Community I accumulate
the revolutionary aims that were compromised, and
make a program for reestablishing social stability. Psy-
chologically this has the advantage for me of making my
radical rejection spectacularly conservative: it protects
me from the danger of simple assertion. Metaphysically,
however, two things: on the one hand there is the
strength of the unfinished situation seeking closure
(and all the better if the "present" is broadened out to
include more past); but on the other hand, is there not
in those accumulations the *built-in* factor of failure,
impossibility? I choose among the events of history
those impossibilities with which I can accuse those who
are successful today. But saying this I am simply defining
the artist: he who reacts against irremediable loss by
denying it, and the question is whether or not he can
make his denial stick.[4]

Here Goodman was artist and therapist and social reformer rolled into one, insisting on his unfinished or incomplete revolutions—so many of them already part of the American self-image—and showing how they were not simply the lost causes of our history but the ongoing neurotic problems of present society, demanding their solutions.

In *Gestalt Therapy* Goodman had criticized the orthodox Freudians for focusing too narrowly on recovering childhood trauma and failing to address the unfinished situation as it presented itself in ongoing behavior. Some of his own critics during the sixties accused him of a kind of political Freudianism, saying that he wanted to go back to a romantic past, but his reply was always this:

> I get a kind of insight (for myself) from the genetic
> method, from seeing how a habit or institution has
> developed to its present form; but I really do understand
> that its positive value and meaning are in its present
> activity, coping with present conditions. Freud, for
> instance, was in error when he sometimes spoke as if
> the man had a child inside of him, or a vertebrate had
> an annelid worm inside. Each specified individual
> behaves as the whole it has become; and every stage of
> life, as Dewey used to insist, has its own problems and
> ways of coping.
>
> The criticism of the genetic fallacy, however, does
> not apply to the *negative,* to the *lapses* in the present,
> which can often be remedied only by taking into
> account some simplicities of the past. The case is analo-
> gous to localizing an organic function, for example,

251

seeing. As Kurt Goldstein used to point out, we cannot localize seeing in the eye or the brain—it is a function of the whole organism in its environment. But a *failure* of sight may well be localized in the cornea, the optic nerve, and so forth. We cannot explain speech by the psychosexual history of an infant; it is a person's way of being in the world. But a speech defect, for example, lisping, may well come from inhibited biting because of imperfect weaning. This is, of course, what Freud knew as a clinician when he was not being metapsychological.

My books are full of one-paragraph or two-page "histories"—of the concept of alienation, the system of welfare, suburbanization, compulsory schooling, the anthropology of neurosis, university administration, citizenly powerlessness, missed revolutions, and so forth, and so on. In every case my purpose is to show that a coerced or inauthentic settling of a conflict has left an unfinished situation to the next generation, and the difficulty becomes more complex with new conditions. Then it is useful to remember the simpler state before things went wrong; it is hopelessly archaic as a present response, but it has vitality and may suggest a new program involving a renewed conflict. This is the therapeutic use of history. As Ben Nelson has said, the point of history is to keep old (defeated) causes alive. Of course, this reasoning presupposes that there is a nature of things, including human nature, whose right development can be violated. There is.[5]

After *Growing Up Absurd* Goodman's next book of social criticism was *Utopian Essays and Practical Proposals,* work primarily written in the late fifties and early sixties and relying on the whole range of his expertise—politics and psychology, education, planning, literature, philosophy, religion. The title was accurate and revealing. Continuing in his new role as sociotherapist, Goodman was applying further ideas of Gestalt therapy to the social neuroses. It was important to recognize the unfinished situations he had listed in *Growing Up Absurd,* but merely drawing attention to them was not enough. His own psychology had always been quite actively pragmatic, not merely in the Jamesian philosophical tradition but literally a therapy of experiment and action, creative adjustments that took the world into account as part of what needed changing. Paying attention to the incomplete reforms and revolutions of history gave some indication of where the problems were. To solve them one did not turn to the past, however, but experimented practically and hopefully in the present. Goodman liked the word "utopian," a label his critics often used to throw cold water on his enthusiasms. If they called it utopian, he said, it meant they were afraid it might be practical; that is, people might regard it as desirable, the first step to action. He enjoyed thinking up little schemes that fit this model, and he was extremely fertile in them. "We could try this," he was always saying.

The point, he would remind his readers, was not that his proposals were feasible (maybe they were) but that they gave hope and engagement. The chief problem was the feeling of powerlessness that modern conditions even at their best were likely to produce. Creative adjustment was never achieved by accepting some idea handed down from on high—not even if Uncle Paul was the one promoting it. There must be something to explore, some new possibility or attitude that would catch the imagination. People had to create their own solutions. A utopian proposal might not work in the sense that it might not fit the case as it eventuated, and yet at the same time it might be quite practical as a means of stirring to action and discovery. This was exactly the approach he had taken with his patients. Let me quote from the essay "Utopian Thinking" with which he began his new book.

> Utopian ideas may be practical hypotheses, that is, expedients for pilot experimentation. Or they may be stimuli for response, so that people get to know what they themselves mean. The fact that such ideas go against the grain of usual thinking is an advantage, for they thereby help to change the locus of the problem, which could not be solved in the usual terms. . . . Further, if a utopian expedient seems *prima facie* sensible, directly feasible, and technically practical, and is nevertheless unacceptable, there is a presumption that we are dealing with an "inner conflict," prejudice, the need to believe that nothing can be done, and the need to maintain the status quo.[6]

Change a few of the terms and this passage could have come out of *Gestalt Therapy*.

"Whatever the subject," he wrote, "I try to keep it *imbedded in its social-psychological causes*, relying heavily on the familiar authors in psychoanalysis, functionalist anthropology, and social history. . . . The reader will see that by and large I prefer the language of pragmatism and, best, an organism/environment psychology of novelty, excitement, and growth."[7] This last triad, of course, was the title he had given to his section of *Gestalt Therapy*.

Goodman's pragmatic utopianism was of a piece with his deep-seated conviction regarding all the humane arts and natural sciences—namely, that although there might be useful theorizing as well as conceptually valuable practice, there could not be any thoroughgoing systematizing that did not distort reality and rigidify experience. Thus the theoretical chapters in *Gestalt Therapy* were not an attempt to pin down human nature in some final definitions and norms, even though he believed there was such a thing as human nature. Similarly his anarchist sociology did not provide a *model* of the good society but an *attitude* toward political and economic life, one that was communicated more readily by example and rules of thumb than by logical analysis or the systematic elaboration of plans and protocols. "There is likely no possible sociology of creative action," he asserted.[8] It was precisely system, and especially the organized system, that created the problems we faced. "This is the crux of the argument over utopian thinking. It *is* true that the organized American system has invaded people's personalities, even though it protects every man's individuality, privacy, and liberty of choice. For the system has sapped initiative and the confidence to make fundamental changes. It has sapped self-reliance and therefore has dried up the spontaneous imagination of ends and the capacity to invent ingenious experiments."[9] People had to learn how to do this once again, but not by the application of still more finely tuned institutions or shrewder planning by experts. As Goodman put it elsewhere, "my social ideas are temperamentally mine, but they do not derive logically from my biases, as a doctrine. I would abhor a politics, pedagogy, or town-planning deduced from metaphysics or epistemology, or even scientifically deduced, rather than being pragmatic and not immoral. One must not manipulate real people because of an idea or a confirmed hypothesis. Indeed, I say 'not immoral' rather than 'moral' because positive morality, when used as a principle for action, can be more abstract and imperial than anything. There are far too many missionaries among my friends."[10]

Goodman said that he believed there was such a thing as human nature, even if the "science" of it could not be like mathematics or logic, self-consistent and valid. Sometimes his critics put him in the tradition of Rousseau and charged that his view of human nature was foolishly optimistic, and many of his disciples did indeed defend optimism as a correct and healthy attitude toward humanity. The complaint usually came from the so-called experts, committed to varieties of positivism that regarded people as finished products and experimental data. But Goodman retorted, "I keep trying to see people whole and beginning—still growing—and then they seem less limited than they do to sociologists or psychologists, politicians or journalists. But it doesn't much matter whether one has an 'optimistic' or a 'pessimistic' outlook, for the question still remains, Now what?"[11]

Goodman's own outlook was in fact pessimistic. The decentralist strain in his anarchism was not just a function of his abhorrence of the doctrinaire, but also took into account that human nature and culture were the result of evolutionary trial and error—with lots of error. It was therefore risky to organize or standardize very much of life, just as it was dangerous to become too specialized. Some expert was bound to make a gigantic little mistake. Let it not be someone whose hand was on the levers of power! People are greedy and callous. Let them not be responsible for the welfare of others whose need or suffering is far away and may seem merely a jiggle on the dials of the social order!

During the early years of the sixties Goodman was classified as an educator by those who wanted an easy label for him. It would have been more accurate to say that he had always been in love with the young. In any case, his educational views were certainly far from those of the academic educators. He thought most people would be better off without any schooling whatsoever, and his program of reform began by doing away with most of the apparatus and institutions. But there were some schools and teachers that Goodman approved of. *Utopian Essays and Practical Proposals* was dedicated to his friend from Gestalt therapy days Elliott Shapiro. His next book, *Community of Scholars*, was dedicated to Ben Nelson, whose immense learning and earnest teaching Goodman admired. *Compulsory Mis-education* was dedicated to his friend Mabel Chrystie, founder of the First Street School, where George Dennison (whom she later married) and Goodman's own daughter Susan were among the teachers.

Like so much else in his social thought, Goodman's educational views were grounded in his psychology. Although he was impressed by the Summerhill experiment of A. S. Neill, with its emphasis on the Reichian principle of self-regulation, his own bias was Deweyan, a focus on learning by doing. He had once taught at a progressive school in that tradition, as well as at the University of Chicago, New York University, Black Mountain College, and Sarah Lawrence—a wide spectrum of educational schemes, including some of the best. He had critical things to say about every institution he had worked for, primarily that they all paid too much attention to their own ongoing enterprise *qua* institution—setting the curriculum, staffing, keeping order, licensing, and so forth—and there was not enough concern with the interests and needs of the young. What he liked about Mabel Dennison's school was its benign neglect of the usual educational bookkeeping, and its engagement with the whole lives of its students, inside and outside its doors. George Dennison's account in *The Lives of Children* makes it clear that what was going on there was a version of group therapy, with private sessions for special cases, and academic subjects pursued not as tasks and goals but as practical experiences in the actual culture surrounding them—and all carried out with plenty of physical contact and affection. The adults at the school explicitly and intentionally took the idea of creative adjustment as their guide to what they were doing, providing the children with interesting and worthwhile occasions and challenges, and dealing with individual hindrances by exaggerating them, or by letting them work themselves out in safe emergency situations.

Goodman's special concern with elementary education has sometimes been lost sight of, because there is more intellectual history to be made of his stand on role of the colleges. As he himself often put it, there is nothing to say about elementary education—it is important but uninteresting. He sometimes laughed at the phrase "alternative education," as if to say there is only one subject matter, the whole of human culture and history, so what is the alternative? The simplicity of his view—to stand out of the way of children, while having a few adults around who know something—could seem to belie the importance of it.

But for schools on the usual model Goodman had little hope, though he characteristically proposed group therapy for the seniors as a utopian measure of minimal reform in the high schools and colleges. At whatever level, the usual curriculum made no sense unless it met student "need, desire, curiosity, or fantasy." All else was parroting and conditioning, either promptly forgotten after the examination, or worse, introjected as part of self-control and conforming to authority. And up to age twelve there was "no point to formal subjects or a prearranged curriculum. With guidance, whatever a child experiences is educational. Dewey's idea is a good one: It makes no difference *what* is learned at this age, so long as the child goes on wanting to learn something further."[12]

None of this meant that Goodman had abandoned the arts and sciences. But it was not apparent to him that higher education actually taught these successfully, not to the majority of students at least. Nor did he think that the academy was such a good home for cultural values and the liberal arts. Pedagogues should look again at the cultural justification for all education: "both youth and adults live in a nature of things, a polity, an ongoing society, and it is these, in fact, that attract interest and channel need."[13] In the history of the world, very few societies had ever handed over their classics and wisdom to a mandarin class without paying a great price.

Goodman did not stand apart from the institutions he criticized, taking pot shots at them from the safe distance of *The New York Review of Books*. He accepted semester-long teaching jobs at a number of colleges during the sixties, in addition to his constant round of lectures and panels on the campuses. Like his hero in *The Empire City*, he even joined the PTA and sat on the local school board where he helped prepare the ground for the decentralization of the New York City school system that began in 1970 and continues to this day. His favorite proposal, for "mini-schools" on the model of the First Street School—a couple of dozen children and a few teachers in a neighborhood storefront—has never been taken seriously by the public schools; but there is little doubt that he made a real difference in the education of the young in his native city.

Young people dissatisfied with lockstep education naturally gravitated to someone like Goodman who understood their problems and made himself their advocate. He warmed to this role because he himself had refused to grow up, was noisy and rebellious, and angry that the adult world was in such a mess. But the mood of the decade changed as the Vietnam War became more and more the focus of all the discontents of the radical young. The violence of the state abroad produced violent reactions at home. For several years pacifist leadership, which included Goodman, managed to keep the antiwar movement both nonviolent and activist, but this high ground slowly eroded as the war spread and escalated. To be sure, there remained a large nonviolent core of peace activists in the movement—perhaps a majority—but the ideological drift among the younger self-styled "cadre" was toward state socialism and Leninist vanguardism. There were calls for violent revolution.

For a time Goodman referred to himself as a "Dutch uncle" of the young, by which he meant to suggest the spirit of good will with which he gave hard advice or unwelcome criticism. He knew how he sounded to them. By 1968 the lines had been

drawn more severely between revolutionaries and nonrevolu-
tionaries. "If you're not part of the solution, you're part of the
problem!" Goodman never gave in to this all-or-nothing demand. Although in his younger days he had often fallen into a
defiant antinomianism himself, and had thereby gotten himself
blacklisted and shunned by respectable people, he had spent
many years learning to be satisfied with less than paradise:
"though I am still not impressed by the wisdom or morality of
righteous society," he wrote near the end of his life, "I am no
longer tempted to deny what I think I do know, nor to act
imprudently on principle."[14]

It was just his prudence and good sense that infuriated some
of the young radicals who had once been his "crazy allies." He
was *against* their revolution, nothing but a liberal, genre of
Arthur Schlesinger, Jr. In fact Goodman's hopes for a better
society had never been based on revolutionary change, though
he sometimes fell into that language in the early sixties before
he saw how seriously the young took such rhetoric. His view of
the society was much like his view of his patients when he was
a therapist. There might be some dramatic breakthroughs now
and then, but these were not to be relied on as new stages of
health. Gradual changes over longer periods—new habits,
more awareness, mutual aid, patience and fortitude—were
what counted. In any case neither the patient nor the therapist
could force a cure.

In politics Goodman's estimate of the possibilities was the
same. The point was not to live in the Golden Age but in a
tolerable society. To be sure, society was *not* tolerable if moral,
cultural, and aesthetic affairs that belong by rights to the community were sold off as if they were merely commodities;

261

"giving access to the young, conserving the environment, helping the needy . . . these are necessary for the society to be tolerable at all."[15] But it was not required to turn society upside
down to achieve these. Goodman began calling himself a conservative; he wrote: "The great conservative solutions are those
that diminish tension by changing 2 percent of this and 4 percent of that. When they work, you don't notice them. Liberals
like to solve a problem by adding on a new agency and throwing money at it, a ringing statement that the problem has been
solved. Radicals like to go to the root, which is a terrible way
of gardening, though it is sometimes sadly necessary in den-
tistry."[16] In fact Goodman said he was not a political person and
had no utopian vision. All he wanted was "that the children
have bright eyes, the river be clean, food and sex be available,
and nobody be pushed around."[17] He titled the novel he wrote
during the sixties *Making Do*. That was the way he had been
brought up, in "decent poverty"—one of the things that the
organized system had abolished. By the same token, 2 percent
of this and 4 percent of that might very well restore his minimal standards. When he said that a marriage was tolerable if
there were *three* good hours a week, that was not an ideal marriage; there was no such thing. Neither was society likely to
become the New Heaven and New Earth, though some of the
young might think they wished it.

Goodman was not squeamish. The revolutionary fantasy did
not repel him because he could not tolerate disorder. On the
contrary, he liked a certain amount of chaos in society, and pre-
dicted more. He did not want to see useless bloodshed and
repression, but there was already much too much law and order
in the United States, and a need for more healthy confusion. It
was not exactly the safe emergency situation of Gestalt therapy,

but it had its therapeutic analogies. When routines break down, sometimes important discoveries are made, or at the very least there could be the wave of relief that comes from relaxing one's grip on things. This was a very deeply rooted tenet in the Taoist corner of Goodman's psychology.[18]

Goodman was not a quietist; his Taoism never had that tinge. He was a troublemaker. It appalled him that most people were so well behaved and content in their abstract idea of liberty. "It's a free country" seemed to mean, "Don't bother me, I'm enjoying my privileges." Guarantees of freedom might be desperately needed in a totalitarian society where there was overt and brutal oppression, but the commodity culture of the "free world" seemed to make people their own jailers. Goodman believed in a society of law and often spoke of the great heritage of the common law, which he thought perfectly compatible with anarchist principles. He was an enthusiast for the Bill of Rights, and an advocate of a rather old-fashioned civil society (not the same as civil order), and even the "statuses and privileges" of earlier communities. "It [would be] better if every person and his community of interest had far more rights, privileges, and immunities," he said.[19] Goodman's anarchism stressed autonomy more than freedom, and he thought it was more important to be able "to invent and initiate a task and do it one's own way" than to possess a set of abstract and unexercised rights.[20] The analogy to psychotherapy was important here. How to make people more self-reliant and independent?

These notions might seem to make Goodman an individualist in the anarchist tradition of Max Stirner or Benjamin Tucker, but in fact he was far from it. One of the primary principles of his philosophical anthropology was that social existence precedes individual existence, prior in development in the organism and prior in culture. "We exist mainly, though not altogether, in community relations. To be a private individual is largely pathological." Then he added immediately, "For a society to act as a collective is largely pathological."[21] Here was another of the quarrels he had with the young, who accepted so many Leninist notions that seemed to Goodman perversions of communitarian and libertarian ideals. The collective was another abstract delusion running roughshod over actual people. His own anarchist faith was in Kropotkin's "mutual aid."

Just as he did not believe in the collective advocated by some of the radicals, so he did not believe in the personified ruling class. This delusion was part of what led to fantasies of revolution. The organized system was not something that could be stabbed to the heart. "I have tried to show," he said,

> that in a complex society which is a network rather than a monolith with a head, a piecemeal approach can be effective; it is the safest, least likely to produce ruinous consequences of either repression or "success"; it involves people where they are competent, or could become competent, and so creates citizens, which is better than "politicizing"; it more easily dissolves the metaphysical despair that nothing can be done. And since, in my opinion, the aim of politics is to produce not a good society but a tolerable one, it is best to try to cut abuses down to manageable size; the best solutions are usually not global but a little of this and a little of that.[22]

In an important way Goodman did not consider himself a political person, though of course he was leading a political life all through the sixties. It went against the grain of his character: "I cannot lead and find it hard to follow."[23] Distrusting both ideology and vanguardism, he insisted that all true politics was "remedial politics."[24] Its proper aim was "to increase autonomy, and so it is mostly undoing," giving people room to exercise their ordinary human powers rather than filling the world with programs and functionaries.[25] Goodman spent the last dozen years of his life doing his citizenly duty as he saw it because he could not look the other way: "I, like any body else, see outrages that take me by the throat, and no question of not identifying them as mine. Insults to the beauty of the world that keep me indignant. Lies, triviality, and vulgarity that suddenly make me sick. . . . It is a moral disaster to suppress indignation, nausea, and scorn; it is a political (and soon moral) disaster to make them into a program. Their right political use is negative, to band together to stop something."[26] Yes. But to devote oneself to criticism and acts of compassion for so many years was draining and dispiriting. Paul Goodman's decade as a therapist had been a burden, but at least there was some closure, a case terminated, groups dissolving back into their everyday lives with renewed vitality. At the end of the sixties, however, the cure of society was not in sight.

Goodman continued his social criticism long after he had lost the euphoric energy that came with the initial success of *Growing Up Absurd*. His yearning for an audience and "to be of use" carried him through the first five or six books, up to 1965 or so, but after that he began to write little poems like this one:

> *If I undertake to say*
> *the conscience of my country,*
> *I only do my duty.*
> *But, Lord, it was not I*

> *who chose it, but the hungry heart*
> *and level look that you allotted*
> *to me when you did burden*
> *with different gifts different men.*[27]

Just as he had profited in his own character from his practice as
a therapist in the fifties, so now his emergence as a public figure brought new lessons and fulfillments. He was not a new
man; rather his life kept adding up, building on itself. In the
thirties he had studied the philosophers; in the forties he had
settled his relations to the state and its wars by embracing anarchism and pacifism; in the fifties he had been converted to his
religion, psychotherapy, and combined theological work with
pastoral service; now in the sixties he took his place in the
forum as one of the elders of the community and a sage of the
New Left, calling on thirty years of experience with ideas and
values that had at last found their time and place.

Gestalt therapy was not superseded in Goodman's thought
by New Left politics, but rather served as that politics' grounding in a theory of human nature and face-to-face community
that included the young. Indeed, one might say that his harping on the importance of scale, of bringing social institutions
down to proportions that could be responsive to individual initiative, was simply his way of arguing for a society of ongoing
group therapy: self-regulation and conservation of basic nature,
creative adjustment and utopian experiment in safe emergency
situations, with pragmatism and phenomenology informing
ethical choices, and with mutual aid and direct action serving
as the fundamental mechanisms of citizenship—all this was
translatable from Gestalt theory to educational practice to
New Left politics.

For himself Goodman again discovered that there was a place for him in the world after all, more genuine fellowship than he had expected, and tasks that used his talents and burnt off his anxiety in something other than sheer defiance. He was not such a sourpuss any more, though he would never recover the buoyancy of his youth. His family relations settled down to comfortable routines and mutual respect. He had little time for cruising the streets for sex and much less inclination. A few love affairs, of diminishing absorption, filled the appetite that had once been insatiable. He spent more time with his real peers than with disciples, at the Institute for Policy Studies, on the editorial board of *Liberation*, in panel discussions and conferences across the country. It would not be accurate to say that all this made him happy, but he was justified.

CHAPTER TEN

"My Only Son
Fell Down and Died"

Playing too happily
on the slippery mountainside
my only son fell down and died.
I taught him how to talk honestly
and without stalling come across
but I could not teach him the cowardice
and hesitation necessary
to live a longer life unhappily.

—FROM *NORTH PERCY*

IN 1967 GOODMAN'S twenty-year-old son Mathew was
killed in a fall while hiking in the White Mountains. No parent can suffer such a blow without terrible grief, and the Goodmans were shaken to the core. I shall not speak of Sally's agony.
Paul's mourning was perhaps not so different from that of any
father, yet the fact that he lived a public life, and that of a
writer, brings it before our eyes more compellingly. Part of the
way he coped with his loss was to write an elegy for Mathew,
North Percy (the name of the mountain he died on), which is
among the most moving in our language. Goodman had always

dealt with suffering and confusion in poems. It did not exorcise his grief, but it was what he *could* do: patience, fortitude, and go about your business. Reading *North Percy* and the memorial essay, "A Young Pacifist,"[1] which he also wrote about Matty, one glimpses the depths of his despair, and begins perhaps to understand more fully the abyss he had peered into when his daughter was struck down by polio. His self—not his self-image or ego but his very self—was at stake. It was not lightly that he had compared the very best moments of therapy to the attention and rewards of rearing children. For a man whose problem in life had been to find and give unconditional love, caring for his children was the very keystone of selfhood, the grounds of faith in any world at all.

It was not that Goodman was an ideal father—is there such a thing? With each of his children he had established a different and special connection, with its own virtues and complications. Since he was at home so much of the time, and not locked behind a study door, he had been in their company more than most fathers ever are. One would not say he doted on them, but he certainly loved them, was proud of them, and expected great things from them. He was caught in a web of identifications with his children and could not lose one of them without feeling it as a threat to his own being. Indeed his health began to decline after Matty's death. The wounds of bereavement grew familiar and began to scar over, but then death pointed at him too. There were those who said that his son's death had broken his heart. In any case, his heart was giving out.

No one finds it easy to face death, whether the loss of a child or one's own mortality. The nonattachment of saints is not a goal for most people, and if sometimes admired it is no less wondered at. Yet at the same time age does bring its lessons and relief; life teaches us to let go—if we live long enough. But Goodman was only fifty-five when Mathew died and not yet sixty when he suffered his first heart attack. It was against the natural order for a child to die first, and the twilight came too soon and too suddenly.

Perhaps he would never have reached the point where mortality could be accepted. Goodman had resisted every new stage of life, unwilling to grow up, unwilling to leave home, unwilling to take on the gravity and burdens of an adult and citizen. But he *had* done all this, and indeed, had done it with extraordinary passion and remarkable effect in the world. In his youth he had thought that all he wanted was to be in love. Life had unfolded in ways that surprised him, and troubled him at every rung of Plato's "Ladder of Love," the maturing of the erotic impulse that Freud had called sublimation but that Goodman found more congenially accounted for by the ancient Greek text.

"How accurate Plato's analysis proved to be!" he wrote at the end of his novel *Making Do*. "I used to think it was only literature."

[Plato] said that, as a man grows, he is first attracted to the beautiful bodies he sees; and I had certainly been wondrously attracted to them, though with indifferent success in ever getting to touch them.

But then, he said, a man begins to fall in love with the virtuous characters of people that behave in those bodies and give them the beauty that shines on their faces. It was true. I had found it to be so.

And then, he said surprisingly, a man's eros turns to the institutions and the customs of the city, that educate

character and nurture physical beauty; and now his
lively concern is with these. I should never have
believed it when I was younger! But as I grew up, I found
that it was true. My crowded days were this love affair
with my city, a thorny adventure, but often I was so busy
at it that I didn't know whether I was unhappy or happy,
and that meant, I suppose, that I was sometimes happy.

But at last, said Plato, a man begins to have intima-
tions of God in whom the city exists, and he comes to
love Him. And presumably God comes across. I had not
yet found it so. At this rung I was frozen on the ladder. I
did not feel any peace of God, if it is peace that one
feels—how would I know? There was a risk that I was
afraid to take. I did not trust to let the nature of things
be, although it certainly worked out according to its
nature, in spite of all my efforts.[2]

Whether or not it was this last elusive hope for God's peace
that was dashed by his son's death, I do not really know. Whatever it was, the mourning labor was never over. He wrote the
passage on Plato's ladder in 1963, long before the death of his
son. Almost ten years later, five years after Matty's death and at
the very end of his own life, he was still brooding on the problem of God's peace:

[A]s I grow old, I inevitably see more and more the
death of my colleagues and dear ones, and I'm confused.
I understand that all flesh is as the grass, and very good.
I see, too, the ever unique woe the survivors suffer—
what we knew as moving and responding and initiating
movement, is a worthless corpse, and it is too late for

271

many things; yet I understand, I *understand* that we must try to mourn it through. I understand these two ideas but I cannot grasp them in one vision. It is too sublime for my finite experience and I become confused.

Prayer is the opposite exercise. I gather together my finite experience that is scattering in confusion. Here it all is, like an offering. Thus I disown my experience and again come face to face with nothing.[3]

For a very long time, in stories and poems that stretch back to his early manhood, Goodman had been fascinated by the question of how people cope with irremediable loss. Again and again he wrote about the mourning labor of the bereaved, and more than once he retold the classic tales of rescue from death—"Orpheus in the Underworld," "Alcestis," "The Death of Aesculapius," "The Galley to Mytilene"—which in his versions always ended in transcendence through art, the best that mortality could do. There had been some very great losses in his own life, the earliest and certainly the most telling being the loss of his father, who had abandoned the family before Goodman was even born. As he grew older, the mourning labor of requiem and elegy more and more had death itself as its occasion, and yet it was not until Mathew's death that he seems to have really looked mortality in the face and felt his own frailty. In the notes for his Gestalt seminar "What Is Man?" he had asked himself, "Is there a great distinction between the thought of one's own death and the experience of the other's death with its threat to oneself?"[4] To be born fatherless made the world seem fallen and alien, and Goodman had grown up thinking of himself as outcast, a fate he met with defiance. To lose a child was a more palpable diminishment and an intimation of final reckoning. Fear of this was surely part of his initial psychotic reaction to his daughter's illness, which he frantically tried to disown, and all the more so behind his response to Matty's accident, which he took as the death of hope itself. In the passage just quoted, the two things he cannot grasp "in one vision" are how to be accepting of mortality and at the same time full of grief. So long as he is "understanding" about death, "philosophical," he suffers no grief, but when he feels his woe, he cannot be philosophical. God's peace would allow him to hold both in awareness; he prays for that peace, but it will not come.

Goodman wrote these words in his last book, *Little Prayers and Finite Experience*. Like *Kafka's Prayer*, which he wrote at the very beginning of his career as a psychotherapist in 1947, this book too was a meditation on theological subjects couched in psychological language. As he repeated over and over, psychotherapy was "the nearest I know to formal religious exercises."[5] His final estimate of the use that therapy had been to him is summed up in these pages. On the one hand, he could say that "there is something sweet in religious routines, once drained of the virulence of belief." They gave "a good background for guiltless sex and common-sense pacifism," like the "cozy religiosity of the Danes." But much of his own experience had the obsessional character of religious ritual, its real meaning repressed. Therapy might bring some of that meaning to light, and even dissipate it, "but it is harsh and imperious toward oneself to try to root out one's archaic symbols."[6] He was who he was. One of the tenets of Gestalt therapy held that neurosis was always an important defense against suffering, not to be given up without great anxiety and risk, though sometimes the risk was worth it. He must be satisfied with what faith he had. The Bible verses rang true to him: "To them who have shall be given; from those who have not shall be taken away even that which they have." He had seen how the "muscular lad plays rough and gets still stronger," or the "lovable person is loved and becomes still more open, radiant, and lovable." But these were not him. "A person who is not anxious profits from psychoanalysis; an anxious person can afford to profit very little."[7] For an anxious person he had climbed very far on the ladder, but not to the top where he imagined the view spread serenely to the horizon. And yet he could see to the limits of his own finite experience, and he understood well enough that it *was* finite. If he was not a saint or a buddha or an archangel, nonetheless he was a sage.

CHAPTER ELEVEN

A Memorial Service for Fritz

THE GESTALT INSTITUTE had persisted as a center for training and visibility in the profession, but like Goodman, most of the original members had gone on to other things in the sixties, with exceptions like Laura Perls and Isadore From, who guided scores of new therapists through *Gestalt Therapy*. Elliott Shapiro was devoting himself to school reform. One could read about him in *The New Yorker* where Nat Hentoff published a profile of "The Principal." Shapiro still saw Goodman occasionally at movement rallies or panel discussions of education, but they were in different worlds. In the middle sixties, when a number of Goodman's young friends and disciples asked his recommendation to a therapist, he sometimes sent them to Laura Perls but more of them went to Shapiro. This was a kind of contact too, a bow from the distance.

George Dennison was another authority on schools whom Goodman rarely saw anymore. They had the same Gestalt perspective, they quoted one another, they even had the same publisher, but Dennison was going through his own Sturm und Drang, and it entailed a great anger and bitterness toward Goodman, whom he seemed to feel had stolen away his youth.

Although each of them made attempts to repair this breach, Dennison's struggle to reconcile art and love and domestic life kept him touchy and ready to explode. Sometimes he wanted to sweep Goodman out of existence with the rest of his wastrel past.

Goodman and Paul Weisz had also been cool toward one another for several years, but in the middle sixties they made contact again and seemed eager to take up their friendship. It had been a long time since Sally Goodman had been in therapy with Weisz, and the intervening years had erased the bad feeling which that had occasioned. The Goodmans had had another child, Daisy, and their family life was happier with a merry little three-year-old to care for, though Paul was old enough to be her grandfather.

Paul Weisz died of a heart attack in the middle of a conciliatory dinner at the Goodman's apartment. This was a few years before Goodman's own series of heart attacks, but he was well aware of the history of angina in his family, and Weisz's sudden death in front of his eyes gave him pause. He wrote this poem.

> Tonight a man passed away
> in my house, in my own bed.
> He rather happily was playing
> with my merry daughter
> yet he was dead within the hour.
> His heart broke. Now my own
> body is like an enemy
> waiting for me in ambush.
>
> I am smoking the tobacco that he left
> and picking up the shoes that he left.
> Two men are carrying out

276

the body that he left.
My merry daughter is asleep
in the other room.
I must be deep in shock
for it is like a dream.[1]

Weisz had always worn a bow tie. When they carried him out, it was not just his tobacco and shoes they left behind, but also the bow tie. Goodman, who almost never wore ties, carefully put it away in a drawer.

Death. The end of every story. His colleagues, his dear ones, himself. Allison Montague killed himself, taking care first to dispatch his dog, Sonny.[2] And finally, it came to Fritz. When the news of Perls's death reached Goodman in March of 1970, he was visiting one of the institute-spas of the sixties—not the Esalen Institute in California which Fritz had made famous, but Ivan Illich's Center for Intercultural Documentation (CIDOC) in Cuernavaca, where Goodman was giving talks on "free schools" and basking in the Central American sunshine—feeling his age at 5,000 feet. He had not yet had his first heart attack, but it would not be long now. Laura Perls called to tell him the news and asked him to be the principal speaker at a memorial service to be held in New York in April. He wrote Sally that he wished Laura had "picked on somebody who had more empathy with him than I," but concluded, "I'll do my best."[3] When the time came, there were others besides Goodman who wished Laura had chosen another eulogist, but in fact he did Fritz considerable justice.

Perls had gone on from New York to found one institute after another, first in Florida and then in California, where he became a kind of Pan among the redwoods in his goatish old age. By the time that he died there were two Gestalt therapies, East Coast and West Coast, and in his last writings—based on tape recordings and soundtracks from films—he had all but repudiated the book on which both therapies were both founded and never mentioned his one-time collaborator.

This parting of the ways is worth dwelling on, for it epitomizes the very different contributions Perls and Goodman made to Gestalt therapy and may help us understand the nature of its influence since then, which has been very great, far beyond the spread of its ideas within the profession. The literal parting of the ways had not been abrupt or decisive. Although Perls was no longer living with his family in New York after 1955, he kept coming back, as if to touch base. For instance, there was a period in 1957—it was while Goodman was on his European voyage—when Perls was in Manhattan again, considering a real estate investment that would include a performance hall for The Living Theatre.[4] Had that eventuated, he and Goodman would have crossed paths many times. But the right deal never turned up, and Perls put his money in other schemes. Then he too left the country on a long foreign holiday, and he too returned to a new career in the sixties. Yet what a different trajectory was his!

During the winter of 1963–1964, when Goodman was a fellow of the Institute for Policy Studies, the radical think tank for post-Kennedy politics in Washington, D.C., Perls was establishing himself at the Esalen Institute in Big Sur, where he presided over the transformation of Gestalt awareness exercises into a panoply of demonstration techniques and cultish slogans—"the hot seat," "the empty seat," "lifescript," "top dog/

under dog," "mindfucking," "elephant shit," and so on—with help from mind-expanding drugs and audiovisual technology.

When the student movement erupted in Berkeley at the end of 1964, one could see elements in it that would appeal to both Goodman and Perls, New Left and hippie, sometimes in conflict but often happily coexisting in the same person. The tidal wave of youth rebellion pulled both of them into its currents; every campus wanted to hear how to reform the university and actualize the self. Their styles were as different as their messages, though it was all part of the same ferment. Goodman came with notes scribbled on the backs of envelopes. There was nothing flashy or arresting about him, he simply talked. Often he would get into dialogue with the audience, much as he had done in his Cleveland workshops. He enjoyed face-to-face polemics with hecklers. Perls also came apparently unprepared—no notes at all—and he too thrived on interaction and spontaneity, but in his case it was more like a bravura performance in the theater. He would invite someone on stage, as a hypnotist brings out his subject, for a bout of instant therapy. "I feel best," he said, "when I can be a prima donna and can show off my skill of getting rapidly in touch with the essence of a person and his plight."[5] The results were often breathtaking, so much so that people wanted to film these encounters and use them as training aids. They were high drama. But where did that leave the person after the show was over? Thank you; you may now return to your seat. By contrast, Goodman genuinely talked to his interlocutors, perhaps leaving them exactly where he found them, but with interesting results for others in the audience. His conversation "elucidated a habit of mind," as one observer put it.[6] This was precisely his idea of both therapy and politics—to convey an attitude, to try out another point of view. No astounding transformations but perhaps some insight into the here and now and next.

When Perls visited Manhattan his demonstrations were now media events. On one occasion he asked Elliott Shapiro to be the final commentator on a program with two or three hundred spectators. There were movies from Esalen and then a demonstration of the hot seat technique with a woman in the audience who had been one of the subjects in the film—and who was applauded just like a movie star. At some point a Reichian in the audience stood up and asked why there was so much attention to the upper part of the body and so little to the lower. Shapiro thought Fritz brushed the question off too dismissively, and he felt inauthentic in his own comments at the end of the evening when he refrained from pointing out how much was being glossed over. That was obviously not what people wanted to hear. Where *did* this audience come from? he wondered. They seemed like a college crowd, well-dressed, in their mid twenties. Apparently they were Fritz's disciples, in a transference relation with him that he had no impulse to resolve.[7]

There was a sense in which Perls's boast was true: "I believe that I am the best therapist for any type of neurosis in the States, maybe in the world."[8] He certainly had a genius for bringing his patients to theatrical breakthroughs. He was no fool, however, and understood "that those so-called miracle cures are spectacular but don't mean much from the existential point of view."[9] Although he could not resist performing them, Perls was more or less immune to the temptation to ask further questions about the source of his power or the nature of his feats. Such philosophizing, including "high level discussion on religion, Gestalt therapy, existential philosophy," was what he called *Geistscheissen*—"wisdom-shitting."[10]

This skepticism may have had its virtues, but it also expressed Perls's awareness as he worked on *In and Out the Garbage Pail* that he was no writer. He was producing this testament in the late sixties when Goodman went down to see him in his pastoral setting at Big Sur. The two famous men, shamans of separate tribes, displayed their feathers and avoided any serious confrontation. One of their younger colleagues from the early days of the institute happened to be present, and was taken aback to see them in the same room together again—and so polite! The give-and-take of their work on *Gestalt Therapy* was long past, but so was the hammering at one another that had been characteristic of their interactions as colleagues.[11] They were national figures now, with dignities to maintain, such as they were. And they were getting along in years, Perls already in his middle seventies; soon both of them would be dead. When Goodman next met Isadore From, he reported on their mutual friend and his book-writing activities: "Pathetic." A little later From had occasion to see Perls, who reported on Paul's visit. It too was "Pathetic."[12]

A restless bird to the very end, Fritz finally left Esalen and his weekend "circuses," as he called them, for a new experiment, a "Gestalt kibbutz" in the woods on Vancouver Island, where he planned to make more training films and fly in therapists for sessions of retreat and study. He himself would fly out periodically to make personal appearances at openings of his films. It had been a long time since he had taken on a private patient. Perhaps this commune was for Perls what the old farmhouse Goodman had acquired in northern New Hampshire was for him, not just a refuge from the demands of fame and followers, but also a kind of shedding of superfluities. For Goodman, at least, as he grew older the simpler satisfactions of life seemed more absolutely necessary—friends, family, work in comparative solitude, rural comforts and austerities.

The East Coast memorial service for Perls took place on April 5; his West Coast followers had already put together a memorial based on specific instructions Fritz himself left for the ceremony, including a performance by his friend and former patient Anna Halprin, who danced to the music of Mahler, Fritz's favorite composer. The New York arrangements, which Laura had placed in the hands of Isadore From, would be very different. Most of the West Coast disciples were satisfied with their own service and did not come East, but the hall was full and the mourners included many of Perls's trainees, from before and after Esalen days, who identified with his brand of Gestalt therapy rather than with that of the New York institute. It did not turn out to be an occasion of reconciliation.

When everyone was seated, a cellist played Bach, not Mahler, followed by a showing of the movie *Fritz*, made at the peak of Perls's fame. Then Goodman stepped forward, dressed in coat and tie, his hair combed—"handsome," said one observer. He spoke from a single page of typed notes. For those who knew the whole twenty-year history of Gestalt therapy, it was a telling moment, not merely the summing up of Fritz's remarkable career but of an epoch. You could see people reaching into their pockets for paper and pencil. Sally Goodman thought it was the best address she had ever heard Paul give.

Yet others found it intolerable. There had been a plan to record what was said for a later radio broadcast, but something went wrong. Some say that the tape was purposely destroyed by an offended "Fritzite." Nonetheless there were many present who never forgot what was said.[13]

Goodman first spoke of the place of Gestalt therapy in philosophy and psychology; then he turned to Fritz as a figure in the history of modern times. What one could see immediately was that, although Perls had come to disown the book they had written together, for Goodman it was still the essential truth about psychotherapy and its possibilities. He described the "weak point" in psychoanalysis, as he and Fritz had agreed in 1950, the theory of the self. Freud, Reich, Adler, Rank—all had partial, limping views of ego and will. The contribution of Gestalt therapy was in its account of awareness "as a positive act, doing something," and in its locating this awareness at the organism/environment boundary, so that the self could be seen as the very process of creative adjustment, active "contact" in this ongoing field. Goodman reminded his audience of the many ingredients and influences on their theory—Taoism and Yoga as well as Aristotle and Kant, existentialism ("but practicable and in ordinary situations"), Zen ("with more than esthetic surface, including body and social scene"), and pragmatism ("with passions and feeling").

He then spoke of the intellectual milieu in which Gestalt therapy found its early nurture, noting that a good many of the original community of believers in the audience, once unknown, were now among the heroes of the sixties in several fields besides psychotherapy. He drew attention to Fritz's own peculiar contribution to classical psychoanalysis, his specialty in dental aggression and the concepts of introjection and assimilation he had evolved on the model of biting and chewing. Goodman pointed out the advance on Melanie Klein's view of hostility: Fritz accepted aggression as part of health, the "normal destruction" entailed in growth and change. Here he compared Fritz's daring to that of Nietzsche, and praised him for his "callousness," his willingness to risk isolation and being frozen out of orthodox circles for the sake of an idea.

These thoughts served as transition to the second half of his address, which began with a characteristic Goodman analysis of the current scene: "dehumanizing institutions, role-playing, impersonality, squeamishness and racism, lack of affect, fragmented community, generation gap," and so forth. All of these losses and failings added up to a need for religious meaning, a view Goodman had been exploring in recent articles and was now about to publish in a book, *New Reformation*. People in general, but particularly the young, were desperate for some message to redeem what seemed a senseless world.

In his own opinion, this hunger translated into a passion for "answers" from those who had "made it," and helped explain the tremendous appeal of charismatic figures like Timothy Leary, Maharishi Mahesh Yogi, D. T. Suzuki, Buckminster Fuller, and of course Fritz. It accounted for the enthusiasm for new sacred texts and holy sacraments, including some of Fritz's favorites—consciousness-expanding devices like audiovisual technology, nitrous oxide, or LSD on the one hand, and on the other the techniques of psychodrama, encounter groups, and sensitivity training, which functioned like religious observances at Esalen and in every free university curriculum.

Goodman located such phenomena alongside other sixties developments. Fritz's "hit-and-run" demonstration style had parallels in both education and theater. One might see in it a fusion of Elliott Shapiro's community-based pedagogy for the oppressed and The Living Theatre's theater of participation, the former with roots in Reich and A. S. Neill, the latter stemming from Erwin Piscator and Bertolt Brecht.

The trouble with Fritz's "educational guerilla theater"—and it was a danger in other radicalizing techniques as well—was the lack of follow-through. It had to be said that Fritz's was not a physicianly character. His taste was for the one-night stand. And although his performance was "often beautiful," he could not bring it under continuous scrutiny, he could not "write it"—it was as if all tongues were foreign to him when it came to writing. Similarly he had "no memory," he was "not a scholar," and too often his "new discovery" was "said better 20 years ago, 10 years ago." In short, Goodman concluded, Fritz was a hippie.

But he had the virtues of these defects. After all, his "free-wheeling" style constituted much of his attractiveness. Although he lacked the gifts of a leader, his admirers could not resist following him. The times brought him into prominence, and his own restless nature, his inability to be satisfied by what the world offered him, combined with his powerful sense of the moment, the here and now of every situation, made him the natural if somewhat unwilling guru of a very large part of the counterculture. Like a "lonely, restless father," he could not show them "the way," for to a great extent he had lost the way himself, but there was no doubt that the flower children were his children. He joined them, adopted their costume and their sacraments, danced their dance.

Goodman refrained from saying the word that had offered itself when he visited Big Sur—"pathetic"—but he might as well have said it in his closing remarks on the virtues of Fritz's failings. That was precisely Goodman's attitude toward the hippies themselves. His final view of Fritz was also colored by a good deal of projection from his own case—his own sense of restlessness, of being an unwilling guru, and of having failed. Before he had finished there were already murmurs of discontent in Goodman's audience. Even among the old guard, the first and second generations of Gestalt therapy's founders in New York, there were some who thought he had made too much of the contributions of Paul Weisz and Laura Perls to Gestalt therapy, paring away at Fritz's primacy. He had specifically compared Fritz and Laura, saying that, after all, it was she who was the intellectual, as a way of characterizing Fritz's style of always leaping to the insight instead of patiently building a case. Even if this were true—it depended on what was meant by "intellectual"—some people took it as pointless degrading of Fritz to promote Laura. It is interesting that no one thought Goodman was running Fritz down in order to boost his own claims as the theoretician of the movement. Indeed there were some in the audience who had never even read *Gestalt Therapy*, and whose sense of the rival camps had more to do with personal experiences than with ideas. Those who knew the history of psychoanalysis and of Fritz in all his guises were in a better position to understand the kind of justice being done to his story, but even among them there were some who were disturbed by the impropriety of speaking harsh truths of the dead. As the rustle of discontent grew in the room, one man rose to protest—he had been Fritz's first patient in the United States and had therefore a special right to say it: "We all know that Fritz was a *character*," he said, "but that's not what we came to hear."

Many voices shouted their agreement; many others affirmed the truth of Goodman's assessment. He had taken the occasion as something more than a conventional memorial ceremony, and the impulse of his audience was to debate the matter, as if it were now time for questions and answers. But Goodman sat down unperturbed, and the cellist and pianist now played the adagio from Beethoven's Sonata in D Major. Afterwards people stood and argued for a long time.

CHAPTER TWELVE

Neither Guru nor Sacred Text—the Gestalt Way

IN HIS MEMORIAL ADDRESS Goodman had spoken of the fascination of the young with figures like Fritz Perls who had "made it," who had somehow achieved the presence and visibility of culture heroes. Modern society did not provide much in the way of careers for the young to look forward to or models to admire and imitate. Those who claimed to know what had gone wrong, the prophets and healers Ben Nelson had once foretold, were therefore hearkened to as much for their wisdom about how to live as for their critique of the culture and its institutions. If the community no longer had elders to guide it, at least it had its gurus. Goodman too had such a following, and in the two years remaining to him after Perls's death he devoted a good deal of his time to a series of essays on "how I go about it," a kind of *credo* for the young who "often asked me how I *am*. . . . Because of the well-known alienating conditions of modern times, they are baffled how anybody can do anything, and I—in their eyes—have 'made it.'"[1]

His major attempt to spell out how he went about it was in a course he gave at the University of Hawaii in the fall of 1971, after his first heart attack and with the awareness that death was not far away. These talks were eventually published in *Little*

Prayers and Finite Experience, a book that appeared in the fall of 1972, a few months after Goodman's death. The very last thing he wrote for publication was the description for the dust jacket of this book, where he spoke of it as "a phenomenology" of his anarchist way of life.

I have quoted many passages from this book already, for it contains Goodman's final words on Gestalt therapy as well as on anarchism, art, and other chief concerns of his life. Although he never mentions Perls here, he speaks repeatedly of the treatise they wrote together, using it as a reference point for views he still holds. Yet at the same time his scope is wider, and *Gestalt Therapy* is only one of a number of works which he regards as his "program": "The critical question for me is how to have, or make, those abstractions 'Organism,' 'Environment,' 'History,' so that they can possibly interact to reconstitute primary experience. I have written ten books on this question in various contexts. 'To have an environment and not to take it as an object, is Tao,' said Chuang-tzu. Sometimes I state my program in the form, 'How to take on Culture without losing Nature,' but that is already too abstract."[2]

What Goodman says here about culture and nature could be illustrated from the pages of any of his books, but let us consider the matter from another angle. The memorial service for Perls ended in controversy between two camps of Gestalt therapists, which we might roughly identify as the East Coast and the West Coast contingents. On the one hand there were those who adhered to the New York institute and its original conception of theory and practice, developed both in Gestalt therapy's primary text and also in the early years of intellectual give-and-take among the founders. On the other hand there were those who adhered to the showier paradigm Fritz Perls had gone on to create at Esalen, with its elements of spiritual conversion and evangelism. To some extent these two camps have persisted ever since, though it is no longer defensible to distinguish them so crudely as East and West Coast, or indeed by any other pair of terms. Over the years various twists have been given to the division. In its most simplistic form it has been reduced to a dispute over who contributed the essential ideas of Gestalt therapy, Perls or Goodman. This can also be understood as a debate over what the core of the movement actually is— "whose ideas?" being a way of saying "which ideas?" At times the debate has become quite acrimonious, but by and large I think it has been fruitful, and in any case it is probably unavoidable, for the issues involved reflect some of the deepest dilemmas of modern times. The Gestalt therapy movement has not buried these conflicts along with its founders but kept them in awareness. New practitioners and patients can try to sort them out and learn from them, whether or not they take sides.

Considering the debate as it was joined in 1970 when Perls died, one might take it as reflecting the split in the youth movement between hippies and political radicals. Although it is certainly true that there was such a split, then growing wider at every moment, and that the sides were justifiably labeled East Coast and West Coast, exceptions were everywhere apparent. In Berkeley in 1970, for example, both "Eastern" radicals and "Western" hippies could be found, a West-Coast simulacrum of the national schism, mirrored again by the plain fact that the dichotomy could often be seen animating a single person. The crisis of the late sixties tended to polarize people and to separate out certain issues as tests of allegiance, but at every stage of the New Left phenomenon, from its origins to its longterm legacy, in individuals and in groups, there was a fusion of political and cultural rebelliousness that marked the epoch as nothing else did.

No doubt we all know what Goodman meant in calling Fritz a hippie in his memorial address, yet at the same time it is evident that Perls was very much a product of the bookish and bourgeois Central European *Kultur* that invented both psychoanalysis and socialism. By the same token Goodman was in his own character not so much a fiery radical in the Bakunin or Kropotkin tradition as a sexy, mischievous street urchin living by his wits in the urban jungle. In fact it was Enlightenment culture that they had in common and were both dissatisfied with. Perls handled the dissatisfaction by disowning a substantial part of his heritage, shedding its trappings for the counterculture style. Goodman tried to find a way of preserving nature—a peculiarly American sort of nature, not so far from the hippie ideal—while holding fast to the tradition of Western culture he was unwilling to give up. In short neither Perls nor Goodman could be summed up in a phrase or category even though they had come to represent emphases and perspectives that were potentially in conflict. And the significant fact persists: whatever their differences they were able to join in the creation of a new kind of psychotherapy and collaborate on its theoretical exposition. Because of this it has seemed worth sorting out the different ingredients that each brought to the project, even polarizing their contributions somewhat and simplifying them against the actual complexity, in order to comprehend more fully the integrating power of the amalgam the two founders achieved.

Perhaps still more to my point, the collaboration of two such different intellects in the founding of a new school of psychotherapy has had the advantage of preventing the typical hardening of theory into a sacrosanct set of doctrines attested to by the seal of a single mind. One does not speak of Perlsianism or Goodmanism the way one speaks of Freudianism or Reichianism. Much of the vitality of Gestalt therapy lies in these unresolved tensions and contradictions, which have kept the movement from shrinking in upon itself and, indeed, have left it prey at the fringes to hybridization, which one hopes is not sterile or monstrous but a healthy growth. While some of the faddish spin-offs are sheer quackery, the spread of basic Gestalt attitudes in the psychotherapeutic community and beyond is surely a favorable sign.

Another way of putting much of this would be to say that Gestalt therapy's central effort to avoid the traditional dualisms—mind/body, objective/subjective, self/external world, biological/cultural, and so on[3]—depended in large part on emphasizing them, not in their characteristic form as abstractions from experience that pose significant problems as standing dilemmas somehow given in the nature of things, but rather as important clues to areas of life where a contextual and phenomenological approach can unbind energy held in polar tension and release the vitality of genuinely creative conflict. It is typical of Gestalt therapy that the healing of a "neurotic split" (as these rigid dichotomies are termed) is not simply a matter of discovering some new integration, though that may be the end in view, but depends first of all on bringing apparent incompatibilities into awareness and allowing "free conflict" to emerge: "since we work in the same world there must somewhere be a creative unity."[4]

I am conflating here, as Goodman and Perls also do at this juncture in their text, the treatment of neurotic splitting in theoretical thinking and in the theorists who think it. In Goodman and Perls's *ad hominem* universe the point was always to acknowledge conflict and to look for unity in the underlying experience—unity that would not be static or final but "creative," an aspect of ongoing "novelty, excitement, and growth," to borrow once again the title of volume two of their book.

With such a conception of conflict in mind we may regard the hubbub that followed Goodman's memorial speech as thoroughly appropriate. Although it is not possible to reconstruct the debate on that afternoon or during the ensuing two decades, a list of some of the more salient oppositions built into the practice of Gestalt therapy may suggest why controversy, keeping the issues alive and unsettled, has proved invigorating:

West	*East*
Hippie	Political
Guru	Text
Therapist-centered	Group-centered
Breakthrough	Follow-through
Technique	Training
Cure	Attitude

Such a list can be used to display the contrasting characters of Perls and Goodman, but close analysis—or debate—regarding any single pair of contraries will produce a much more problematic view of the authors and their respective positions. On the face of it, for example, Perls was surely the guru whose followers treated him like the embodied Buddha himself, whereas Goodman was the writer, the man of letters whose wisdom was preserved and embodied in the text. Yet there is much more to be said about these characterizations. Vivid and famous as

Goodman and Perls were, there was a tendency for enthusiasts to treat them as stars, objects of fantasy and cultish worship from afar. Both of them were somewhat safeguarded by their complete lack of interest in the mirror of fame. Each of them needed an audience to do his proper work, but neither worried much about the figure he cut in front of it so long as he was taken seriously. They had plenty of other foibles, but these too were more likely to undermine adulation and transference than to invite it. Nonetheless, in their different ways, both Perls and Goodman had disciples, some of whom were like Zen acolytes trying to get the discipline into their bones, some of whom were sixties groupies, part of the chorus attracted by the limelight.

The Gestalt Way was not much in evidence or easily acquired in such circumstances, which provided neither the safe emergency situation nor the ongoing mutual aid of group therapy. Yet there was the possibility of breakthrough and conversion for those already teetering on the edge. The question then would be what sort of support and follow-through the community of disciples and the teachings themselves might offer. Always standing in front of audiences rather than running groups, the gurus were too busy with their causes to be of much help. Perls's workshops and Goodman's panel discussions were versions of group demonstrations, not really of therapeutic use to most participants or observers, though of course one could learn something important from them.

Perls was charismatic, to be sure, but as Goodman pointed out in his memorial speech, he was no leader. In any interactive situation he liked to take control, but more for the excitement of the moment than to steer toward a goal or gather disciples. His was the fascination of breaking through facades and touching the quick of things. Although he needed an audience to shine in front of, Perls was neither posing nor crusading. In his own way he was a living embodiment of the Gestalt notion of the self as creative adjustment at the contact boundary: he came to life in direct proportion to the life he could provoke in others. There was a good deal of eros in this mutual excitement.

Actually Goodman was not so different, though more concerned with his message and its long-term effects than with his performance of the moment. Like Fritz, he had no desire to lead. Given Gestalt therapy's emphasis on the here and now, and its reliance on heightened awareness and ongoing creative adjustment—self-regulation and autonomy rather than system or dogma—the notion of a guru who is not interested in leading makes a lot of sense. However, when one looks closely at Perls's personal style, one finds only part of the Gestalt attitude. In Goodman's view the here and now also implied a "next"— one thing led to another and the ground underfoot gave faith for a further step. Perls's aggressive, confrontational impulses were certainly true to the theory of dental aggression that was his primary contribution to psychotherapeutic thought, but physicianly compassion, respect for the autonomy of others, and even the habits of awareness and openness to experience were undeveloped in his character. There is plenty of testimony to his sharp eye and fearless pounce, to his relish for life, and to a streak of playfulness in him, all of which might well be qualities worth cultivating, but they do not add up to the attitude one associates with the Gestalt movement. Rather these are the techniques and talents of psychodrama and the encounter group, Esalen-style shedding of convention and the plunge into role-playing and contact.

If we turn to the other pole of our dichotomy, the sacred text, we find another mixed case. There has been some temptation among Perlsian adepts of the here and now to derogate the second and third generations of the New York and Cleveland institutes who, in the adepts' view, treat *Gestalt Therapy* too worshipfully, as if it encoded all there is to know of theory and practice. "Religions of the book" are typically proselytizing and excluding, doctrine and conversion serve as gateways rather than paths, and there is much stamping out of heresy. However, it is doubtful that *Gestalt Therapy* has been used that way very often, nor have Goodman and Perls's psychological writings been belabored with sectarian commentary in anything approaching the quantity or intensity devoted for instance to Freud or Reich.

Although Perls was always willing to take credit for *Gestalt Therapy*, in his Esalen years he rarely mentioned it and clearly regarded the book as outmoded by his later work—much in the way that Reich considered *Character Analysis* or *The Sexual Revolution* perfectly sound and important writings, but of no stature next to the books he wrote after the discovery of the orgone. Goodman, however, did not change his mind about the insights of their book, and in other major works—*Growing Up Absurd*, for instance, or *Little Prayers and Finite Experience*—he is still quoting *Gestalt Therapy* in formulations that he might now improve on, stylistically, but which suited his intellectual purposes as thoroughly as the day he first wrote them. By the same token, he wrote too many other books to worry about *Gestalt Therapy*'s status as a sacred text.

Has the book been used as dogma? It is certainly true that over the years some therapists from the East Coast camp, which might be called the founding tradition, have complained that the ideas and practices of therapists of the "heretical" West Coast are not Gestalt therapy—implying deviation from some doctrinal norm—while those so accused have a similar perception, though viewed from the opposite heights. But all this is mere froth, even though it sometimes gets in people's eyes. East and West here are not serious labels, and whatever their local allegiances, advocates of Perls's primacy as the fountainhead of the movement are just as likely to claim a greater share of the book for him as they are to minimize its significance.

More to the point perhaps is the practical fact that for so many years the training of Gestalt therapists has been centered on a meticulous study of the book. Isadore From, who trained so many current practitioners, made a sentence-by-sentence discussion of the theoretical half of Gestalt Therapy his cornerstone.[5] Whoever went through his mentoring would know that part of the book backwards and forwards. Yet his purpose was not doctrinal so much as pedagogical. Just as the first half of the book with its sequence of do-it-yourself exercises had in view the assimilation of the Gestalt attitude, so the second, theoretical half was also conceived as a regimen. The authors themselves spoke of their approach as a kind of ad hominem argument designed "to bring into the picture the total context of the problem, including the conditions of experiencing it, the social milieu and the personal 'defenses' of the observer," with the goal of improving clinical practice while also providing "insights for us all toward a creative change in our present urgent crisis."[6] That is, the method was indeed catechistic, but its aim was psychic restructuring and autonomy rather than orthodoxy. As From saw it, a large part of Goodman's achievement was to write about Gestalt therapy "in a way that reasonably prevents introjection."[7] It had to be worked through, and in the process a reader would be changed. This conception of the relation of the text to training and practice is completely compatible with the notion just offered of the Gestalt guru, whose stance toward disciples is that of a master craftsman, or perhaps an Oriental sage, but not a systematizer or prophet.

The point again is that one can find elements of the same attitudes in both East and West, Goodman and Perls, even though their primary dispositions are so obviously different. This overlap is as true for other polarities on the list as for the dichotomy of guru and text. Perls, for example, was very much a therapist-oriented practitioner, from the days when he sat behind the couch to the days when he starred in his own demonstration films. But then too, Gestalt therapy was in certain ways a therapist-centered movement no matter where we look. Goodman himself made it clear that the aim was to treat every patient as a trainee, a potential therapist, that is, to work toward dissolving the difference between therapist and patient. This was part of Goodman's rejection of psychotherapy as "a prophetic vocation."[8] The therapist, like the patient, was to be his or her "ordinary self," and that implied anyone in the group might be the therapist, depending on the dynamics of the moment.

Perls was also his ordinary self in every situation, though his was a very different character type. He too ultimately focused on the training of other therapists, first at Esalen and then at his Gestalt utopia in Canada. His films and other demonstrations of technique were always conceived as training aids, and his starring role in them was as much a means of transcending self as it was a self-conscious performance. He said of himself,

"When I work I am not Fritz Perls. I become nothing, no-thing, a catalyst, and I enjoy my work. I forget myself and surrender to you and your plight." But he also added, "And once we have closure I come back to the audience, a prima donna demanding appreciation."[9]

Or take it from the other side. If Goodman was always group-oriented in his therapy, developing his notions of the Gestalt community of patients along anarchist lines of mutual aid and direct action, Perls seems not so very far behind. By the end of his life Perls was saying that individual therapy was "obsolete," and envisioning "Gestalt communities as an efficient means for producing real people."[10] Lake Cowichan in British Columbia was his fantasy of the first Gestalt kibbutz. Looking a little more closely, however, we meet again the fundamental differences between Perls and Goodman. Just as their trainees in Cleveland had observed that their styles of self-presentation were utterly opposed—Perls the "magician," Goodman the ordinary "member of the community"[11]—so too in their conceptions of communal life they were at odds, Perls's notion of the Gestalt kibbutz being a hazy blend of the Esalen counterculture with the patriarchal communes of the utopian tradition in nineteenth-century Europe and America, whereas Goodman's idea of community was grounded in a view of human nature and its social bonds that went back to Aristotle and in a politics that included the citizenly ideals of the Greek *polis* and the gritty day-to-day life of American towns and urban neighborhoods.

Similarities and distinctions like these may be found in every aspect of Gestalt therapy's two traditions, though forty years of controversy and assimilation have muted the contrasts. Perls's predilection for technique, breakthrough, and cure—a set of methods and aims that surely had its value—has been moderated by Goodman's insistence on training and follow-through, essential if the patient is to acquire the new attitude toward experience and the ability to go on making creative adjustments that is the Gestalt movement's therapeutic goal. Perls seems closer to his predecessors in these matters, especially Reich, and Goodman more the rebel and innovator, though if we take the broader view of cultural history it is Goodman's emphasis that conserves the traditional view of human nature and life in community. Like Reich, Perls tended to believe that if people were only cured, everything else would take care of itself; whereas Goodman regarded therapy as an ongoing part of life, its attitude widely and continually applicable whether or not we are in desperate straits. Yet it is not the whole of life, which includes much that is not psychological at all and many real problems that therapy cannot solve.

In general we may say that the contribution of Gestalt therapy to the psychoanalytic tradition has been primarily a matter of fusion and synthesis. Not only was its development full of eclecticism and cross-fertilization, but its place in history, at the moment of tremendous shifts in the intellectual relations of Europe and the United States, and at the point when the first generation of psychoanalysts was dying, guaranteed that many broken threads would be waiting to be woven into a new pattern, including some strands that would keep coming unraveled in any theory. Freud had dealt with dualisms like mind/body or self/society in ways that reactivated their tensions, but his focus on childhood trauma, repression, and the *psycho*-neuroses rather than *actual*-neuroses gave short shrift to whatever was not part of the self—or the Ego, Id, and Superego. Reich in his turn had paid much attention to some of the areas Freud tried to finesse, the body's share in selfhood, the vicious circle of repressive social institutions and anxious citizens, but in the end he too relied on a model (biological determinism) that shrank human nature to one dimension, "against all the evidence," as Goodman put it, "of the humane sciences, art, history, and so forth."[12] *Gestalt Therapy* was an attempt to save as much of the conflicting appearances as possible in a new synthesis built on a phenomenological account of experience viewed as prior to the awareness of subject and object. The self was conceived as creative adjustment of organism and environment, including all the nontherapeutic and nonpolitical work and sociality of the world. The here and now was defined as a field for ongoing experiment with the unfinished situations of the character and the unfinished revolutions of the social order. In this new formulation Goodman and Perls borrowed from the Gestalt psychologists, especially Kurt Goldstein, from Otto Rank, from Buber and Lao-tzu, from Aristotle and Kant and William James, as well as from the central tradition in which they saw themselves, that of Freud and Reich. On the one hand they attempted to find ways of contextualizing and integrating the wisdom of these philosophers of human nature; on the other hand they affirmed an attitude of creative conflict, a refusal to systematize, that kept open new possibilities of insight and invention. As Goodman said, the goal was always to "take on Culture without losing Nature." For Goodman, this implied a cycle of unending novelty, excitement, and growth.

In *Gestalt Therapy*, I reason my way into the subject as follows: If we envisage an animal moving, continually

seeing new scenes and meeting new problems to cope
with, it will continually have to make a creative adjustment. Selecting, imitating, shaping, in order to appropriate the novelty of the environment to itself, and
to screen out what would destroy homeostasis. Adjusting, because the organism's every living power is actual-
ized only in its environment. And the environment, for
its part, must be amenable to appropriation and selec-
tion; it must be plastic to be changed and meaningful to
be known. The precipice that you fall off is not your
environment.[13]

There is nothing in this passage, written a year and a half
after Perls's death, that Perls would not have agreed with, but
Goodman's concern for continuity, looking forward and back
from the present moment, was an impulse almost totally missing in Perls, whose fascination was with the here and now. For
Goodman it was here and now and next. The world did not
depend on his awareness of it; beyond the horizon still more life
awaited his discovery: "Faith is having a world-for-me. That my
experience is given. That it will continue to be given: the Next
is not the brink of a precipice. Its structure has consequences
that I can draw; there might be evidence to clarify the meaning
if I attend. By faith I am not caged in my finite experience; it has
an horizon rather than bars; so I speak of it as 'roomy enough.'"[14]

Ultimately this concern with what is not-yet or no-longer
is a religious attitude, and Goodman's psychological thinking
joins here with the long history of wisdom literature, sacred and
profane inquiries into the nature of the human spirit. He
observed in *Little Prayers and Finite Experience*:

302

NEITHER GURU NOR SACRED TEXT—THE GESTALT WAY

I notice that I sometimes use the language of psychoanalysis and rarely a few terms of existential philosophy,
but on the whole I prefer the language of orthodox theology to talk about the invisibles. Using words like faith,
hope, love, paradise, purgatory, nonattachment, vocation, Way, Creation, koan, holy spirit, mana, Messiah,
idol, Void, God, Karma, incarnation—mostly from the
West, with a scattering from the East or from primitive
religions.

These theological terms have been in use for thousands of years far and wide. We must assume that they
have met a need, and they have certainly been polished
by handling. Naturally they are resonant in a poet's
vocabulary. They are very ambiguous and have been tor-
mented by interpretation—though perhaps not more so
than recent psychoanalytic and philosophical terms—
but the contrasting interpretations are themselves
ancient and have been spelled out in schisms and here-
sies. Hundreds of fine brains have been busy about it,
with millions of adherents, and much bloodshed to show
that they meant something or other.

Goodman goes on to note that "young people these days
like this palaver, which seems meaningful to them, though
their language is rather more eclectic than mine. But there is a
difference from my own youth when such talk was considered
moronic and we had no language at all to describe our hopes or
troubles. (I hit on psychoanalysis.) In the peculiar historical crisis they are now in, some of the young are so alienated that
they finally germinate crazy ideas and will add to the history of

theology, if there is any further history of anything."[15] There have been many remarkable changes in the world since Goodman wrote these words over twenty years ago, and perhaps the theological hope he discerned in the young looks more like despair today, but youth is not a historically bound phenomenon so much as an ever-renewable resource, part and parcel of human nature itself. It was a virtue of Goodman's philosophy to understand this and allow for it. There *will* be further history, a next, even if our here and now is dim and dispiriting. Goodman sometimes thought of himself as Adam:

> *Like Adam firmly walking to*
> *the farm-work that he knew to do*
> *in deep confusion, for the grim*
> *news of everyday to him*
>
> *happened each thing by surprise*
> *like a fist between the eyes*
> *—so let me day to day work on*
> *in the thick cloud that has sunk down.*[16]

But he was also the author of "Noah's Song."

> *What is that lovely rainbow that abides*
> *upon the dripping moments till it fades?*
> *God promised me, though I am old,*
> *if I will work this new-washed field*
>
> *while my future vanishes past,*
> *something will come of it at last.*
> *This is the rainbow that abides*
> *on the dripping moments—till it fades.*[17]

Notes

Chapter One

1. Paul Goodman, *Little Prayers and Finite Experience* (New York: Harper-Collins, 1972), p. 59.

2. *Little Prayers and Finite Experience*, p. 77.

3. Paul Goodman, "The Political Meaning of Some Recent Revisions of Freud," *Politics* (July 1945), 2, p. 201; reprinted in Taylor Stoehr, ed., *Nature Heals: The Psychological Essays of Paul Goodman* (New York: Free Life Editions, 1977), pp. 53–55. Goodman quotes from Erich Fromm, *Escape from Freedom* (Troy, Mo.: Holt, Rinehart & Winston), 1941, pp. 271–272.

4. "The Political Meaning of Some Recent Revisions of Freud," p. 201.

5. Paul Goodman, *The Empire City* (New York: Bobbs-Merrill, 1959), p. 387. *The Empire City* is made up of four related, sequential novels: *The Grand Piano or, The Almanac of Alienation* (originally published 1942), *The State of Nature* (originally published 1946), *The Dead of Spring* (originally published 1950), and *The Holy Terror*.

6. *The Empire City*, p. 96.

7. Taylor Stoehr, ed., *The Galley to Mytilene: Stories 1949–1960*, vol. 4 of *The Collected Stories of Paul Goodman* (Santa Rosa, Calif.: Black Sparrow Press, 1980), p. 47.

8. Paul Goodman, *Five Years* (New York: Brussel & Brussel, 1966), p. 101. The original manuscript notebooks of Goodman's journals, kept between 1955 and 1960 and ultimately printed as *Five Years*, are part of the collection of his papers at the Houghton Library of Harvard University. In many cases the manuscript entries differ from and are often fuller than the printed versions. For the sake of representing Goodman's first thoughts, set down at the time he had them, I have used the manuscript texts when available (a few of the notebooks are missing) though my citations are to the pages of the published journal. A number of manuscript readings are also reprinted in

Nature Heals, under the heading "Notes from a Journal," pp. 234–248. Unless otherwise noted, all quotations from Goodman's manuscripts are by permission of the Houghton Library.

9. Author's interview with Henry Kaiser, March 11, 1976.

10. *Five Years*, p. 36.

11. *The Empire City*, p. 125.

12. *The Empire City*, p. 376.

13. See, for example, *Little Prayers and Finite Experience*, pp. 103–105.

14. See Paul Goodman, "Great Pioneer But No Libertarian," *Liberation* (Jan. 1958), *2*, pp. 7–9; reprinted in *Nature Heals*, p. 85.

15. Author's interview with Alexander Lowen, December 4, 1974. For six months in 1946 and 1947, and continuing much less programmatically as late as 1950, Goodman filled over a hundred pages with free associations, dreams, memories, and interpretive conjectures. These pages have survived, and I have consulted them in reconstructing his self-analysis, which I will discuss in my forthcoming biography of Goodman. Although his self-analysis naturally forms part of the background of his psychoanalytic thought, it was virtually complete—so far as this phase of it is concerned—before Goodman's work with Fritz Perls on the theory of Gestalt therapy, and I have therefore only mentioned it in passing here, just as I have touched only briefly on Goodman's early acquaintance with the work of Freud and Reich. Although the main body of Goodman's manuscripts in the Houghton Library of Harvard University may be consulted there, the papers that make up the self-analysis are not yet available to scholars.

16. *Five Years*, p. 41.

17. *Five Years*, p. 10.

18. Paul Goodman, "On Being a Writer," in *Nature Heals*, pp. 213–215.

Chapter Two

1. Author's interviews with Holley Cantine, November 13, 1974; David Koven, March 25, 1975; and Dachine Rainer, June 29, 1977.

2. For Fritz and Lore Perls's early history together, see the interview with the latter, in Joe Wysong and Edward Rosenfeld, eds., *An Oral History of Gestalt Therapy* (Highland, N.Y.: The Gestalt Journal, 1982) and other transcriptions of conversations and interviews with Lore Perls in *Keeping the Flame: Laura Perls and Gestalt Therapy*, in *Voices* (Summer 1982), *18*, pp. 5–37, and in the early pages of Jack Gaines, *Fritz Perls: Here and Now* (Millbrae, Calif.: Celestial Arts, 1979). For an account more narrowly from Fritz Perls's perspective, see Frederick S. Perls, *In and Out the Garbage Pail* (New York: Bantam, 1972), p. 40 and elsewhere; originally published by Real People Press, 1969, unpaginated.

3. For an account of Reich's work, see Myron Sharaf, *Fury on Earth: A Biography of Wilhelm Reich* (New York: St. Martin's Press, 1983).

4. *In and Out the Garbage Pail*, p. 50.

5. Frederick S. Perls, Ralph F. Hefferline, and Paul Goodman, *Gestalt Therapy: Excitement and Growth in the Human Personality* (New York: Julian Press, 1951), pp. 246–247.

6. Letter from Goodman to his friend Benjamin Nelson [spring 1948], in the Benjamin N. Nelson Collection, Columbia University Libraries. Not all letters to and from Goodman carry dates; I have supplied them in brackets where possible. This and further letters from Goodman to Nelson are quoted by permission of the Columbia University Libraries.

7. "Great Pioneer But No Libertarian," in *Nature Heals*, p. 84.

8. F. S. Perls, *Ego, Hunger and Aggression* (London: Allen & Unwin, 1947), pp. 79, 124. U.S. edition published by Vintage, 1969.

9. Interview with Isadore From, in *An Oral History of Gestalt Therapy*, p. 28.

10. Author's interview with Jerry Raphel, July 15, 1974.

11. *In and Out the Garbage Pail*, pp. 90–91.

12. Interview with Isadore From, in *An Oral History of Gestalt Therapy*, pp. 12, 27, 28.

13. For Lore Perls's contributions to *Ego, Hunger and Aggression*, see *An Oral History of Gestalt Therapy*, p. 13, and *Voices* (Summer 1982) *18*, p. 9. The manuscript that provided the impetus if not literally the germ for *Gestalt Therapy* is said to have been a hundred pages long. It apparently still exists although not available to scholars at the present time. From study of Fritz Perls's other writings, and from what people who saw it have said, it is possible to form a reasonably trustworthy idea of its contents and character, though of course one wishes it could be examined.

14. *In and Out the Garbage Pail*, p. 264.

15. *In and Out the Garbage Pail*, p. 264. Compare the interview with Laura Perls, in *An Oral History of Gestalt Therapy*, p. 15.

16. Interview with Laura Perls, in *An Oral History of Gestalt Therapy*, pp. 8, 28.

17. Author's interview with former patient, August 16, 1974.

18. *Complex* (Winter 1953/1954), 9.

19. Interview with Laura Perls, in *An Oral History of Gestalt Therapy*, pp. 5, 7, and elsewhere.

20. *Ego, Hunger and Aggression*, p. 5.

21. "The Food We Eat," *Resistance* (May/June 1948), 7, p. 14; "Gandhi," *Politics* (Winter 1948), 5, p. 15.

22. Author's interviews with Laura Perls, October 16 and November 30, 1974.

23. Letter from Goodman to Benjamin Nelson [late winter 1948], Columbia University Libraries.

24. Letter from Goodman to Benjamin Nelson [spring 1948], Columbia University Libraries.
25. Author's interview with Goodman's sister-in-law, Naomi Goodman, November 27, 1975; author's interview with Jane Gapen, November 14, 1974.
26. *Gestalt Therapy*, p. 432.
27. This is said of Arabelle, the "Laura Perls" character in Goodman's roman à clef *Making Do* (New York: Macmillan, 1963), p. 82.
28. *Gestalt Therapy*, p. 304.
29. Paul Goodman, *Kafka's Prayer* (New York: Vanguard, 1947); Sander Katz, ed., *Freud: On War, Sex and Neurosis* (New York: Arts & Sciences Press, 1947).
30. *Kafka's Prayer*, p. 5.
31. *Kafka's Prayer*, p. 6.
32. *Kafka's Prayer*, p. xii.
33. *Freud: On War, Sex and Neurosis*, p. v.
34. *Freud: On War, Sex and Neurosis*, pp. vii–viii.

Chapter Three

1. Author's correspondence with Alexander Katz. "Revolution, Sociolatry and War" appeared in *Politics* (December 1945), *2*, pp. 376–380; and formed part of "The May Pamphlet," reprinted in Taylor Stoehr, ed., *Drawing the Line: The Political Essays of Paul Goodman* (New York: Free Life Editions, 1977).
2. Paul Goodman, *Stop-Light: 5 Dance Poems* (Harrington, N.J.: The 5 X 8 Press, 1941); Paul Goodman, *Art and Social Nature* (New York: Vinco, 1946).
3. Letter from Alexander Katz to Dwight Macdonald, November 23, 1949, in the Dwight Macdonald collection of the Yale Collection of American Literature, Beinecke Rare Book and Manuscript Library, Yale University, quoted by permission. Author's correspondence with Katz.
4. Letter from Goodman to Benjamin Nelson [March? 1950], Columbia University Libraries.
5. Frederick S. Perls, "The Anthropology of Neurosis," *Complex* (Summer 1950), *2*, pp. 19–27; Laura Perls, "The Psychoanalyst and the Critic," *Complex* (Summer 1950), *2*, pp. 41–47. Announcements of future contributors were printed in *Complex* (Spring 1950), *1*, p. 64.
6. "Unpublished 'Editors' Note' for First Issue of *Complex*," in *Nature Heals*, p. 89.
7. Letter from A. S. Neill to Wilhelm Reich, July 30, 1951, in Beverley R. Placzek, ed., *Record of a Friendship: The Correspondence of Wilhelm Reich and A. S. Neill* (New York: Farrar Straus Giroux, 1981), p. 327.

8. A. S. Neill, "Self-Regulation and the Outside World," *Orgone Energy Bulletin* (Apr. 1950), pp. 69–70.

9. "Self-Regulation and the Outside World," p. 70.

10. Letter from A. S. Neill to Alexander Katz, April 27, 1950. Quoted by permission of Ena Neill and Zoe Readhead (Neill). I am indebted to Jonathan Croall for directing my attention to this letter.

11. Letter from Wilhelm Reich to A. S. Neill, May 10, 1950, in *Record of a Friendship*, p. 279.

12. Letter from A. S. Neill to Wilhelm Reich, January 10, 1946, in *Record of a Friendship*, p. 153.

13. Letter from Goodman to *The Village Voice*, November 14, 1963; published in *The Village Voice* (November 21, 1963), 9, p. 4.

14. See *Record of a Friendship*, pp. 288–297; and Sharaf, *Fury on Earth*, pp. 362–363.

15. Letter from Goodman to A. S. Neill, n.d., Houghton Library.

16. Letter from Wilhelm Reich to A. S. Neill, June 29, 1950, in *Record of a Friendship*, pp. 281–282.

17. Letter from A. S. Neill to Goodman, June 13, 1950, Houghton Library, quoted by permission of Ena Neill and Zoe Readhead (Neill).

18. George Orwell, "Politics and the English Language," *Horizon* (Apr. 1946); reprinted in Sonia Orwell and Ian Angus, eds., *The Collected Essays, Journalism and Letters of George Orwell*, vol. 4 (Orlando, Fla.: Harcourt Brace Jovanovich, 1968), pp. 128–129.

19. Author's observation. Goodman told friends that the question of sexual privacy was also a live issue in his home (author's interview with Honore Valincourt Elkus, July 17, 1975).

20. "The Anthropology of Neurosis," p. 20; slightly altered when published in *Gestalt Therapy*, p. 308.

21. "The Anthropology of Neurosis," p. 21; slightly altered when published in *Gestalt Therapy*, p. 310.

22. "The Anthropology of Neurosis," p. 20; slightly altered when published in *Gestalt Therapy*, p. 309.

23. Letter to author from Alexander Katz, July 23, 1976.

24. G. William Domhoff, *The Mystique of Dreams: A Search for Utopia Through Senoi Dream Theory* (Berkeley: University of California Press, 1985).

Chapter Four

1. *In and Out the Garbage Pail*, p. 39; compare pp. 33–34, 37.

2. *Ego, Hunger and Aggression*, p. 192.

3. *Ego, Hunger and Aggression*, pp. 195–196.

4. Interview with Erving Polster, in *An Oral History of Gestalt Therapy*, p. 55.

5. Elliott Shapiro, in "An Oral History of Gestalt Therapy: Part Four: A Conversation with Elliott Shapiro," interview by Joe Wysong, *Gestalt Journal*, (Fall 1985), 8, p. 16; also, interview with Laura Perls, in *An Oral History of Gestalt Therapy*, pp. 13–14.

6. Interview with Isadore From, in *An Oral History of Gestalt Therapy*, p. 31.

7. Interview with Laura Perls, in *An Oral History of Gestalt Therapy*, p. 14; interview with Arthur Ceppos, in *Fritz Perls: Here and Now*, pp. 37–38.

8. Two letters from Goodman [about March 1950] to Benjamin Nelson, Columbia University Libraries.

9. Author's interview with Benjamin Nelson, July 10, 1974.

10. "Project for a Modern Jewish Museum," *Commentary* (Feb. 1946), 1, pp. 15–20. See also Benjamin Nelson's letter to Goodman, June 7, 1945, Columbia University Libraries.

11. Author's interview with Percival Goodman, July 9, 1974.

12. Interview with Isadore From, in *An Oral History of Gestalt Therapy*, p. 30.

13. See, for example, *Gestalt Therapy*, p. 220.

14. *Gestalt Therapy*, p. 247.

15. Manuscript notes for Cleveland workshops, Houghton Library. Compare *Gestalt Therapy*, pp. 228, 231.

16. *Gestalt Therapy*, p. 228.

17. *Gestalt Therapy*, p. 229.

18. On Smuts, Friedlaender, and Federn, see *Ego, Hunger and Aggression*, pp. 13–14, 26–27, 143; on the ego as a function, see pp. 71, 138.

19. On Perls's familiarity with Gestalt texts, see *In and Out the Garbage Pail*, p. 62.

20. *Gestalt Therapy*, pp. 258–259.

21. Interview with Isadore From, in *An Oral History of Gestalt Therapy*, p. 35; compare interview with Laura Perls, in *An Oral History of Gestalt Therapy*, p. 20.

22. See, for instance, "Reflections on the Anarchist Principle," *Anarchy* (Apr. 1966), 62; reprinted in *Drawing the Line*, pp. 176–177.

23. *Ego, Hunger and Aggression*, pp. 101–102.

24. *Gestalt Therapy*, p. 430.

25. *Gestalt Therapy*, pp. 443–444.

26. *Five Years*, p. 207.

27. *Ego, Hunger and Aggression*, pp. 101–102. Gordon Wheeler points out in *Gestalt Reconsidered* (New York: Gardner Press and The Gestalt Institute of Cleveland, 1991), p. 45, that Perls speaks of Zeigarnik's experiments as if they were Lewin's; in fact the Gestalt community generally regarded these experiments as part of Lewin's research program, though actually carried out by his student. See, for instance, Wolfgang Köhler, *Dynamics in Psychology* (New York: Grove Press, 1960), p. 44; originally published in 1940. Zeigarnik's arti-

cle attempts to quantify the influence on short-term memory of tensions experimentally induced by interrupting subjects as they performed simple manual and mental tasks. Whatever its significance for Lewin's theorizing about the way need organizes a field of perception, Zeigarnik's research could hardly be regarded as a stimulus to Goodman's adoption of "unfinished situation" as the pivotal term in his reformulation of Freud's theory of repression. The Zeigarnik-Lewin experiment was one of the few Gestalt studies that Perls claimed familiarity with; see *In and Out the Garbage Pail*, p. 62. For the article itself, see Willis D. Ellis, ed., *A Source Book of Gestalt Psychology* (London: Kegan Paul, 1938), pp. 300–314.

Chapter Five

1. Letter from Alice Goodman to Oscar Shaftel, October 12[?], 1934. I am grateful to Oscar Shaftel for sharing his file of letters from Paul and Alice Goodman with me.
2. See *Little Prayers and Finite Experience*, pp. 15, 21.
3. Letter from Wolfgang Köhler to psychologist Molly Harrower, who had transmitted the galleys to Köhler, December 8, 1951, Houghton Library.
4. Letter from Goodman to Wolfgang Köhler [December 1951], Houghton Library.
5. Interview with Laura Perls, in *Voices*, p. 7.
6. Author's interview with Jerry Raphel, July 15, 1974.
7. Interview with Laura Perls, in *An Oral History of Gestalt Therapy*, p. 13.
8. Manuscript notes for Cleveland workshops, Houghton Library.
9. *Ego, Hunger and Aggression*, p. 206.
10. *Ego, Hunger and Aggression*, p. 209.
11. *Gestalt Therapy*, p. 424.
12. *Gestalt Therapy*, p. 377.
13. *Little Prayers and Finite Experience*, p. 7.
14. *Ego, Hunger and Aggression*, pp. 138–139.
15. *Ego, Hunger and Aggression*, p. 143.
16. *Ego, Hunger and Aggression*, pp. 216–219, 253–257.
17. *Gestalt Therapy*, pp. 380, 389–390.
18. *Little Prayers and Finite Experience*, p. 91.
19. Paul Goodman, "*De Anima* and the *Posterior Analytics*," unpublished student paper, p. 4. Many of Goodman's student papers are in the Houghton Library.
20. Paul Goodman, *The Structure of Literature* (Chicago: University of Chicago Press, 1954), dedication page.
21. "On the Soul," in Richard P. McKeon, ed., *Introduction to Aristotle*, 2d ed. rev. and enlarged (Chicago: University of Chicago Press, 1973), p. 219.

McKeon used J. A. Smith's translation for his edition: see W. A. Ross, ed., *Works of Aristotle*, vol. 3, (Oxford: Clarendon Press, 1931).

22. *Gestalt Therapy*, p. 227.

23. *Gestalt Therapy*, p. 229n.

24. "Music as Invention," *Musical Mercury* (June 1936), 3, p. 17.

25. *Columbia Review* (Mar. 1937), 18, p. 32.

26. *Little Prayers and Finite Experience*, pp. 7–9.

27. *Little Prayers and Finite Experience*, p. 15.

28. *Little Prayers and Finite Experience*, pp. 11–13.

29. *Gestalt Therapy*, p. 418.

30. See *Little Prayers and Finite Experience*, p. 91.

31. Richard King, *The Party of Eros: Radical Social Thought and the Realm of Freedom* (Chapel Hill: University of North Carolina Press, 1972).

32. Letters from Goodman to Richard King, March 31, 1969; May 14 and 30, 1972. I am grateful to Richard King for sharing his Goodman files with me.

33. Kurt Goldstein, *Human Nature in the Light of Psychopathology* (Cambridge, Mass.: Harvard University Press, 1940), p. 5.

34. William James, *Psychology: Briefer Course* (New York: Collier Books, 1962), p. 226; originally published 1892.

35. *Gestalt Therapy*, pp. 280–281.

36. Otto Rank, *Will Therapy* and *Truth and Reality*, trans. Jessie Taft (New York: Knopf, 1947), p. 39; the original German edition of *Will Therapy* was first published in two parts in 1929 and 1931 and the original German edition of *Truth and Reality* in 1929; Taft's English translations of both works were first published in 1936.

37. Otto Rank, *Art and Artist* (New York: Knopf, 1932), p. 100; *Truth and Reality*, p. 212.

38. *Gestalt Therapy*, pp. 230–231.

39. *Gestalt Therapy*, p. 247.

40. *Gestalt Therapy*, p. 235.

41. *Gestalt Therapy*, p. 248.

42. *Gestalt Therapy*, p. 245.

43. See interview with Isadore From, in *An Oral History of Gestalt Therapy*, pp. 37–38, on Perls's knowledge of Rank.

44. *Gestalt Therapy*, p. 321

45. *Gestalt Therapy*, pp. 323, 325.

46. *Gestalt Therapy*, p. 324

47. *Gestalt Therapy*, pp. 325–326. Compare "On a Writer's Block," *Complex* (Winter 1952), 7, pp. 42–50; reprinted in *Nature Heals*, pp. 193–201.

48. Author's interview with Benjamin Nelson, July 17, 1974.

49. *Gestalt Therapy*, p. 193.

Chapter Six

1. *In and Out the Garbage Pail*, p. 214.
2. Information on this period from interview with Isadore From, in *An Oral History of Gestalt Therapy*, pp. 29–30; interview with Laura Perls, in *Voices*, pp. 38–39; author's interviews with Jerry Raphel, July 15, 1974; Richard Kitzler, April 21, 1975.
3. Interview with Laura Perls, in *Voices*, p. 5; Interview with Gestalt therapist Pat Kelly, in *Voices*, p. 41; author's interview with Elliott Shapiro, October 15, 1974.
4. "A Conversation with Elliott Shapiro," *Gestalt Journal* (Fall 1985), 8, pp. 6–10; author's interview with Elliott Shapiro, October 15, 1974; author's correspondence with Elliott Shapiro, April 10 and 22, 1986.
5. "A Conversation with Elliott Shapiro," p. 17; author's interview with Elliott Shapiro, October 15, 1974; author's interview with Richard Kitzler, April 21, 1975.
6. *In and Out the Garbage Pail*, p. 113; author's interview with Richard Kitzler, April 21, 1975.
7. Author's conversations with George Dennison, from 1972 to 1987.
8. *The Empire City*, pp. 512–513.
9. Untitled manuscript (unfinished), in Houghton Library.
10. *Five Years*, p. 12.
11. Manuscript notes for Cleveland workshops, p. 5, Houghton Library.
12. Information on Goodman's groups comes from author interviews with about a dozen people who were regular group members or visitors, as well as various colleagues, trainees, and other observers, including some who were private patients not in the groups.
13. Letter from Goodman to George Dennison, July 25, 1954, in George Dennison Collection of the Houghton Library of Harvard University. This and other letters from Goodman in the Dennison Collection are quoted by permission of the Houghton Library.
14. *Five Years*, p. 65.
15. Author's interview with Jerry Raphel, July 15, 1974; interview with Isadore From, in *An Oral History of Gestalt Therapy*, pp. 29–30, 32–33; see also interview with Laura Perls, in *Voices*, pp. 5–6 (where the dates are wrong).
16. Interview with Laura Perls, in *An Oral History of Gestalt Therapy*, p. 12; "A Conversation with Elliott Shapiro," p. 13; author's interview with Richard Kitzler, April 21,.1975.
17. Author's interview with group member, July 29, 1975; author's interview with Elliott Shapiro, October 15, 1974; author's correspondence with Elliott

Shapiro, April 22, 1986; interview with Laura Perls, in *Voices*, pp. 5–6; interview with Laura Perls, in *An Oral History of Gestalt Therapy*, p. 14; interview with Isadore From, in *An Oral History of Gestalt Therapy*, pp. 33–34.

18. "A Conversation with Elliott Shapiro," p. 14.

19. "A Conversation with Elliott Shapiro," p. 15.

20. Author's interview with Richard Kitzler, April 21, 1975.

21. Author's interview with Richard Kitzler, April 21, 1975.

22. "A Conversation with Elliott Shapiro," p. 15.

23. Interview with Laura Perls, in *An Oral History of Gestalt Therapy*, pp. 5–6; author's interview with Elliott Shapiro, October 15, 1974.

24. Houghton Library. Note Goodman's idiosyncratic spelling of Shakespeare.

25. "Free University: How to Make a College" [a dialogue with Alvin Duskin], *Despite Everything* (Mar. 1965), *2*, p. 26.

26. Letters from Goodman to George Dennison, February 1, 1954; November 25, 1954, Dennison Collection, Houghton Library.

27. Manuscript notes for Gestalt seminar, Houghton Library.

28. Manuscript notes for Gestalt seminar, Houghton Library.

29. Description in the brochure announcing the seminars, Houghton Library.

30. Letter from Goodman to George Dennison [late October 1953], Dennison Collection, Houghton Library. The phrases in parentheses were afterthoughts inserted by Goodman.

31. Letter from Goodman to George Dennison, February 1, 1954, Dennison Collection, Houghton Library.

32. Letter from Goodman to George Dennison, November 25, 1954, Dennison Collection, Houghton Library.

33. Printed in *Nature Heals*, pp. 249–259.

34. Journal entries bearing directly on psychological topics are collected, in their original versions where recoverable, in *Nature Heals*, pp. 234–248, but see also the entries Goodman grouped under the rubric "Method" in *Five Years*.

35. Paul Goodman, *Utopian Essays and Practical Proposals* (New York: Random House, 1962), p. xiii.

36. *Nature Heals*, pp. 249, 252, 254.

37. *Nature Heals*, p. 250.

38. *Nature Heals*, p. 253.

39. *Nature Heals*, pp. 256–257.

40. Letter from Goodman to George Dennison, November 15, 1954, Dennison Collection, Houghton Library.

41. *Nature Heals*, p. 258.

42. Author's conversation with George Dennison, April 21, 1983.

43. *Nature Heals*, pp. 257–259.

Chapter Seven

1. Manuscript notes for Cleveland workshops, p. 16, Houghton Library.
2. Interview with Laura Perls, in *Voices*, p. 21; *In and Out the Garbage Pail*, pp. 281–282.
3. *Gestalt Therapy*, p. 310.
4. Author's interview with group member, July 29, 1975.
5. Author's conversation with George Dennison, October 6, 1973.
6. Manuscript notes for Cleveland workshops, p. 7, Houghton Library.
7. Author's interview with group member; unpublished journal entry [winter 1957–1958], Houghton Library.
8. Manuscript notes for Cleveland workshops, p. 7, Houghton Library.
9. Author's interview with group member, July 29, 1975.
10. *The Diaries of Judith Malina: 1947–1957* (New York: Grove Press, 1984), p. 314; entry for February 22, 1954.
11. Letter from Goodman to George Dennison, February 1, 1954, Dennison Collection, Houghton Library.
12. Author's interviews with Elliott Shapiro, October 15, 1974; Laura Perls, October 16, 1974; and psychotherapist Marilyn Hamilton, January 27, 1976.
13. Abraham S. Luchins, Review of *Gestalt Therapy*, *American Journal of Psychology* (Jan. 1953), 66, pp. 165–166.
14. Author's interview with Leo Raditsa, November 28, 1975.
15. Author's interview with Benjamin Nelson, July 20, 1975; interview with Benjamin Nelson, conducted by Robert Merideth, December 1972 (I am indebted to Robert Merideth and to Toby Huff for assistance in recovering this interview).
16. *Saturday Review of Literature* (Aug. 2, 1947), 30, p. 15.
17. Merideth's interview with Benjamin Nelson.
18. Benjamin Nelson, ed., *Freud and the 20th Century* (New York: Meridian Books, 1957), p. 7.
19. *Psychoanalysis and the Future* (New York: National Psychological Association for Psychoanalysis, 1957), p. x.
20. Author's interview with subject, November 7, 1979.
21. Author's interviews with Naomi Goodman, November 27, 1975; Sally Goodman, December 3–6, 1975.
22. Termination, yes, but was it a cure? While the swing at Paul may have helped, it took years of special exercises to clear up the bursitis. Though Percy experienced some relief after his angry flare-up, his morning exercises were necessary to prevent recurrence and eventually to cure his ailment. No Perlsian "instant cure" after all, though Paul might like to think so in this case. (Author's correspondence with Naomi Goodman, July 9, 1992.)

23. Manuscript notes for Cleveland workshops, p. 6, Houghton Library.

24. Author's interview with Richard Kitzler, April 21, 1975.

25. Interview with Laura Perls, in *An Oral History of Gestalt Therapy*, p. 14; interview with Isadore From, in *An Oral History of Gestalt Therapy*, pp. 34–35; interview with Erving Polster, in *An Oral History of Gestalt Therapy*, p. 48.

26. *Diaries of Judith Malina*, p. 310.

27. Author's interview with group member, July 16, 1974; letter from Goodman to George Dennison [late 1953?], Dennison Collection, Houghton Library.

28. *Diaries of Judith Malina*, p. 180.

29. Author's interview with group member, July 29, 1975.

30. *Diaries of Judith Malina*, pp. 314–315.

31. Interview with Erving Polster, in *An Oral History of Gestalt Therapy*, pp. 54–55.

32. Manuscript notes for Cleveland workshops, p. 5, Houghton Library. By opposing "Differential friends" to "Profession" Goodman meant that a Gestalt therapist like himself would not maintain professional distance and dignity nor would his patients all get the same degree of attention and concern from him—there would be differences, as among friends.

33. Interview with Isadore From, in *An Oral History of Gestalt Therapy*, p. 35; interview with Erving Polster, in *An Oral History of Gestalt Therapy*, p. 54.

34. Manuscript notes for Cleveland workshops, p. 8, Houghton Library.

35. Letters from Goodman to Sally Goodman [various dates in summer of 1957], Houghton Library.

36. Author's interview with Paul Mattick, May 17, 1976.

37. Letter from Goodman to George Dennison, June 8, 1954, Dennison Collection, Houghton Library.

38. Manuscript notes for Cleveland workshops, p. 7, Houghton Library.

39. Letter from Goodman to George Dennison [late 1953?], Dennison Collection, Houghton Library.

40. Manuscript notes for Cleveland workshops, pp. 7, 16, Houghton Library.

41. Author's interview with Karl Bissinger, December 4, 1975.

42. Author's interviews with former patients, January 26, 1976; November 25, 1978.

43. Author's interview with Marilyn Hamilton, January 27, 1976.

44. Paul Goodman, "The Continuum of the Libido," in Taylor Stoehr, ed., *A Ceremonial: Stories 1936–1940*, vol. 2 of *The Collected Stories of Paul Goodman*, (Santa Rosa, Calif.: Black Sparrow Press, 1978), p. 158.

45. Author's interviews with Ray Rosenthal, April 19, 1975; Richard Kitzler, April 21, 1975.

46. *Diaries of Judith Malina*, p. 285.

47. George Dennison, "Memoir," in Taylor Stoehr, ed., *Collected Poems of Paul Goodman* (New York: Random House, 1973), pp. xix–xx.

48. George Dennison, "Memoir," p. xx.

49. Author's interview with Richard Kitzler, April 21, 1975.

50. Author's interviews with group members, July 15, 1974; July 29, 1975.

51. Author's interview with group member, July 29, 1975.

52. Author's interview with Karl Bissinger, December 4, 1975.

53. *Diaries of Judith Malina*, p. 295; entry for September 21, 1953.

54. Author's interview with group member, July 29, 1975.

55. Manuscript notes for Cleveland workshops, p. 8, Houghton Library.

56. Author's interviews with Sally Goodman, May 19, 1973; March 4, 1992.

57. Author's interviews with Isadore From, August 21, 1974; Laura Perls, October 16, 1974.

58. *Five Years*, p. 51.

Chapter Eight

1. "The Politics of Being Queer," *Nature Heals*, pp. 218–219. First published, in a slightly different version, as "Memoirs of an Ancient Activist," *WIN* (Nov. 15, 1969), 5, pp. 4–7.

2. *Nature Heals*, pp. 220–221.

3. *Nature Heals*, pp. 223–224.

4. The friend was William Poster; see *Five Years*, p. 182.

5. "On Being a Writer," in *Nature Heals*, pp. 204–215. "On a Writer's Block" was first published in *Complex* (Winter 1952), 7, pp. 42–50; reprinted in *Nature Heals*, pp. 193–201. "Advance-Guard Writing, 1900–1950" was first published in *Kenyon Review* (Summer 1951), 13, pp. 357–380; reprinted in Taylor Stoehr, ed., *Creator Spirit Come! The Literary Essays of Paul Goodman* (New York: Free Life Editions, 1977), pp. 154–164.

6. *Nature Heals*, p. 205.

7. *Five Years*, p. 28. Compare the poem Goodman also wrote on this theme, *Collected Poems*, p. 378.

8. Letter from Goodman to George Dennison, July 25, 1954, Dennison Collection, Houghton Library.

9. All of these stories are to be found in Taylor Stoehr, ed., *The Galley to Mytilene: Stories 1949–1960*, vol. 4 of *The Collected Stories of Paul Goodman* (Santa Rosa, Calif.: Black Sparrow Press, 1980).

10. Goodman had never been willing to spend the money to have his dissertation typed, and so had no formal degree. The revised book also bore a new title.

11. Letters from Goodman to George Dennison, October 1 and November 25, 1954, Dennison Collection.

12. "Paul Goodman: A Conversation" [interview by Robert W. Glasgow], *Psychology Today* (Nov. 1971), 5, p. 90.

13. "Paul Goodman: A Conversation," p. 90.

14. Unpublished journal entry [winter 1957–1958], Houghton Library.

15. *The Empire City*, p. 407.

16. *The Empire City*, p. 544.

17. *The Empire City*, p. 503.

18. *Five Years*, p. 148.

19. Unpublished journal entry [early 1960], Houghton Library.

20. *Five Years*, p. 148.

21. *The Empire City*, pp. 590–591.

22. *The Empire City*, p. 589.

23. Letter from Goodman to George Dennison, February 17, 1955, Dennison Collection, Houghton Library.

24. *Five Years*, p. 62.

25. Unpublished journal entries, Houghton Library.

26. *Little Prayers and Finite Experience*, p. xviii.

27. Unpublished journal entry, Houghton Library.

28. Unpublished journal entry, Houghton Library.

29. *Five Years*, p. 64.

30. Unpublished journal entry, Houghton Library.

31. Author's conversation with Edwin Nevis and Erving Polster, April 4, 1992. Laura Perls, Elliott Shapiro, and Isadore From knew nothing of Goodman's situation at the time.

32. The correspondence with Albany is in the Houghton Library.

33. Information from Goodman's tax returns.

34. Author's correspondence with Susan Goodman, March 13 and August 1, 1992.

35. *Collected Poems*, p. 422; the version printed here is from the original manuscript in the Houghton Library.

36. Unpublished poem, May 1947, from the manuscript in the Houghton Library.

37. *Collected Poems*, p. 385; the version quoted here is from the manuscript in the Houghton Library.

38. *The Galley to Mytilene*, p. 73.

39. *Five Years*, p. 71. The original manuscript notebook is lost. This published version may have been revised after the fact, when Goodman had begun to recover from his panic.

40. *Five Years*, p. 73.

41. *Five Years*, p. 77.

42. *Little Prayers and Finite Experience*, p. 113.

43. *Five Years*, p. 86.

44. *Five Years*, pp. 95–96.

45. *Five Years*, p. 84.

46. *Five Years*, p. 100.

47. *Five Years*, p. 113.

48. *Five Years*, p. 118.

49. *Five Years*, p. 134.

50. *Five Years*, p. 136.

51. *Collected Poems*, pp. 405–406; the version quoted here is from the manuscript in the Houghton Library.

52. *Five Years*, p. 132.

53. *Five Years*, p. 138.

54. *Five Years*, pp. 154–155.

55. *Five Years*, p. 164.

56. *Gestalt Therapy*, p. 309.

57. *Gestalt Therapy*, p. 311.

58. *Gestalt Therapy*, p. 318.

59. *Gestalt Therapy*, p. 318.

60. *Gestalt Therapy*, p. 354.

61. *Gestalt Therapy*, p. 358.

62. *Five Years*, p. 161.

63. *Five Years*, p. 161.

64. Author's interview with Leo Raditsa, November 28, 1975.

65. Author's interview with Leo Raditsa, November 28, 1975.

66. Information from Goodman's tax returns.

67. *Five Years*, p. 190.

68. *Five Years*, p. 198.

69. *Time* (June 1, 1959), 73, pp. 88–89.

70. *Five Years*, pp. 221–222.

Chapter Nine

1. *Art and Social Nature*, pp. 1, 19; reprinted in *Drawing the Line*, pp. 3, 18.

2. *The Empire City*, pp. 386–387.

3. *Little Prayers and Finite Experience*, pp. 39–41.

4. *Five Years*, p. 208.

5. Paul Goodman, *New Reformation: Notes of a Neolithic Conservative* (New York: Random House, 1970), pp. 206–207.

6. *Utopian Essays*, pp. 19–20.

7. *Utopian Essays*, pp. xiv–xvi (Goodman's emphasis).

8. *Utopian Essays*, p. 112.

9. *Utopian Essays*, pp. 9–10.
10. *Little Prayers and Finite Experience*, p. 43.
11. *Utopian Essays*, p. xiv.
12. "Freedom and Learning: The Need for Choice," *Saturday Review* (May 18, 1968), *51*, p. 73.
13. "Freedom and Learning," p. 73
14. *Little Prayers and Finite Experience*, p. 83.
15. *Little Prayers and Finite Experience*, p. 65.
16. *Little Prayers and Finite Experience*, p. 77.
17. *Little Prayers and Finite Experience*, p. 75.
18. See Paul Goodman, "Confusion and Disorder," *Earth* (Aug. 1971), *2*, pp. 57–61; reprinted in *Drawing the Line*, pp. 233–245.
19. *Little Prayers and Finite Experience*, p. 69.
20. *Little Prayers and Finite Experience*, p. 47.
21. *Little Prayers and Finite Experience*, p. 65.
22. *New Reformation*, p. 204.
23. *Little Prayers and Finite Experience*, p. 43.
24. *Little Prayers and Finite Experience*, p. 41.
25. *Little Prayers and Finite Experience*, p. 49.
26. *Little Prayers and Finite Experience*, p. 45.
27. *Little Prayers and Finite Experience*, p. 52.

Chapter Ten

Epigraph: Paul Goodman, *North Percy* (Santa Rosa, Calif.: Black Sparrow Press, 1968); revised version in *Collected Poems*, pp. 132–151.
1. Paul Goodman, "A Young Pacifist," *Liberation* (Sept./Oct. 1967), *12*, pp. 75–79; reprinted in *Drawing the Line*, pp. 145–155.
2. *Making Do*, p. 274.
3. *Little Prayers and Finite Experience*, p. 121.
4. *Nature Heals*, p. 259.
5. *Little Prayers and Finite Experience*, p. xvii.
6. *Little Prayers and Finite Experience*, pp. 83–85.
7. *Little Prayers and Finite Experience*, pp. 93–95.

Chapter Eleven

1. *Collected Poems*, p. 14.
2. Author's interview with Richard Kitzler, April 21, 1975.
3. Letter from Goodman to Sally Goodman, March 19, 1970, Houghton Library.

4. *Diaries of Judith Malina*, pp. 404, 429.

5. *In and Out the Garbage Pail*, p. 2.

6. Author's Interview with Jim Nixon, March 23, 1975. Nixon was one of the leaders of the San Francisco State College student body, which hired Goodman as its first student-appointed faculty member in 1966.

7. Author's interview with Elliott Shapiro, October 15, 1974.

8. *In and Out the Garbage Pail*, p. 228.

9. *In and Out the Garbage Pail*, p. 228.

10. *In and Out the Garbage Pail*, p. 210; compare interview with Laura Perls, in *Voices*, p. 21.

11. Author's interview with Glenn Lewis, August 9, 1974.

12. Author's interview with Isadore From, August 21, 1974.

13. Richard Kitzler's memory of the event was particularly vivid. So too was Joe Wysong's. Author's interview with Richard Kitzler, April 21, 1975; author's correspondence with Joe Wysong, October 8, 1992. The page of notes from which Goodman gave his address is in the Houghton Library.

Chapter Twelve

1. *Little Prayers and Finite Experience*, p. xviii.

2. *Little Prayers and Finite Experience*, pp. 37–39.

3. The full list appears in *Gestalt Therapy*, pp. 240–243.

4. *Little Prayers and Finite Experience*, pp. 244–245.

5. Interview with Isadore From, in *An Oral History of Gestalt Therapy*, p. 35.

6. *Gestalt Therapy*, pp. 243, 250.

7. Interview with Isadore From, in *An Oral History of Gestalt Therapy*, p. 36; compare. p. 45.

8. *Five Years*, p. 12.

9. *In and Out the Garbage Pail*, p. 228.

10. *In and Out the Garbage Pail*, pp. 24, 289.

11. Interview with Erving Polster, in *An Oral History of Gestalt Therapy*, p. 55.

12. *Gestalt Therapy*, p. 392.

13. *Little Prayers and Finite Experience*, p. 39.

14. *Little Prayers and Finite Experience*, pp. 91–93.

15. *Little Prayers and Finite Experience*, pp. 103–105.

16. *Little Prayers and Finite Experience*, p. 14.

17. *Little Prayers and Finite Experience*, p. 68.

Selected Bibliography

Selected Books by Paul Goodman

Stop-Light: Five Dance Poems. Harrington Park, N.J.: 5 X 8 Press, 1941.

The Grand Piano or, The Almanac of Alienation. Vol. 1 of *The Empire City*. San Francisco: Colt Press, 1942.

With Meyer Liben and Edouard Roditi. *Pieces of Three*. Harrington Park, N.J.: 5 X 8 Press, 1942.

The Facts of Life. New York: Vanguard Press, 1945; London: Editions Poetry London [Nicholson & Watson], 1946.

Art and Social Nature. New York: Vinco, 1946.

The Copernican Revolution. Saugatuck, Conn.: 5 X 8 Press, 1946.

The State of Nature. Vol. 2 of *The Empire City*. New York: Vanguard Press, 1946.

Kafka's Prayer. New York: Vanguard Press, 1947.

With Percival Goodman. *Communitas: Means of Livelihood and Ways of Life*. Chicago: University of Chicago Press, 1947.

The Break-Up of Our Camp and Other Stories. New York: New Directions, 1949.

The Dead of Spring. Vol. 3 of *The Empire City*. Glen Gardner, N.J.: Libertarian Press, 1950.

With Frederick S. Perls and Ralph E. Hefferline. *Gestalt Therapy: Excitement and Growth in the Human Personality*. Vol 2., *Novelty, Excitement and Growth*, entirely by Goodman. New York: Julian Press, 1951.

Parents' Day. Saugatuck, Conn.: 5 X 8 Press, 1951.

The Structure of Literature. Chicago: University of Chicago Press, 1954.

The Empire City. Indianapolis, Ind., & New York: Bobbs-Merrill, 1959.

Growing Up Absurd: Problems of Youth in the Organized System. New York: Random House, 1960; London: Victor Gollancz, 1961.

Our Visit to Niagara. New York: Horizon Press, 1960.

With Percival Goodman. *Communitas: Means of Livelihood and Ways of Life.* (rev. 2nd ed.) New York: Vintage Books, 1960.

The Community of Scholars. New York: Random House, 1962.

Drawing the Line. New York: Random House, 1962.

The Lordly Hudson: Collected Poems. New York: Macmillan, 1962.

The Society I Live in Is Mine. New York: Horizon Press, 1962.

Utopian Essays and Practical Proposals. New York: Random House, 1962.

Making Do. New York: Macmillan, 1963.

Compulsory Mis-education. New York: Horizon Press, 1964.

People or Personnel. New York: Random House, 1965.

Three Plays: The Young Disciple, Faustina, Jonah. New York: Random House, 1965.

Five Years. New York: Brussel & Brussel, 1966.

The Moral Ambiguity of America. Massey Lectures, Sixth Series. Toronto: Canadian Broadcasting Corporation, 1966. Published in the United States as *Like a Conquered Province: The Moral Ambiguity of America.* New York: Random House, 1967.

Hawkweed: Poems. New York: Random House, 1967.

Adam and His Works: Collected Stories. New York: Vintage Books, 1968.

North Percy. Santa Rosa, Calif.: Black Sparrow Press, 1968.

The Open Look. With photographs by Stefan Congrat-Butlar. New York: Funk & Wagnalls, 1969.

Homespun of Oatmeal Gray: Poems. New York: Random House, 1970.

New Reformation: Notes of a Neolithic Conservative. New York: Random House, 1970.

Tragedy & Comedy: Four Cubist Plays. Santa Rosa, Calif.: Black Sparrow Press, 1970.

Speaking and Language: Defence of Poetry. New York: Random House, 1971.

Little Prayers and Finite Experience. New York: HarperCollins, 1972.

Collected Poems of Paul Goodman, ed. Taylor Stoehr, with a memoir by George Dennison. New York: Random House, 1973.

The Writings of Paul Goodman, ed. David Ray and Taylor Stoehr. *New Letters*, Winter/Spring 1976, 42, entire special double issue.

Creator Spirit Come! Literary Essays of Paul Goodman, ed. Taylor Stoehr. New York: Free Life Editions, 1977.

Drawing the Line: Political Essays of Paul Goodman, ed. Taylor Stoehr. New York: Free Life Editions, 1977.

Nature Heals: Psychological Essays of Paul Goodman, ed. Taylor Stoehr. New York: Free Life Editions, 1977.

The Break-Up of Our Camp: Stories 1932–1935. Vol. 1 of *The Collected Stories of Paul Goodman*, ed. Taylor Stoehr. Santa Rosa, Calif.: Black Sparrow Press, 1978.

A Ceremonial: Stories 1936–1940. Vol. 2 of *The Collected Stories of Paul Goodman*, ed. Taylor Stoehr. Santa Rosa, Calif.: Black Sparrow Press, 1978.

Don Juan; or, The Continuum of the Libido, ed. Taylor Stoehr. Santa Rosa, Calif.: Black Sparrow Press, 1979.

The Facts of Life: Stories 1940–1949. Vol. 3 of *The Collected Stories of Paul Goodman*, ed. Taylor Stoehr. Santa Rosa, Calif.: Black Sparrow Press, 1979.

The Galley to Mytilene: Stories 1949–1960. Vol. 4 of *The Collected Stories of Paul Goodman*, ed. Taylor Stoehr. Santa Rosa, Calif.: Black Sparrow Press, 1980.

Crazy Hope and Finite Experience, ed. Taylor Stoehr. San Francisco: Jossey-Bass, 1994. Augmented edition of *Little Prayers and Finite Experience*.

Format and Anxiety: Paul Goodman's Critique of the Media, ed. Taylor Stoehr. Brooklyn: Autonomedia, 1994.

Decentralizing Power: The Social Criticism of Paul Goodman, ed. Taylor Stoehr. Montreal: Black Rose Books, 1994.

Work Edited by Paul Goodman

Seeds of Liberation. New York: Braziller, 1964.

Selected Interviews

Morgan Gibson and Barbara Gibson. "Highlights of an Interview with Paul Goodman on *The Empire City.*" *Kulchur*, Summer 1965, 5, 2–15.

Robert W. Glasgow, "Paul Goodman, A Conversation." *Psychology Today*, Nov. 1971, 5, 62–65, 90–96

Studs Terkel. "What Is a Man's Work?" *WFMT Perspective*, Aug. 1962, 2, 29–35.

Bibliographies

Tom Nicely. *Adam and His Work: A Bibliography of Sources by and about Paul Goodman (1911–1972)*. Scarecrow Author Bibliographies, no. 42. Metuchen, N.J.: Scarecrow Press, 1979.

Tom Nicely. "Adam and His Work: A Bibliographical Update." In Peter Parisi, ed. *Artist of the Actual: Essays on Paul Goodman*. Metuchen, N.J.: Scarecrow Press, 1986, pp. 153–183.

Selected Critical Works

Hayden Carruth. "Paul Goodman and the Grand Community." *American Poetry Review*, Sept./Oct. 1983, 12, 22–32.

George Dennison. "The Ways of Nature." *Inquiry Magazine*, Mar. 6, 1978, 1, 20–22. This issue also contains pieces on Goodman by Michael Rossman, Lewis Perry, and Emile Capouya; see also Dennison's "Memoir" in Goodman's *Collected Poems*.

Lewis Fried. "Paul Goodman: The City as Self." In Lewis Fried, *Makers of the City*. Amherst: University of Massachusetts, 1990, pp. 159–206.

Geoffrey Gardner. "Citizen of the World, Animal of Nowhere." *New Letters*, Winter/Spring 1976, 42, 216–227.

Richard King. "Paul Goodman." In Richard King, *The Party of Eros: Radical Social Thought and the Realm of Freedom*. Chapel Hill: University of North Carolina, 1972, pp. 78–115.

Peter Parisi, ed. *Artist of the Actual: Essays on Paul Goodman*. Metuchen, N.J.: The Scarecrow Press, 1986.

Leo Raditsa. "On Paul Goodman—and Goodmanism." *Iowa Review*, Summer 1974, 5, 62–79.

Theodore Roszak. "Exploring Utopia: The Visionary Sociology of Paul Goodman." In Theodore Roszak, *The Making of a Counter Culture*. New York: Doubleday, 1969, pp. 178–204.

Taylor Stoehr. "Paul Goodman and the New York Jews." *Salmagundi*, Winter/Spring 1985, 66, 50–103.

Taylor Stoehr. "Adam and Everyman: Paul Goodman in his Stories." In Taylor Stoehr, *Words and Deeds: Essays on the Realistic Imagination*. New York: AMS Press, 1986, 149–164.

Taylor Stoehr. "*Growing Up Absurd*—Again: Rereading Paul Goodman in the Nineties." *Dissent*, Fall 1990, *37*, pp. 486–494; see also Stoehr's introductions to his editions of Goodman's essays.

Bernard Vincent. *Paul Goodman et la reconquête du présent*. Paris: Editions du Seuil, 1976.

Bernard Vincent. *Pour un bon usage du monde: Une réponse conviviale à la crise de l'école, de la ville et de la foi*. Tournai, Belgium: Desclée, 1979.

Colin Ward, "Planning: Patrick Geddes and Paul Goodman." In Colin Ward, *Influences: Voices of Creative Dissent*. Bideford, Devon, U.K.: Green Books, 1991, pp. 114–132.

Kingsley Widmer. *Paul Goodman*. Boston: Twayne, 1980.

David Wieck. "Paul Goodman: *Drawing the Line*," *Telos*, Spring 1978, *35*, 199–214.

Index

INDEX

329